BIOGRAPHICAL MEMOIRS OF FELLOWS, IV

PROCEEDINGS OF THE BRITISH ACADEMY · 130

BIOGRAPHICAL MEMOIRS OF FELLOWS IV

Published for THE BRITISH ACADEMY
by OXFORD UNIVERSITY PRESS

Oxford University Press, Great Clarendon Street, Oxford OX2 6DP

Oxford New York
Auckland Bangkok Bogotá Buenos Aires Cape Town Chennai
Dar es Salaam Delhi Hong Kong Istanbul Karachi Kolkata
Kuala Lumpur Madrid Melbourne Mexico City Mumbai Nairobi
São Paulo Shanghai Singapore Taipei Tokyo Toronto

British Library Cataloguing in Publication Data
Data available

ISBN 0–19–726350–X   978–0–19–726350–1
ISSN 0068–1202

Typeset in Times
by J&L Composition, Filey, North Yorkshire
Printed in Great Britain
on acid-free paper by
Antony Rowe Limited,
Chippenham, Wiltshire

The Academy is grateful to Professor P. J. Marshall, CBE, FBA
for his editorial work on this volume

Contents

ISAIAH BERLIN

Isaiah Berlin
1909–1997

ISAIAH BERLIN had such a varied career that his biographer should be a committee, and what follows should be a book. He had such a talent for friendship that his biographer should be above all a committee of his friends. Berlin's death inspired some remarkable tributes from those friends, among them Lord Annan's address at the Memorial Service held at the Hampstead Synagogue in January 1998 and those of Sir Stuart Hampshire and Sir Bernard Williams at the Sheldonian Theatre some two months later. Their affectionate eloquence was matched by the eloquence of Isaac Stern's violin and Alfred Brendel's piano. Almost any account of Berlin's achievements must come lamely in the wake of such tributes. Berlin's own talents as an obituarist and memorialist were, of course, extraordinary; he was a master of the *éloge*, and more than one reader thought that the collection printed in *Personal Impressions* was the best of his writing. His friends often wondered what he would say about them when the time came, or indeed what he had already written about them for future readers of *The Times* It is to be regretted that unlike Bertrand Russell, Berlin did not pen his own obituary, not even one written tongue in cheek as Russell's was.

Berlin's fascinating early life was well described in Michael Ignatieff's biography, and only a reminder is needed here. He was born in Riga, Latvia on 6 June 1909. He was an only child; a sister had been still-born, and his mother, Marie, had been warned against another pregnancy. Berlin's left arm was permanently damaged by the forceps of the attending doctor. Whether he might otherwise have had athletic tastes is doubtful, but his

Proceedings of the British Academy, **130**, 3–20. © The British Academy 2005.

favoured place was certainly the sofa, not the mountain track. His family were upper middle-class Jews; his father was a descendant of the founder of the Lubavitcher sect, but the immediate family were thoroughly Europeanised, and their passions were musical and literary. Berlin took a wry pleasure in the fact that Menachem Schneerson, the 'Lubavitcher Rebbe', was a distant cousin. The Lubavitcher Rebbe's view of the connection is not known.

The family's comfortable life was disturbed by the First World War, which provoked anti-Germanism and anti-Semitism; the family moved to Petrograd in 1916, and there encountered the Russian Revolutions of February and October 1917. Although they suffered no violence, and not much deprivation, Berlin's parents saw what might happen after the Civil War of 1920–1, and made their way to England early in 1921. Mendel Berlin, Berlin's father, was a timber merchant with commercial ties to Britain, and greatly admired British decency and toleration. Ian Buruma has described Isaiah Berlin's acquisition of a wholly English *persona* as an astonishing act of self-creation. This perhaps underestimates Mendel Berlin's role in the process. Appropriately, the family first settled in Surbiton before they moved to Kensington.

Arriving with little English in a wholly strange environment, the 12-year-old Berlin thrived. A suburban preparatory school was followed by St Paul's, where he followed the traditional classical syllabus. In 1928 Berlin went on as scholar to Corpus Christi College, Oxford. He by-passed Honour Moderations and took a First in Greats in 1931 and another in PPE in 1932. He made many friends, and his flair for conversation was a great resource in so doing. Late 1920s Oxford was snobbish and mildly anti-Semitic, but it sheltered a society that was less attached to its social prejudices than to cleverness and charm. Both of these the young Berlin had in abundance. In 1932, he was elected to a Prize Fellowship at All Souls, the first Jew to be elected in its five-hundred-year history, an achievement that brought congratulations from the Chief Rabbi and lunch with Lord Rothschild.

Until 1938, Berlin held his All Souls Fellowship in combination with a lecturership in philosophy at New College; after the Prize Fellowship had expired, he was from 1938 to 1950 a Fellow in philosophy at New College, though absent for six years on war service. He later said that he found pre-war New College deeply boring. It was a view shared by the Warden, H. A. L. Fisher, who described the college on his return to it in 1925 as 'one - vast - mau - so - leum'. A decided compensation was the visitors Berlin met in the Warden's Lodgings, including as they did

Virginia Woolf—Fisher's cousin—and Elizabeth Bowen. The former wrote a maliciously funny account of their meeting, but Bowen became a good friend, with whom he carried on a vivid correspondence for many years.

As a young teacher and scholar, Berlin would have been harshly judged by the appraisal committees of the present age. He always said that he could not have been a member of any academic community more tightly structured than the Oxford of his day; the ability to pursue his own interests in his own way was indispensable. He was endlessly courted by American universities after the Second World War, but he could not have survived the departmental organisation of American university life, let alone the early-morning classes common in the United States. He was reluctant to leave his bed before mid-morning, and passed the time during tutorials playing with mechanical toys or with the wind-up gramophone whose enormous horn was remembered by generations of pupils. In spite of this seeming uninterest in their work, almost all his pupils, and by no means only the cleverest, found that they learned more philosophy from Berlin than from their more orthodox instructors.

He was recalled with particular affection by students who had been terrified by, or entirely uninterested in, philosophy. The contrast with H. W. B. Joseph was much in his favour. New College students were terrified of Joseph: Maurice Bowra used to say that he had found artillery bombardments in the First World War much less frightening than the tutorials that put him off philosophy for life. The undergraduates of the 1930s were the first of many generations who found Berlin an astonishingly kindly and generous teacher. He was a rarity among university teachers in the later twentieth century in finding young people irresistible; well into his eighties, he was endlessly available to naive and vulnerable graduate students from all parts of the world, who would sit at his feet for an afternoon, and leave in a happy daze.

In the 1930s Berlin was part of a small group of young and iconoclastic philosophers that included John Austin, Stuart Hampshire, and A. J. Ayer. It was his good fortune that at All Souls and elsewhere, he had close friends of his own age and intellectual weight. They met in Berlin's rooms in All Souls and thrashed out their puzzles in debate. Berlin later regretted that they had been too introspective to publish their conclusions; their passion was for the excitement of the chase, and their chief desire to convince one another. Once they had settled a problem to their own satisfaction, they saw no reason to broadcast the answer. They were broadly in sympathy with what became the linguistic turn in philosophy, but as their later careers showed, were otherwise far from being of one mind. Ayer was an early convert to logical positivism, Austin, Hampshire and Berlin were not.

A favourite move within logical positivism was to translate propositions that were held to be epistemologically dubious for one reason and another into propositions felt to be more secure; statements about the past, about the future, about the contents of other minds, and about persisting material objects, were parsed as hypothetical propositions about verifiable facts about our own experience. Berlin wrote three original and powerful criticisms of this central tactic of logical positivism, 'Verification', 'Empirical Propositions and Hypothetical Statements', and 'Logical Translation', the first published in 1939, and the others in 1950. Berlin himself always said that these essays gave no clue to his later interests and work; indeed in the 1978 Preface to *Concepts and Categories*, he claimed that he could not bring himself to read them. This is somewhat at odds with the chronology: only one of them was written before the War, two were published in 1950, and a later paper on *Equality*, delivered as the Presidential Address to the Aristotelian Society in 1956, is an impeccably 'analytical' essay.

Bernard Williams had perhaps a better understanding of the matter than Berlin himself. It is true enough that Berlin's assaults on the implausibility of assorted forms of phenomenalism were deft statements of what became the orthodox view—that the supposedly more reliable propositions into which we were to translate statements about the past, about physical objects, and about other minds in fact presupposed the truth of statements about these allegedly dubious entities. But Berlin was more concerned with something rather different. He always thought of philosophy as a discipline concerned with uncovering the hidden presuppositions of our everyday claims about the world and ourselves. This rather Collingwoodian view of the subject implied from the first an interest in the history of ideas, the context of inquiry, and the intellectual temper of the philosopher whose ideas are being scrutinised. The passion for bringing thinkers vividly to life that Berlin's work exhibited after the Second World War was implicit in his work much earlier.

More important in the longer term was the commission from Fisher and Gilbert Murray in 1933 for an account of the life and ideas of Karl Marx for the Home University Library. Berlin was not the publisher's first choice for a project that had already been turned down by the Webbs, Frank Pakenham, and Harold Laski, and it took him a long time to finish the book. Although Berlin was a notoriously rapid talker, he was a slow producer of manuscripts. He was an inveterate tinkerer with his text and reluctant to hand it over to be published. Both the manuscript and the typescript of *Karl Marx* display his passion for rewriting up to, and frequently after, the last possible moment, and they induce some surprise that *Karl Marx* ever saw the light of day at all. In the event, *Karl Marx* was a publishing success and a double landmark in Berlin's life. It was one of the first works in English to treat Marx objectively—neither belittling the real intellectual power of his work, nor descending into hagiography. And it revealed Berlin's talent as a historian of ideas—or more exactly as a biographer of ideas. Berlin was no admirer of Marx, and deplored the political consequences of his ideas, but he entered into the mental world of Marx and his contemporaries as few biographers have known how to do.

It was a decidedly lop-sided book inasmuch as Berlin never took any interest in Marx's economics; when he revised the book thirty years later, it was to write more kindly of Marx's theory of alienation, not to provide a beginner's guide to the transformation of values into prices. What Berlin was interested in was the philosophical frame of mind in which intellectuals embraced utopian schemes for the regeneration of mankind. The fact that he thought of himself as almost wholly devoid of religious sensibility did not prevent him finding the utopians of the nineteenth century endlessly, but appallingly, fascinating. Like Carl Becker, whose *Heavenly City of the Eighteenth-Century Philosophers* lies behind a good many of Berlin's post-war essays on the Enlightenment and its critics, Berlin thought that many a secular rationalist had been nourishing in his bosom an essentially religious hankering after a timeless harmony— social, intellectual, and psychological. The five years of reading and reflection on the ideas and allegiances of the radical intelligentsia of nineteenth-century Europe that were needed to write *Karl Marx* fur- nished Berlin with the resources he employed in his later accounts of the Enlightenment, of Romanticism, and of the ideas of the Russian radicals whom he brought to wider notice in the 1940s and 1950s.

Berlin's career was first interrupted and then spectacularly accelerated by the outbreak of the Second World War. Initially, he was stranded. He was not fit for military service, and as a Latvian by birth he was suspect to the intelligence services, who vetoed his application for a humble desk job. In the summer of 1940, Guy Burgess persuaded him to accompany him to Moscow. Who had authorised the trip—if anyone—is still unclear. Later events suggested that if it was not Harold Nicolson, it was Burgess himself, and that he had not even tried to persuade his superiors to endorse the scheme. He and Berlin arrived in the United States after an unpleasant Atlantic crossing, and Burgess was promptly recalled to London. Berlin's efforts to get to Moscow were then vetoed by Sir Stafford Cripps, the British Ambassador. Meanwhile, Berlin began to charm the political and newspaper élites of Washington and New York to whom he was introduced by Felix Frankfurter, the Supreme Court Justice whom he had met in Oxford a few years earlier. Friends suggested to Lord Lothian that a job should be found for Berlin, and he was set to work analysing American press reports of the British war effort. This went so well that he was given a permanent post in the British Information Office in New York. After a few weeks back in Britain to settle his affairs, Berlin returned to the United States in January 1941, and spent the remainder of the war there.

After a year in New York he was poached by the British Embassy in Washington, and for the remainder of the war drafted dispatches for transmission to London for his Ambassador, Lord Halifax. (A selection was published by H. G. Nicholas in 1981 as *Washington Despatches 1941–1945.*) They were much admired by Winston Churchill and many others. The usually remote Halifax —'a creature from another planet' in Berlin's recollection—was fond of his colleague from All Souls and gave him his head. Through Frankfurter, Berlin met most of the Democratic administration, along with coming young journalists such as Joseph Alsop, and the publishers of the *Washington Post,* Philip and Katherine Graham, all of whom remained friends for life. Berlin walked with great skill the fine line between exact reporting and colouring the news to enhance the prospects of a desired policy. It was a skill that he especially needed to preserve relations with Chaim Weizmann and other Zionist friends. Berlin did what he could to keep doors to both the American and British governments open for them, but he was acutely aware of Foreign Office doubts about Zionist aspirations and the limits beyond which he could not go. He neither betrayed his friends nor destroyed his own use-fulness by becoming an object of suspicion to his employers, even though in the course of 1943 he was instrumental in obstructing a joint British-American declaration against the establishment of a post-war Jewish state.

The years in Washington brought Berlin into close contact with the makers of American foreign policy and reshaped his sense of what he might do with his life. Even more important were his postwar encounters with Russian poets, novelists, dramatists and other intellectuals in the winter of 1945–6. He finally got his wish to work in Moscow, and spent six months there at the end of the war. Just what happened is hard to recapture, even though Berlin wrote several accounts of his experiences, but he was evidently persuaded of two things. The first was that he was as much a Russian intellectual as an Oxford don; the other was that Stalin's near-destruction of Russian cultural and intellectual life was appalling, not only because of the cruelty and thuggishness involved in all Stalin's actions, but because there had been a vitality and originality in Russian literature and political thinking from the 1840s onwards that made them more vivid and more engrossing than anything in the West. At a personal level, it was Anna Akhmatova and Boris Pasternak who persuaded him of this; at a more austerely intellectual level, it was Alexander Herzen and Ivan Turgenev.

Berlin decided that if he was to remain in England and Oxford, it could not be as a post-war incarnation of the philosophy tutor he had been before the war. He did not immediately abandon philosophy for the history of ideas, nor did he immediately abandon undergraduate teaching. It was not until 1950 that he resigned his fellowship at New College and returned to All Souls. Indeed, he half-jokingly claimed that the move had been forced upon him when he was sacked by an economy-minded bursar of New College who had counted the philosophy tutors and decided that Berlin was one too many. But his intellectual tastes had in any case changed. He turned to the history of ideas, political theory, and what may be termed 'cultural commentary'. The change was signalled in 1953 by the publication of *The Hedgehog and the Fox*, the long essay on Tolstoy's theory of history that made famous a hitherto obscure tag from Archilochus: 'The fox knows many things, but the hedgehog knows one big thing.' Tolstoy, on Berlin's view of the matter, was a fox who tried to turn himself into a hedgehog, a man whose genius lay in his understanding of the infinite variety of human character, and who drove himself almost mad by trying to cramp that genius into a single recipe for salvation.

In 1954, Berlin gave the Northcliffe Lectures on 'A Marvellous Decade' that brought to an English audience the ideas of Herzen and Belinsky and other romantic radicals of the Russian 1840s. Their impact on British intellectual sensibilities was indirect but powerful. On the one hand, the lectures demonstrated that liberalism could no longer be thought of as an Anglo-American possession presented to the world by John Locke and John Stuart Mill; on the other, they showed that the contrast between a naturally despotic Russia and a naturally liberal western Europe had to be given up. In the Soviet Union, Berlin's revelation of the romantic, liberal Herzen was heretical; in Soviet ideology, Herzen was approved of as a populist, though criticised for the inadequate, pre-Marxist view that underlay his populism. The loathing with which Herzen would assuredly have greeted the Soviet regime was not something Soviet commentators cared to have dwelled on.

During the 1950s Berlin became an important figure outside academic life in the broader cultural life of Britain, as a speaker on the BBC Third Programme and as a commentator on political and intellectual life in the context of the Cold War. To the surprise and occasionally the anger of critics, Berlin wrote nothing about the Holocaust, and little about German anti-Semitism as such. Nonetheless, he wrote at length and vividly about what one might call Jewishness in the modern world. After several decades in which political theorists have endlessly discussed multiculturalism in all its varieties, the dilemmas of what one might call 'Enlightenment Judaism' have become better understood; but Berlin was an important originator of the debate about where the middle ground lay between assimilation and exclusion—whether that be self-exclusion or exclusion by the wider society.

One of his more surprising insights was that the existence of the state of Israel was a necessity for Jews everywhere, but not as a place of refuge for the survivors of the Holocaust or future victims of persecution in the Middle East or the Soviet Union. He explained the importance of the existence of the state of Israel for Jews outside Israel in his essay on 'Jewish Slavery and Emancipation'. A state that Jews anywhere in the world could regard as a second home protected Jewish freedom everywhere else. Berlin himself certainly experienced the existence of Israel as an element in his conviction that he could choose to stay in England without facing a stark choice between assimilation and emigration. Although he was urged by his Zionist friends to join them in Israel, there was no real prospect of his doing so. He felt too English to make his home among Middle Eastern Jews, and in any event disliked a good many of the most significant figures in the new state, and was unhappy about the role of terrorism in its creation.

Nonetheless, he remained a confirmed liberal Zionist, and he remained a good friend of Chaim Weizmann, the first President of Israel, and the subject of one of Berlin's most heartfelt *éloges*. An interesting insight into Berlin's view of Israel is provided by an another *éloge*, this time of his cousin Yitzhak Sadeh (born Isaac Landoberg), who was a noted general in the Israeli War of Independence. Berlin recalled him as 'a huge child', who did more for Israel than his exploits on the battlefield alone might suggest. In Berlin's words, he 'introduced an element of total freedom, unquencheable gaiety, ease, charm, and a natural elegance, half bohemian, half aristocratic, too much of which would ruin any possibility of order, but an element of which no society should lack if it were to be free or worthy of survival'. The moral for Israeli politics was the more powerful for being unstated. In something of the same way, his famous essay on Moses Hess's slow and reluctant movement from assimilationism to a liberal Zionism provided a further perspective on Berlin's own state of mind. It would be going too far, however, to try to extract further insights from perhaps the most unlikely—but wonderful—short double-biography of all time, his essay on Karl Marx and Benjamin Disraeli as exemplars of mid-Victorian London Jewishness.

In 1953 Berlin spent some months teaching at Bryn Mawr, and there gave a set of lectures entitled *Political Ideas of the Romantic Age* which were intended to provide the basis of a series of talks for the BBC with the same title. The unfinished and ill-organised typescript of these lectures contains in embryo almost all the most important essays on topics in political theory that Berlin published over the next two decades, and in particular *Two Concepts of Liberty*. As a political theorist he was concerned with Stalinist totalitarianism rather than Nazism. His interest lay in the way in which the rationalist and reformist impulses of the Enlightenment, sometimes in perverse combination with the anti-Enlightenment forces of Romanticism, had produced millenarian and totalitarian movements that had set back the cause of liberal, pluralist, humanitarian progress by a century and more. It was this concern that gave him an undeserved reputation as an anti-Enlightenment thinker himself. He was, as he himself said, a cautious defender of Enlightenment.

It was in arguing on behalf of a pluralist, indeterminist, open-ended version of Enlightenment that he invoked those figures in the history of ideas that he particularly made his own. Berlin described himself as having abandoned philosophy in order to pursue the history of ideas. He gave two different reasons for the change of intellectual allegiance. Sometimes, he suggested that he had become bored with philosophy as practised in Oxford and Harvard. He often quoted the deflationary observation of C. I. Lewis: 'There is no a priori reason for thinking that the truth, once discovered, will necessarily prove interesting.' Berlin did not wish to spend his life accumulating boring truths. More often he said that he had come to believe that there was no progress in philosophy and that he had wanted to work in a field where he could expect to know more by the time he died than he had known when he started. This is the version of events that he recounts in the Preface to *Concepts and Categories* where he ascribes his change of course to a conversation with the

Harvard logician H. M. Sheffer; Sheffer had said that the only areas of philosophy in which unequivocal progress could be made were logic and psychology—the latter being capable of empirical development. Whether Berlin made the transition that either of these explanations suggest is doubtful.

He certainly did not become the kind of historian of ideas that his second account implied that he should have become. He was not interested in the quotidian history that lay behind the ideas by which he was fascinated. Bold ideas and original, quirky, and imaginative thinkers interested him. When more historically minded historians of ideas observed that ideas are transmitted by the derivative and the second-rate, Berlin did not turn to the derivative and the second-rate. He occasionally rescued the intellectually second-rate from obscurity, but only because he found them interestingly underivative. It sometimes seemed to be out of a sense of historical justice that he rescued them; because they had had no impact, he wished to bring them to the attention of their descendants, to rescue them from the condescension of history.

Berlin found the politics of the 1960s and 1970s more difficult than those of the 1950s; the uninhibited defence of Anglo-American liberalism against Stalinist oppression was a good deal easier than knowing just what to say about the Vietnam War. Nonetheless, the intellectual apparatus on which he relied and the allegiances in whose service it was employed were firmly in place by the early 1950s, and what happened thereafter was more application than innovation. Before turning to Berlin's career as Chichele Professor of Political Thought, President of Wolfson College, Oxford, Fellow and President of the British Academy, and trustee of the Royal Opera House, the National Gallery, and a host of other institutions, we may profitably ask what Berlin's renowned 'pluralism' amounted to, and how it was connected to the way he practised the history of ideas. We may leave to the end of this account a last look at the kind of liberalism Berlin defended.

One might in no unkind spirit wonder why Berlin invoked the historical figures he did to draw the morals he wished to draw. If Berlin wished to argue that values are many not one, that the future is open not closed, and that the quest for Utopia is more likely to arrive at Hell than Heaven, he needed no help from the dead. These are issues in philosophy or matters of political prudence that he could have argued on his own behalf, and without appealing to anyone else for support. Many essays did indeed argue the case with less historical reference. Understood as an essay in analytical political philosophy, 'Two Concepts of Liberty' might seem heavily encrusted with historical allusion; but it is not an essay in the history of ideas. 'From Hope and Fear Set Free' is similarly light on historical reference, while 'Historical Inevitability' argues against determinist theories of history with relatively little further reference.

Nonetheless, all these essays rely for their effect on a historical framework and a network of historical allusion. The question is why this approach was so frutiful. The answer perhaps lies with Berlin's discovery of Giambattista Vico. Berlin was seized by Vico's concept of *fantasia*, and he took over Vico's thought that human society was a historical phenomenon, that an understanding of the human mind was to be sought by an active effort of positive, imaginative recreation, and that understanding the moral and political concepts by which we make sense of our existence, both individual and collective, is a historical activity.

This suggests yet another reason to reject a sharp separation between the philosophical and the historical understanding of the concepts of political philosophy. They are, on this view, best understood as the reflection of transitional, if not necessarily transitory, attempts by human cultures to grasp their moral and political experience and to mould it in ways they desire. The other feature of the concept of *fantasia* that provides the clue, not so much to the content as to the dazzling rhetorical form, of Berlin's work in the history of ideas is its emphasis on the *re-enacting* of past thought as it was thought by past thinkers. I have in other contexts over-used the image of Berlin taking his hearers to a party in the Elysian Fields; but the thought that conveying a full understanding of another writer is very like bringing the reader into the physical presence of that writer is, with due allowances made, hard to escape. Berlin's account of the kind of knowledge that Vico had identified was that it was the sort of knowing that participants in an activity possess as against mere observers: the knowledge of actors rather than the audience, that it was the 'inside' story rather than one obtained from some 'outside' vantage point. It was, he said, the kind of knowledge involved when a work of the imagination or of social diagnosis or a work of critcism or scholarship or history is described not as correct or incorrect, but as profound or shallow, realistic or unrealistic, perceptive or stupid, alive or dead.

Thinking our way through the dichotomies of 'pluralism/monism,' 'freedom/authoritarianism,' and 'indeterminism/determinism' is on that view part of a conversation with writers, many of whom happen to be dead, and it is an activity that requires us to imagine our own society pictured against others, in order to illuminate its virtues and vices. To know why we believe in—if we do believe in—negative liberty, for instance, is to know what we would want to say to Pericles about his beloved Athens, and what we would want to say to Benjamin Constant about the contrast he drew between the liberty of the ancients and the liberty of the moderns. Seen in that light, Berlin's handling of the figures about whom he wrote becomes easy to understand.

By the same token, the pluralism that Berlin defended was multi-dimensional, and one whose character emerged in the course of a dialogue with writers who were themselves sometimes pluralists and sometimes monists, and often both at once. Machiavelli's pluralism was not that of Benjamin Constant, and neither was a pluralist in the same sense as Herder. How best to characterise Berlin's own understanding of pluralism is not easy to know. It is, after all, a fairly banal thought that in the world as we have it, not everything that we want can be had simultaneously, and Berlin was certain that pluralism was not banal. For Berlin, it was a deep truth that good lives were many not one; Tolstoy's search for the one saving truth may have been misguided, but his mistake, if it was a mistake, was not silly, but tragic. By the same token, the idea that we can accommodate the tensions of multiple demands upon us by a strategy of 'mix and match' will do for lifestyle choices and will not do for anything more serious.

What Berlin wrote was still philosophy rather than history, but he almost reversed the old tag that history is philosophy teaching by examples. It was rather that philosophy is history raised to self-consciousness. Ideas come to life in a process that Berlin self-consciously understood as a re-enactment of the original author's thinking. The ideas in which Berlin was interested, particularly the central concepts of politics such as freedom, equality and progress can only be understood historically and comparatively in the light of the way they have been understood in different societies and cultures. They are also pre-eminently ideas that take their colouring from the personality of the thinkers who explore them; Berlin's talent for gossip was the everyday social counterpart of an unusual talent for exploring the psychology of his favourite thinkers.

Critics sometimes complained that Berlin projected more of himself than was proper onto the figures he most admired, but the effect was certainly to bring to life neglected thinkers as well as to illuminate well-known ones in novel ways. It also meant that his natural form of expression was the lecture and the essay rather than the monograph, which gave him an unjustifed reputation for being reluctant to publish. He published a great deal, but it was often in fugitive journals and out of the way places, as though he disliked the thought of freezing an unfinished conversation by committing himself in too public a fashion, and was happier to be overheard than read.

It was not only Berlin's intellectual life that prospered in the 1950s. Berlin enjoyed the company of women, but thought himself sexually unattractive, and believed until his late thirties that he was destined to remain a bachelor. All Souls was a more than comfortable setting for the bachelor life, and Berlin's affection for his mother was such that he need neither be driven into marriage by the discomforts of single life nor lured into it by the need for stronger emotional attachments than the unmarried life provided. It was to the surprise of his numerous friends that in 1956 he married Aline Halban, the daughter of Pierre de Gunzbourg. He thereby acquired step-children as well as a beautiful and well-connected wife. They established themselves in Aline's substantial and elegant house on the outskirts of Oxford: Headington House, nicknamed 'Government House' by Berlin's more left-wing friends, and there they lived and entertained—or, as the same friends had it, held court—for the next forty years. Although he left marriage late, Berlin never ceased to recommend the married condition, and his happiness was a persuasive advertisement for what he preached.

In 1957 he was elected to the Chichele Professorship of Social and Political Theory. The next twenty years were the high tide of Berlin's career. He was elected to the British Academy in the same year, was Vice-President from 1959 to 1961, and President from 1974 to 1978; he was a member of the Board of Directors of the Royal Opera House, Covent Garden, from 1954 to 1965, and again from 1974 to 1987, and a Trustee of the National Gallery from 1975 to 1985. He had received the CBE for his wartime service in 1946, was knighted in 1957, and awarded the Order of Merit in 1971. These positions and honours, more than enough for most people, do not capture the richness of Berlin's existence, nor his impact on British, American and Israeli social and cultural life. He was in constant demand as a lecturer; and he gave dazzling performances in settings obscure and famous. He described himself in self-deprecating terms as an intellectual taxi-cab: when he was hailed, he went. Yet, even though he was a figure who seemed more at home in the streets of Jerusalem and New York than in the English countryside, he found Oxford indispensable, and still resisted the urgings of Israeli or American friends who thought he should abandon his phlegmatic and slow-moving English university for more adrenalin-charged environments. They failed to see that Berlin was not the cosmopolitan figure they thought; his view was that most of us need a base in some particular place and attachments to particular persons and opinions if we are to understand other places, persons, and opinions. Perhaps he was conscious of the insult of 'rootless cosmopolitan' that was the commonplace of Soviet anti-Semitism; at all events, it was a rooted cosmopolitanism that he espoused.

Berlin's loyalty to Britain needed little theoretical explanation. He had arrived as a small boy; Britain was tolerant and friendly; and it was full of people for whom he felt affection. Although he was instantly at home in New York, or Washington, or Cambridge, Massachusetts, he had no reason to emigrate to places that he could visit as often as he liked without revising his political and personal allegiances. If it was a matter of sheer pleasure, he preferred Italy to any other destination. He and Aline built a house overlooking Portofino, and from there he explored far and wide, frequently in search of half-forgotten *bel canto* operas that were being revived in out of the way places.

In 1966, he became President of Wolfson College. Under the name of Iffley College, this had been a new and under-financed graduate college, created to provide a collegiate base for lecturers, mostly scientists, who had no collegiate attachment, and to provide a community for graduate students who had hitherto been neglected in Oxford. The Ford Foundation and the Wolfson Foundation provided an endowment for the college. It was renamed Wolfson College in acknowledgement of the generosity of Sir Isaac Wolfson's foundation. Berlin toyed with the thought that 'St Isaac's' might be apt, but only in private. With these resources, he secured from the architectural practice of Powell and Moya one of their best large-scale developments, a set of unflinchingly modern collegiate buildings running gently down to the River Cherwell, whose white concrete and granite starkness was not softened but elegantly heightened by the lushness of the gardens and riverside.

Berlin was a very successful founding president, but he had never been enthusiastic about presiding over an established collegiate institution. He was an inventor rather than a manager. Nor did he expect to feel at home in the institution he had created. Berlin wanted Wolfson College to be family-friendly; but All Souls and New College had not provided much training for a world in which married graduate students took this to mean that they should bring their babies to dinner in college. Berlin retired from Wolfson College in 1975, and returned to All Souls as a Distinguished Fellow.

He remained a considerable intellectual figure. His years at Wolfson coincided with the most contentious period of British and American post-war politics. The Vietnam War, and the upheavals of 1968 in France,

Germany, Czechoslavakia and the United States, raised questions about the prospects of liberal politics. Berlin's inaugural lecture as Chichele Professor, 'Two Concepts of Liberty', was second in fame only to *The Hedgehog and the Fox*, and came to occupy a position in late twentieth-century liberalism like Mill's essay *On Liberty* a hundred years earlier. Its ambiguities and unclarities have been explored for half a century, but its simple assertion of the priority of 'negative liberty'—the right to be left alone—over other goals—including those summed up as 'positive liberty'—was irresistible to most and intolerable to many. Written when admirers of the Soviet Union were still insisting that it had achieved a higher form of liberty than the decadent West, 'Two Concepts of Liberty' was seized on by the critics of Soviet Communism, and inevitably became entangled in the arguments between Cold War liberals and their liberal and socialist critics.

Berlin's liberalism remains difficult to characterise. There is a tension at its heart that Berlin never quite addressed. He famously held two views. The first was his pluralism: that the ends of human existence are many not one, they conflict with one another, and that there is no one best life, either for an individual—who must live one only of the possible lives that might suit her or him—or for whole societies—each of which holds a particular set of cultural, social, political, moral, or religious allegiances which bring with them gains and losses peculiar to them. This insistence on the plurality of goods was neither relativism nor scepticism, neither the view that what is good depends on who and where you are, nor the view that there are no real goods or bads. Berlin thought there was a plurality of genuine goods. Yet he also held a second view, that liberty took priority over all other values. On the face of it, this combination is incoherent. If there is no rationally defensible hierarchy of values, liberty cannot be at its summit. There are many ways of softening the conflict between Berlin's liberalism and his pluralism; none is so obviously right that one can assume that it must be what he really thought.

Berlin's liberalism was not in the ordinary sense political. In party terms, it was consistent with voting for any of the main parties in British politics, and implied an allegiance to none of them in particular; in fact, he held moderate Labour views in the 1940s and became more sceptical about social reform as he aged. His liberalism was the defence of a set of cultural and psychological attachments rather than the defence of a particular set of political and legal arrangements. Like the romantics that he invoked in his Mellon Lectures on *The Roots of Romanticism* in 1965, Berlin saw human beings as always unfinished creatures capable of new and unpredictable feats of invention. Like the romantics, he thought it was impossible to write history from the detached perspective appropriate to physics or chemistry, and that it was absurd to pretend to do so. History was not a scientific experiment but a moral drama. The main models for Berlin's literary, cultural, and philosophical engagements were Russian: Belinsky, Herzen, and Turgenev in particular. Berlin translated Turgenev's *First Love* as early as 1950, and twenty years later devoted his Romanes Lecture of 1970 to Turgenev's *Fathers and Sons*.

It was an extraordinarily apt choice. By this time Berlin closely identified with Turgenev. Turgenev sympathised with the young radicals of the 1870s while thinking they were intolerably crude and fanatical; Berlin felt the same about their successors of the 1960s. Turgenev feared that his scepticism and caution in political matters might be mere cowardice; so did Berlin. Such anxieties were heightened by the political quarrels of the 1960s, when Berlin's many American friends took violently opposed sides on the Vietnam War and all expected him to side with them. Berlin had no qualms about describing himself as a 'Cold War Liberal', inasmuch as he had no doubt that the United States and what it represented were worth defending against the threat posed by the Soviet Union. His doubts about the Vietnam War were not high-principled; as a matter of prudence, he was far from certain that American foreign policy was well-advised.

Berlin's talent for friendship means that a roll-call of those who thought of themselves as his good friends would embrace most of the musical world in Europe and the United States, just as it would embrace social and political theorists, philanthropists, journalists, diplomats and politicians. Their affection for him is not surprising; their admiration for him is in some respects more so. Berlin's passion for music was unaccompanied by any technical proficiency; he could not play an instrument, and could not read a score. He was, nonetheless, a friend of Stravinsky, and later a close friend of Alfred Brendel, who said that Berlin was a uniquely illuminating commentator on his performances. He had discussed music endlessly with Theodore Adorno before the war, and his first published essays were on musical performances. He often said that he could not imagine a world without music.

As in many other areas, his intuitive sense of the most important issue at stake was uncanny. He had, like anyone else, blind spots and antipathies; he did not care for Wagner, and disliked the cruelty that lurks in *Turandot* and *Tosca* The operas of Mozart and Italian opera from Bellini to Verdi were where his affections lay, rather in the way his non-operatic passions led him to Mozart and Schubert. The powerful feelings that music provoked made him a very influential Trustee of the Royal Opera House at Covent Garden. His passion was above all for the music; *prima la musica* was his operating principle, though it took exceptional performances to make him forgive cheap or tawdry productions. One achievement was to secure the services of Sir Georg Solti as musical director at Covent Garden. As a Trustee of the National Gallery, he was equally invaluable. When the controversial Sainsbury Wing was being built, he played a vital role in soothing the bruised feelings of the Trustees on the one side, and of their distinguished architect, Robert Venturi, on the other. Characteristically, what enabled him to do this was his discovery that the architect's wife was a Baltic Jew like himself. And he was an impressively fearless President of the British Academy; his intellectual distinction, and his years of mingling with politicians, senior civil servants, and the rich and famous in the worlds of arts and letters, gave him a unique immunity against whatever governments and administrators might try to impose.

It is more puzzling that Berlin was admired by historians and sociologists to whom his unconcern for minute factual detail would, on the face of it, have not endeared him; but only a very few of them could bring themselves to complain that his broad-brush characterisations of movements of ideas in European history omitted much and misrepresented a good deal. The obvious explanation is that even where one might on third or fourth reading come to think Berlin's characterisation of a thinker or a thought was seriously askew, readers were grateful for the stimulus provided by Berlin's fertile imagination. He started hares, flushed the historical coverts for overlooked quarry, and discovered strange, neglected species. By the same token, his success as a college president and his membership of so many governing bodies and committees might seem slightly surprising. He was an enthusiastic conspirator, and enjoyed getting his favoured candidates into positions for which they were not always entirely suited, but he was not one of nature's civil servants.

He did not need to be, since those who were were sufficiently enchanted to carry out his plans. The same qualities kept him on good terms with the publishers who despaired of the books they had been promised, and the editors who got corrections to their proofs long after the last possible moment. This did not go along with a wholly relaxed attitude to his work. His capacity for tinkering with the wording of his text went well beyond the point of diminishing returns, and his self-deprecating estimate of his own abilities did not extend to an equal tolerance of criticism from others. He was notably thin-skinned. It must be said in mitigation that his critics were rarely very friendly; they were made fiercer by Berlin's own eminence and because political allegiances were as much at stake as academic reputations. Berlin died in Oxford on 5 November 1997. Although he was in his late eighties and had been ill for several months, he left a hole in many lives that the years since have not filled.

ALAN RYAN
Fellow of the Academy

Note. Portions of this memoir have been taken from my entry on Isaiah Berlin in the *Oxford Dictionary of National Biography*, 60 vols. (Oxford, 2004), 5, 402–8 and my essay, 'Isaiah Berlin: Political Science and Liberal Culture', *Annual Review of Political Science*, 2 (1999), 345–62. I am grateful to Lawrence Goldman and Nelson Polsby respectively for their kind permission.

CHRISTOPHER HILL

John Edward Christopher Hill
1912–2003

CHRISTOPHER HILL was a great historian. People who question this can point to his apparent limitations. Nearly all his huge output was on the seventeenth-century 'English Revolution' and its origins. He seldom used manuscript records or original letters. He did not write much straight narrative. He said little about art or music or agriculture to add to his huge knowledge of literature. More seriously it was claimed that his Marxism, even when mellowed, led him to ignore evidence that did not support it. The 'bourgeois revolution' was a theme he never quite discarded but its meaning changed uneasily. None of this, even so far as it was valid, diminished his great achievement—to show, largely from one period and country, the role of historical studies in the sum of human knowledge. In at least twenty books and innumerable articles he made two vital additions to the old accounts of his chosen time: the impact of popular movements and the immense range of ideas written and spoken. No seventeenth-century author escaped him. No group and no person was insignificant. His regular technique was to combine close study of an individual, great or obscure, with a forthright account of the social and economic setting. His style was lucid, uncomplicated, enthusiastic. He showed that it was possible for a great historian to have a most pleasing personality, generous and tolerant, warm and humorous. Belief in equality was as essential in his life as in his scholarship even when he rose to a position of power.

John Edward Christopher Hill was born near York on 6 February 1912. His father, Edward Harold Hill, was a prosperous solicitor and a devout Wesleyan Methodist. He is not remembered as forbidding or

Proceedings of the British Academy, **130**, 23–49. © The British Academy 2005.

severe, rather as 'shy and reserved'. He had one great enjoyment—
cycling. Christopher's mother, Janet Augusta Hill, was more relaxed and
lively. A great-uncle, David Hill, had been a well-known missionary in
China. Together the Hill parents were 'kindly, genial, hospitable and
benevolent'. Their life was simple but far from austere. They had a large,
mostly late Victorian, house staffed by a gardener, a cook and a live-in
maid. There was a large library. Its three or four thousand books included
'most of the classics of history, English and philosophy'. Christopher had
unrestricted access to it, though bible-reading was of course compulsory.
On Sundays life became strictly regulated. The whole family twice rode
their bicycles to the Centenary Chapel in York and afterwards discussed
the sermons together. Occasionally Christopher had to follow his father's
example in cycling round the villages delivering leaflets and collecting
money. Methodism in practice took the form mainly of devotion to hard
work and personal morality. Drink and any hint of sexual interest outside
marriage were sin. A misdeed by Christopher after his first term at Oxford
was to take a girl to the theatre. She was his sister, but that made it worse.
Their father was aghast, though there were 'tense silences rather than
shouted anger'.[1]

St Peter's School in York, where Christopher was first a day-scholar
and later a boarder, evidently developed and recognised his brilliance. He
might well have gone, as several of the family had, to Cambridge. Two
Balliol history tutors, Vivian Galbraith and Kenneth Bell, were so
impressed by reports of his quality that they drove to York to persuade
his parents that Balliol must have him. By his own account he did not feel
at all like a star applicant. He was 'a very shy, callow and unsophisticated
boy' who after his interview sat despondently in a cold Balliol room feeling that he had failed. But two tutors 'burst in unannounced' and staged
an argument between themselves in the hope of provoking him to join in.
'What good', said Galbraith, 'ever came out of the Church of England?'
Hill, in a thin small voice, at last intervened with one word: 'Swift'. He
was led to 'improvise a defence of Swift'.[2] Any lingering doubts disappeared: Hill was awarded the main entrance scholarship. That was in

[1] Penelope Corfield, '"We are all one in the Eyes of the Lord": Christopher Hill and the
Historical Meanings of Radical Religion', *History Workshop Journal*, 58 (Autumn 2004),
113–15. Further information on Hill's early life has been generously supplied by Professor
Corfield and her mother, Christopher's younger sister. See also Samuel H. Beer in Donald
Pennington and Keith Thomas (eds.), *Puritans and Revolutionaries* (Oxford, 1978), pp. 1–4.
[2] Christopher Hill, 'Historic Passions: a First-Class Performer', *History Workshop Journal*, 42
(1996), 207–9.

December 1930 and as the academic year would not begin until October there were months to wait. It was probably then that he had a long visit to Freiburg. This was his first escape from the parental home—though his mother went out to see him—and he must have made friends whose opinions were very different from those he had met in the Methodist chapel or the conservative school.

Hill's undergraduate career was as distinguished as expected. Vivian Galbraith was the tutor who appreciated 'how bored I was by the way some parts of history were being taught' and encouraged him 'to combine English literature and history'. He won the University's Lothian Prize with an essay not on his future field but on the French Jesuits of Port Royal. Some of his contemporaries remembered him for a different reason: he scored a decisive try that won the rugby cup for Balliol. ('Heartiness', he once remarked, 'has always been a skeleton in my cupboard.') His brilliant first-class degree was followed by a Goldsmiths' Senior Studentship and, in November 1934, a fellowship at All Souls. Its residence requirements were lax and with the guidance of another Balliol tutor, Humphrey Sumner, Hill decided on a prolonged visit to Russia. He returned with a critical admiration for the Soviet system, a fluent knowledge of Russian and a grasp of Russian historical scholarship that few western academics could have claimed.

Conversion to Marxism was not a sudden event. Early in his undergraduate career he had to admit to his parents that he was now an agnostic, causing them inescapable distress. He was not exceptional in this. Raphael Samuel found other British Marxists, including E. P. Thompson, with a Methodist education. The non-conformist strand in British socialism could be traced back to its earliest days. A very different writer, D. H. Lawrence, described in 1931 how being soaked in the Bible from infancy had made him, like many of his generation, dislike and resent it.[3] Hill did not openly resent. How completely he rejected his Methodist past is a question hidden in the rest of his life. In 1965 his *Intellectual Origins of the English Revolution* was dedicated to T. S. Gregory, acknowledging 'a thirty-five year old debt which can never be repaid'. Gregory had been a fiery Methodist preacher in Yorkshire and was, Hill wrote, the first person who showed him that 'all accepted truths, just because they are accepted, tend to become lies'. Gregory became a Roman Catholic, Hill a Marxist. Asking Hill about the origins of his Marxism allowed him to

---

[3] Raphael Samuel, 'The British Marxist Historians', *New Left Review*, 120 (1980), 41–5. D. H. Lawrence, *Apocalypse* (London, 1931), p. 3.

enjoy giving typically enigmatic replies, such as 'through reading the metaphysical poets'.[4] He certainly read far more widely than most undergraduates. G. D. H. Cole's Left Book Club discussion group put him in touch with the socialist writing of the 1930s. A. D. Lindsay as Master, a Scottish Calvinist and one-time member of the Independent Labour Party, was not then hostile to extreme opinions. But Hill, with his career still uncertain, did not assert his politics too forcibly. During his undergraduate years he joined the Communist Party. There was nothing deeply secret about that. Denis Healey, briefly a member himself, reckoned that by 1939 there were about two hundred undergraduate members in Oxford. 'Not many outstanding undergraduates on the left did not join the Communist Party.' Many more belonged to the predominantly Marxist Labour Club.[5]

Hill could perhaps, on his return from Russia, have found a lasting Oxford fellowship; but Maurice Powicke, after many years at Manchester, recommended a spell at a provincial university. Accordingly in 1936 Hill became an assistant lecturer at Cardiff. Not all his Welsh superiors welcomed the appointment of this product of Balliol and All Souls, especially when he developed a more informal relationship with students than was customary. His lectures on the Reformation were noticeably lacking in Christian belief. Instead of attending chapel, he addressed meetings of the Left Book Club. His application to join the International Brigade fighting in the Spanish Civil War was rejected; but he devoted great energy to helping Basque refugees, even inviting some to York. He lodged on a housing estate with a family reputed to be communist. Gradually his success in teaching and his tactful charm broke down the suspicions. Dorothy Marshall and eventually the Principal, Sir Frederick Rees, were among those who saw him as an outstanding member of the academic community.[6]

In 1938 Balliol was able to bring Hill back as fellow and tutor in history. For the next two years he was, with Richard Southern, Humphrey Sumner, Kenneth Bell and A. B. Rodger, one of an aptly varied group of Modern History teachers. His published work was not at first extensive. Two articles appeared in his first year. 'The 250th anniversary of the "Glorious Revolution"' demolished the accepted idea that 1688 was the great turning-point in English history, of which the Civil War and

---

[4] Hill, *Intellectual Origins of the English Revolution* (Oxford, 1965), p. ix; Penelope Corfield, *History Workshop Journal*, 58, 116.

[5] Denis Healey, *The Time of My Life* (London, 1989), p. 36 in Penguin edn.

[6] Gwendolyn B. Whale in Pennington and Thomas (eds.), *Puritans and Revolutionaries*, pp. 4–6.

Interregnum were unsuccessful precursors. The article would have made excellent reading for undergraduates: but it was in the *Communist International*, 16 (November 1938) under the pseudonym C. E. Gore. Rodney Hilton later recognised in it the characteristics of future Hill writing: it was 'incisive, witty, densely packed with suggestive lines of thought . . . and refreshingly free from jargon'.[7] Then there came a contribution to the *Economic History Review*, a periodical that was safely academic but more enterprising then than later. Under the title 'Soviet Interpretations of the English Interregnum', Hill was able to introduce in a detached form what became some essentials of his own view. Soviet historians had the advantage of familiarity with a social order in some ways like that of seventeenth-century England. Most saw the civil war as a conflict of classes. The old landed aristocracy were in possession; attack came from 'the bourgeoisie' plus the 'progressive country gentry' behind whom stood a peasantry and in London the small masters. The later split between presbyterians and independents was a struggle between commercial and industrial capital. The thorough research of Arkhangelsky led to a less crude analysis that found possession and exploitation of the land behind each of the conflicts.[8]

In June 1940 Hill entered the army. According to an unconfirmed report his nominal attachment to the Field Security Police concealed a scheme to include him in an abortive plan to drop agents into the Baltic states. In 1942, having reached the rank of Major, he was seconded to the research department of the Foreign Office and soon transferred to the Northern Department that handled relations with the USSR. In May 1944 the Foreign Office set up a not very successful Committee on Russian Studies that was to consider the facilities for studying every aspect of Russian culture and institutions. Hill became secretary of one of its sub-committees, on teaching facilities. Forty years later his work at the Foreign Office was the subject of a section in the book by Anthony Glees, *Secrets of the Service*. It suggested, with few unqualified factual allegations, that Hill had concealed his membership of the Communist Party (though the Foreign Office and Intelligence authorities can hardly have been so stupid as not to know this) and had used his position to further his own friendly relationships with Russia. The story, with its numerous obvious errors, was comprehensively demolished by John Saville in

---

[7] Pennington and Thomas (eds.), *Puritans and Revolutionaries*, pp. 6–7.
[8] Hill, 'Soviet Interpretations of the English Interregnum', *Economic History Review*, 8, (1938), 159–67.

his book *The Politics of Continuity*. By using documents released in the Public Record Office, Saville was able to show how Hill, chosen for his knowledge of Russian language and society, held a valuable but not vitally important position in the Foreign Office. Despite all this, Glees was the main source of the absurd stories that were widely circulated as soon as Hill died that he had been a 'spy' or 'mole'.[9]

In 1940 the name of Christopher Hill first became known for a small book. *The English Revolution 1640* (a date chosen for the tercentenary rather than any crucial significance) was not at first intended for a large readership. Hill's seventy-page work was followed by shorter essays by Edgell Rickword and Margaret James.[10] He described it in later reprints as 'a first approximation . . . with all its crudities and oversimplifications'. It was, he explained in 1980, 'written very fast and in a good deal of anger' and aimed to be 'rather provocative'. It was to be 'my last will and testament' since he was convinced that he was about to be killed in the war.[11] Later editions explained how the words 'feudal' and 'progressive' were used in a Marxist sense. They did not explain the word that was to bring endless trouble in years to come—'bourgeoisie'. The wars and interregnum were 'the English bourgeois revolution' but it could not be shown that a simply identifiable class was responsible for it. 'The merchant class' was all-important; but 'England was still ruled by landlords'. The 'capitalist farmers and progressive landowners' had to be treated as part of the bourgeoisie. A new class of 'petty bourgeoisie'—peasants, artisans and journeymen—had interests temporarily identical with those of the capitalist merchants and farmers. This complex class struggle was not liked by Stalinists; for others who had known only the cavalier and roundhead stories of the Civil War it was a revelation. Adam Phillips, when he was sixteen and a 'wishy-washy royalist' found it in a second-hand bookshop. He had, he wrote, discovered 'a new country in a country I knew. . . . It fascinated me without effort.'[12] For most readers it was not Marxist theory that mattered. The sections on 'the economic background' and 'the political background' formed more than half the book.

---

[9] John Saville, *The Politics of Continuity. British Foreign Policy and the Labour Government 1945–6* (London, 1993), pp. 212–17 and notes on pp. 265–5. A. Glees, *Secrets of the Service* (London, 1987), pp. 279–88. Typical of the 'spy' stories is Ian Cobain in *The Times*, 5 Mar. 2003.
[10] Christopher Hill (ed.), *The English Revolution, 1640* (London, 1940), Hill's own essay was often reprinted and translated separately.
[11] Hill, *The English Revolution, 1640* (3rd edn., London, 1955), pp. 4–5.
[12] Adam Phillips, 'Historic Passions: Revolutions and Rebellions', *History Workshop Journal*, 39 (1995), 219–23 at 220.

They covered the whole Tudor and early Stuart period, condemning the orthodox accounts and raising questions 'not usually very satisfactorily answered in the text-books'. One of them was whether the events had 'any significance for us at the present day'. Many readers saw that they had. The rest of the war naturally produced little under Hill's name; but an approved booklet *The Two Commonwealths: the Soviets and Ourselves* (1945) was by the pseudonymous K. E. Holme.

In 1945 Hill was back at Balliol. His success as a tutor did not come from assertions or provocations. Tutorials were cheerful rather than formidable occasions. He could seem interested even in the most tedious essays and he would rather have an argument between a pair of pupils than one with him. (A rare exception was when, it was reported, a monstrous misstatement made him fling up his arms with such horror that he fell backwards off his oddly-shaped chair.) Of the many pupils who went on to academic careers only one or two were lifelong Marxists. It was neither dogma nor scholarly learning that he sought to convey but enthusiasm. He was the most accessible of the fellows, able to talk to undergraduates and postgraduates as friends. In the later 1940s he was, as he put it, 'fairly politically active in the Communist Party', writing 'a lot of more or less hack party stuff'.[13] Some articles on Stalin are now, fortunately, hard to find. At the same time he was beginning the vast accumulation of notes on which his later work was based. Hugh Stretton described how the restricted supply of paper was cut into small squares on which summaries and quotations were recorded in a very small hand even more illegible than his correspondence. The margins and endpapers of the books he acquired were filled in the same way.[14] One work, *Lenin and the Russian Revolution* (1947) in the 'Teach Yourself History' series made some use of his familiarity with Russian sources. It seems an unexpected and fairly subdued item in the Hill bibliography; but it produced a little welcome money.

There were many other activities. Overcoming a mild stammer, Hill became a much-appreciated lecturer both for the university and for the wider audiences he preferred, such as the WEA and the Historical Association. Occasional essays appeared in such periodicals as *The Communist Review, Science and Society* and *The Modern Quarterly*. But the body at

[13] Geoff Eley and William Hunt (eds.), *Reviving the English Revolution: Reflections and Elaborations on the Work of Christopher Hill* (London, 1988), p. 100.
[14] Pennington and Thomas (eds.), *Puritans and Revolutionaries*, p. 13.

the centre of his Marxist life down to 1956 was the Communist Historians' Group.[15] Its origins can be traced back to discussions of A. L. Morton's *People's History of England* (1938) that encouraged the writing of *The English Revolution 1640*. Hill, Morton and Dona Torr were the natural leaders of the informal group. They were soon joined by John Saville, Jack Lindsay, Eric Hobsbawm, Gordon Leff, the young Raphael Samuel and several teachers. Hobsbawm describes meetings at Marx House, Clerkenwell, with its 'physical austerity, intellectual excitement, political passion and friendship'. Hill, unlike any of the others, was able to report discussions in the Soviet Academy of Science, and produced 'Nine Theses on Absolutism'.[16] Ambitious plans for a many-volumed collection of documents covering the whole of British people's history were not completed. Dona Torr, whom Hill regarded as one of the main influences on his development, was to be the editor. One of the four volumes that appeared in 1948–9 was by the unlikely collaboration of Christopher Hill and Edmund Dell, *The Good Old Cause*, with the subtitle *The English Revolution of 1640–60, its Causes, Course and Consequences*. (Dell soon departed to begin the career that made him a right-wing Labour minister.) There was a simple answer to complaints that this was selective evidence: it was meant to be. The purpose was to reproduce 'some of the evidence on which *The English Revolution 1640* had been based, showing 'how one social class was driven from power by another' and an appropriate form of state power replaced the old.[17]

By 1952 the Group had become a fully developed organisation, supported by the Party but allowed to debate freely. Recruits included Edward and Dorothy Thompson, who stayed on the fringe, George Rudé, Victor Kiernan (who was sharply critical of orthodox Marxism) and Rodney Hilton. There was a committee, a secretary, and even some local branches. Large weekend conferences at Netherwood House in Sussex brought active and less active members together. One of these in July 1954, was devoted to the scheme for a large-scale history of British capitalism. A cyclostyled *Local History Bulletin*, later *Our History*, appeared

[15] Accounts of the Group include Eric Hobsbawm, 'The Historians' Group of the Communist Party' in Maurice Cornforth (ed.), *Rebels and their Causes: Essays in Honour of A. L. Morton* (London, 1973) and Eric Hobsbawm, *Interesting Times: a Twentieth-Century Life* (London, 2002), ch. 12 and notes; A. L. MacLachlan, *The Rise and Fall of Revolutionary England* (London, 1996) pp. 116–21; John Saville, *Memoirs from the Left* (London, 2003), pp. 86–9. A good summary of Hill's own comments on the Group is in the interview with Lee Humber and John Rees, 'The Good Old Cause', *International Socialism*, 56 (London, 1992), 131–3.

[16] MacLachlan, *Rise and Fall of Revolutionary England*, p. 116.

[17] Hill and Dell, *The Good Old Cause* (London, 1949), pp. 19–20.

rather uneasily. But the most successful activities were in the period sections. Of these the one on the sixteenth and seventeenth centuries dominated by Hill was outstanding. He recalled the discussions as 'some of the most stimulating experiences I've ever had'. Hobsbawm called the Group 'a continuous Marxist seminar'. Dorothy Thompson, on the other hand, felt that the picture of great minds discussing great thoughts was a myth.[18] Certainly there was tension in the Group, which tended to be between the academics and those led by Harry Pollitt who saw it as a means of celebrating the glory of the Party. Hill's view was clear: the Group would not advocate any crude class interpretation but would encourage debate between non-Marxists and every variety of Marxist. He was even able to introduce an interest in literature. In 1954 the Soviet Academy of Sciences invited Hill and three other historians to Moscow, where their high-powered entertainment was an embarrassment in the 'visibly impoverished country'. There were splendid parties but no serious discussion. They returned depressed.[19]

For one lasting achievement Marxist historians, though not the Party or the Group, were largely responsible. *Past and Present* began in 1952. It was to be a journal where Marxist and non-Marxist historians would share a common outlook. It would have no narrow academic monographs: articles would draw on every place and period and would be in plain English that the non-specialist could understand. The Introduction to the first number quoted a fourteenth-century Arab scholar, Ibn Khaldun: history is 'the record of human society or world civilisation . . . and of all the transformations that society undergoes'. The editor, John Morris, was to be completely independent, though Hill, who at first doubted whether such a publication could survive, joined an 'editorial board' including Rodney Hilton, and, as assistant editor, Eric Hobsbawm. It was hard at first to persuade non-Marxists that it was respectable to write for *Past and Present* and some who had joined the board soon left. The formation of a 'Past and Present Society' with Hill as president helped to extend the list of two hundred subscribers. Hill's own contributions began with his article on 'Puritans and the Poor' and later included occasional debates. The controversies on 'science and society' in 1964–5 and on 'parliament and people' in 1982–3 showed his ability to mix powerful argument with courteous and sometimes ironical

[18] Information on the Group kindly supplied by Dorothy Thompson.
[19] Hobsbawm, *Interesting Times*, p. 97.

readiness to agree as far as he could.[20] From 1958 distinguished historians not of the left, such as Lawrence Stone, Keith Thomas and Joan Thirsk, began to serve on the editorial board. When the hundredth number appeared in 1983 *Past and Present* had won an international status as the liveliest of all English historical journals.[21]

The years 1956–7 were a crucial time in Hill's life. His marriage in 1944 to Inez Waugh had begun very happily but ended distressingly. In his second wife, Bridget Sutton, he now found the ideal partner who shared all his future career. Her optimism and outgoing cheerfulness must have been a salvation in every difficult time. Also in 1956 there appeared his first major book. *Economic Problems of the Church: from Archbishop Whitgift to the Long Parliament* was a title no one could complain of, though the Oxford University Press was a little dubious about publishing work by Hill. While keeping carefully to its theme, it intended to 'throw fresh light on the part played by religion in preparing for the seventeenth-century revolution'. There was no slogan-shouting here and the book was recognised as an academic triumph. After years of preparation it drew on probably a wider range of sources than his later books. The Historical Manuscripts Commission, record societies and county histories had been searched exhaustively. 'I have relied mainly', he explained, 'on printed sources, since my object was to cover as wide a field as possible. But there is room for far more thorough investigation' using the material buried in manuscripts. He kept carefully to the 'non-religious reasons' for the church's difficulties: class interests and capitalism were mentioned only casually. In perhaps a hint of his developing emphasis he noted that 'literary evidence, evidence of opinion has been used, though I hope with caution . . .'.[22] In the same year two essays showed how Hill's international reputation was growing. 'Die geselleschaftlichen und ökonomischen Folgen der Reformation in England' in *Beiträge zum neuen Geschichtsbild* (ed. F. Klein and J. Streisand) was revised in English in *Puritanism and Revolution* (1958). 'A propos d'un article récent sur Cromwell' was in *Annales E.S.C.*, 11 (The article was by Trevor-Roper.) There were the reviews too. Hill had hitherto reviewed occasionally, for publications ranging from the *English Historical Review* to the *Daily Worker*. Now he became a regular reviewer for, of all unlikely weeklies,

---

[20] *Past and Present*, numbers 27, 28, 29 (1964), 31, 32 (1965), 92 (1981), 98 (1983).

[21] *Past and Present*, number 1 (1952) i–iv; number 100 (1983), 3–28.

[22] Hill, *Economic Problems of the Church: from Archbishop Whitgift to the Long Parliament* (Oxford, 1956), pp. ix–xii.

the *Spectator*, which carried some twenty of his contributions in the first year. Perhaps it was a coincidence that the owner and editor, Ian Gilmour, was Hill's former pupil.

In the same short period Hill found himself at the centre of British communist politics, when the Historians' Group led the movement to end the Party's obedience to Moscow. As Eric Hobsbawm pointed out, they were 'the most consistently active and flourishing group of communist intellectuals'.[23] To accept uncritically Soviet suppressions and misstatements would be a betrayal of their principles as historians. For all western communists the problem of Stalin's USSR had grown more acute. What little information emerged on the atrocities could be dismissed as capitalist propaganda and the failures of the Soviet economy blamed on western hostility or natural causes. But the adulation of the dictator before and after his death could only be swallowed for the sake of 'unity'. Then, in February 1956, the twentieth congress of the Communist Party of the Soviet Union heard in a secret session Khrushchev's speech denouncing some of Stalin's abuses of power. It was soon published in the west; but the British Communist Party contrived almost to ignore it. The speech, and the beginnings of 'destalinisation' in Russia and the eastern bloc countries, confirmed what the British historians agreed was 'the most serious and critical situation the Party was in since its foundation'. Hill was now regarded as the most senior member of the Historians' Group. A junior member, Gordon Leff, remembered him as a guarantee against totalitarian attitudes, combining enlightened Marxism with tolerant liberalism. It was after discussion with Hill that Edward Thompson and John Saville inaugurated *The Reasoner*, at first typed and duplicated, demanding full debate within the Party. The national executive banned it. Its third number was almost complete when news came of the Soviet invasion of Hungary. Most of the historians signed a forthright letter of protest at the 'uncritical support given by the Party to the Soviet action'.[24] Protesters faced the choice between resigning (or being expelled) and hoping to reform the Party from within. Many resigned at once, others, including Thompson and Saville, in the next few months. The Party tried to appease the 'little band of bourgeois intellectuals' by permitting a Commission on Inner Party Democracy, with a safe majority supporting the official line. Hill led the opposition and presented to the Party Congress in the spring of 1957 what became known as the Minority

---

[23] Hobsbawm, 'The Historians' Group', p. 30.
[24] Hobsbawm, *Interesting Times*, p. 207. The main part of the letter is printed on p. 425.

34 *Donald Pennington*

Report. It was not until October 1994 that he revealed publicly his regret at Thompson's departure. In the *Times Higher Education Supplement* he suggested that without the resignations the outcome might have been different. The precipitate action of those who resigned had 'ensured that the Party would decline into insignificance'.[25] The Hills and Thompsons remained good friends. After the Congress Hill himself left the Party. Unlike some he never abandoned the principles he held when he joined.

In the following years Hill's prolific pattern of work was established— a major book every two or three years, a great variety of essays and a constant stream of reviews and lectures. During term teaching and friendship with pupils and colleagues left only some afternoons and some evenings for reading and writing. Yet he seldom seemed stressed or exhausted. The next book, *Puritanism and Revolution*, was a collection of essays written, according to the Preface, 'independently on various occasions during the past eighteen years'. The list of where they were originally published shows an impressive range of acceptability: *The English Historical Review* (1940), *The Modern Quarterly* (1946), *Philosophy for the Future* (New York, 1949), *Past and Present* (1952), the Japanese *Journal of Historical Studies* (1953), *History Today* (1953 and 1957), and the BBC Third Programme in 1956. Part One of *Puritanism and Revolution*, on 'Movements and Men', has the long article on the Norman Yoke—the belief that a golden age of equal prosperity existed before 1066—and the varied interpretations of this in the seventeenth, eighteenth and nineteenth centuries until it became 'a stick to beat the modern aristocracy with'. The article is reprinted from *Democracy and the Labour Movement: Essays in Honour of Dona Torr* (1954). In the second half of *Puritanism and Revolution* eight essays announced their method by a dual title on person and topic, such as 'Lord Clarendon and the Puritan Revolution', 'John Mason and the End of the World', 'James Harrington and the People'. 'The people of England', according to a typical Hill aside, was 'a subject one mentions with diffidence.' One of the best chapters, 'Society and Andrew Marvell', written originally in 1946, was an early exploration of the links between literature and society. Marvell's poetry was 'shot through with consciousness of a conflict . . . between the idea and the reality, which it is perhaps not too far-fetched to link up, very indirectly of course' (we can picture the wry smile behind that) 'with the social and political problems of his time'. A final essay on Richardson's *Clarissa*, 'one of the greatest of unread novels', is a proof from fiction of the need

---

[25] Hill, 'The Shock Tactician', *Times Higher Education Supplement*, 7 Oct. 1994.

to understand 'Puritan attitudes towards society, marriage and the individual conscience'.[26]

In 1962 Hill delivered the Ford Lectures. The invitation to do this is generally seen as the foremost distinction the University could confer on historians. *Intellectual Origins of the English Revolution* (Oxford, 1965) was an expanded version. 'I was', he admitted, 'advancing a thesis . . . I therefore picked up evidence which seemed to me to support my case' — a remark which later critics chose to apply unjustifiably to everything he wrote. 'Revolutions are not made without ideas'; but a body of thought 'takes on' when it meets the needs of significant social groups. He was not suggesting a direct relationship between London science and the parliamentary cause. 'Science' meant not just academic theory but the inventions and work of 'the industrious sort of people'. We might suggest 'very tentatively' a link between kinds of interest in science and degrees of political and social radicalism. Parliament 'was believed', for instance, to have support from most medical doctors.[27] The uncertainty was not to be taken too literally. No text could quite convey the moments of ironic humour and self-deprecation that enlivened the lectures.

There were two contrasting books in the early sixties. *The Century of Revolution, 1603–1714* (1961) was intended for sixth-form students, or those whose schools did not ban such a dangerous writer, as well as for a wide public. Its popularity grew and lasted: the latest reprint was in 2002. This was not an ordinary textbook. The narrative that introduced each of four chronological parts was short if not perfunctory. Then came chapters on economics, politics and the constitution—a separation he often deplored. Hidden in these were indications of Hill's modified outlook. Several of his own books were added to the reading-lists in later editions, but not (as A. L. Merson pointed out) *The English Revolution 1640*. 'Feudalism' and 'bourgeoisie' were terms still occasionally used, but cautiously. 'The division in England is not Third Estate versus gentry and peerage but country versus court.' Those excluded from economic privilege looked to parliament and common lawyers to help them to get it. The revolution eventually was 'incomplete'.[28]

Society and Puritanism in Pre-Revolutionary England (1964) confronted another dangerous word. It 'tries to suggest that there might be

[26] Hill, *Puritanism and Revolution: Studies in Interpretation of the English Revolution of the 17th Century* (London, 1958) pp. 26, 367.
[27] Hill, *Intellectual Origins of the English Revolution* (Oxford, 1965), pp. vii, 72, 119.
[28] A. L. Merson, 'Problems of the English Bourgeois Revolution', *Marxism Today*, Oct. 1963, 310–15; Hill, *The Century of Revolution, 1603–1714* (London, 1965), pp. 101 etc.

non-theological reasons for . . . being a Puritan'. The first chapter adds to the countless attempts to define the word. As a term of abuse 'Puritan' could be applied to almost anyone, or at least to any opponent of church or court. But there was 'a mainstream of puritan thought'. It was, as the abundant quotations showed, a living faith and a view of life 'deeply rooted in the English society of its day'. Much of the social content survived when Puritan ideals degenerated into hypocrisy. To appreciate this we must understand the needs, fears, hopes and aspirations of the godly artisans, merchants, yeomen, gentlemen, ministers and their wives.[29] The order in which the groups are listed may be significant: artisans, or the industrious sort of people, came first and are the subject of one of the best chapters. Some ministers kept their ideals; but the priesthood of all believers was ushering in a secular society. The parish was becoming part of the machinery of government rather than a purely church unit; but the household was becoming 'spiritualised', with its head taking on the authority of the priest.

In the years down to 1965 Hill's success as a Balliol tutor continued to grow. One of the pupils and later colleagues who admired him while holding opposite opinions, Maurice Keen, recalled the weekly evening parties. All historians were welcome. 'Christopher and Bridget, a barrel of beer and a large number of people' were always there. It meant that they did not think of him as 'someone on the other side of a barrier of status'.[30] Relations with other fellows were not always as easy as with junior members. Lord Lindsay, whom Hill greatly admired despite many disagreements, resigned as Master in 1949 and was succeeded by the 'stolid traditionalist' Sir David Keir. Almost all reforms of the College were blocked, Lindsay became Principal of the first post-war new university, Keele, where there were prospects of a broader curriculum and a less privileged intake than seemed likely to happen in Oxford. There was a distinct possibility that Hill might go to Keele. But he stayed, and his position in the Senior Common Room improved. To many he was 'the acceptable face of communism'. His unassuming friendliness and his advocacy of the practicable rather than the ideal were appreciated by both younger and older fellows. In 1965, with the retirement of Keir, there arose the possibility that Hill might become Master. It needed some shrewd campaigning before the formally unanimous vote was announced. A few old members, and some in other colleges, were

---

[29] Hill, *Society and Puritanism in Pre-Revolutionary England* (London, 1964), pp. 9, 29, 510.
[30] Pennington and Thomas (eds.), *Puritans and Revolutionaries*, p. 18.

shocked and some newspapers contrived to be alarmed that Oxford should appoint a supporter of the cold-war enemy to such a post. But it was soon apparent that Hill as Master would be a success. Richard Cobb, the only fellow who could rival Hill's scholarly output, enjoyed teasing him as 'Supergod' but was more explosive than others in combining opposition to some reforms with, he wrote, 'affection and respect'.

There were a few immediate indications of change. The new Master's first request was that he would continue to be known, except on the most formal occasions, as Christopher. He chose not to occupy the Master's lodging in College, releasing some rooms for undergraduate residence. He renounced the Master's right to admit some applicants without examination. He soon coped well with routine duties. Ceremonies were lightened by taking the pomp only half solemnly. He could produce whenever it was needed a witty and moderately tactful speech, usually with a few ironic ambiguities for those able to detect them. He nearly always accepted the occasional defeat in College Meetings, though he admitted that he liked a little intrigue now and then. Bigger developments would evidently be gradual. One of Hill's hopes was not in his time quite realised—to have a smaller proportion of entrants from public schools. He made a few unobtrusive visits to grammar schools himself and encouraged some fellows to do the same. He initiated a summer-school for underprivileged sixth-formers, with undergraduates as tutors and guides. (One was Howard Marks, with whom Hill kept in touch.) He upheld cautiously the campaign for the admission of women. 'Can Balliol afford not to admit women?' he wrote in his last annual Master's letter. A series of votes indicated that the College was in favour of this provided nothing was done yet. Female undergraduates first arrived in 1979.

One reform proved easy, Much of the work of the College Meeting was transferred to an Executive Committee on which there were to be undergraduate representatives (though for some purposes the committee met without them). Relations with undergraduate organisations required all Hill's diplomatic skill, especially in the peak years of student rebellion. Balliol had long been reputedly the most left-wing of colleges. Hill's instinctive sympathies were with the undergraduates against what they saw as tyrannical authority; but he accepted his duty to protect the status of the College. He presided equitably over the governing body in its exercise of disciplinary power, and accepted the penalties demanded by a majority of fellows. Afterwards he, or he and Bridget, might quietly help the victim.

The mastership made it even harder than before to understand how Hill could do more in a day than seemed humanly possible. The new burden might well have reduced his literary output; but the only hint of that was that he did not write quite as many reviews. He hardly ever seemed to be in a desperate hurry. College work still included a few tutorials; more afternoons and evenings had to be given up to committees. Somehow there was still time to mix on equal terms in the Senior Common Room, where his wit was sometimes ambiguous but rarely hurtful. There was nearly always time too to see the many people in and outside the College who wanted to talk to him. He often gave major lectures away from Oxford. The Riddell Memorial Lectures at the University of Newcastle upon Tyne became the book *Antichrist in Seventeenth-Century England* (Oxford, 1971). The Barnett Shine Foundation Lecture in the Economics Department of Queen Mary College, London, in 1974 on 'Irreligion in the "Puritan" Revolution' (with significant quotation marks in the title) found sources for a subject that usually 'we hear of only through the reports of its enemies'. The Hobhouse Memorial Lecture (1969) was on 'Reason and Reasonableness'.

An extraordinary range of collections and periodicals can be added to earlier lists. *The Baptist Quarterly*, *The Listener*, *Royal Society Notes and Records*, *The British Journal of Sociology*, *The Texas Quarterly*, the Italian *Historia* and the German *Studien über die Revolution* were a few of them. There was another textbook, *Reformation to Industrial Revolution: a Social and Economic History of Britain 1530–1780* (1967). *God's Englishman: Oliver Cromwell and the English Revolution* (1970) blended a fair amount of revolution into the biography. In these Hill, as Professor Corfield put it, 'quietly shifted his emphasis'. Without diminishing the Revolution he was seeing it 'not as the triumph of capitalism but as a triumph for the conditions that allowed capitalism to flourish'.[31] The outstanding work of the mastership period was *The World Turned Upside Down* (1972) with the subtitle *Radical Ideas during the English Revolution*. Many reviewers rated it as Hill's best book so far.[32] It had frequent reprints and translations and must be the only work of its kind to be made into a play, which the National Theatre performed. The book

[31] Penelope Corfield, *History Workshop Journal*, 58 (2004), 111–26. See also her article 'Il percorso intellettuale di Christopher Hill: dal protestantismo biblico al umanesimo marxista' ('Christopher Hill's Intellectual Trajectory: from Biblical Protestantism to Humanist Marxism'), trans. Paola Redalli, *Italia Contemporanea*, 232 (2003), 401–505.
[32] The book is studied 'in retrospect' by Barry Reay in Eley and Hunt (ed.) *Reviving the English Revolution*, pp. 53–72.

smoothly combines the favoured essay form with a full unity of theme. Three chapters are on the social background in which radical ideas developed. The focus was no longer on a bourgeoisie but on 'the mobile society of early capitalism . . . the crowds of masterless men, vagabonds and urban poor'. Some of the poor had been brought together in the armies, especially the New Model, some in the gathered churches that could now flourish. Theirs was to be a revolution within the revolution. Each of the subsequent chapters is an essay in itself, exploring the variety of radical ideas and people who expressed them. Hill does not add to the abundant studies of the Agitators but investigates 'something vaster if more inchoate', the multitude they hoped to lead. London is not the exclusive interest: almost every county appears somewhere in the book. In one region, the north and west, 'the dark corners of the land', some of the most revolutionary schemes begin. In towns remote from the south-east Ranters were most easily found. Fourteen specimens of northern and western radicals are listed. There are other beliefs too: astrology, magic, and alchemy contributed to the radical outlook. 'Base impudent kisses' have a chapter, as do other sins—and hell. At every opportunity Hill's most characteristic method takes over: generalisations are linked to individuals, some famous, others unknown to most of us.[33] An admirer who talked to Hill on long car journeys remarked that he discussed everyone he had written about as if they were his own friends.

There was one outstanding figure in *The World Turned Upside Down*. Gerrard Winstanley was Hill's lasting hero. He had written briefly about Winstanley in an introduction to a selection of the writings in 1944. In 1973 he brought out his own edition of the main works and in 1978 a *Past and Present Supplement* on 'The Religion of Gerrard Winstanley'. The unchanging belief of Winstanley in the equality of all mankind was also Hill's ideal. In the theological tracts Winstanley developed a solution to some problems of bible-centred Puritanism that had been touched on by other nearly-heretical writers: scriptural stories could be allegories or myths. God was within every man and woman. 'The ascension so called' was the rising of the spirit of the Father, which is pure reason. Clergy and the state church were barriers to accepting the God within us, barriers which governments for their own ends maintained. Secular ideas became more prominent in later Winstanley works than the purely theological.

[33] Ch. 9 includes sections on William Erbery, Abiezer Coppe, Lawrence Clarkson, Joseph Salmon, Jacob Bauthumley, Richard Coppin, George Foster, John Pordage and Thomas Webbe. Chs. 11 and 12 are on Samuel Fisher and John Warr.

He was 'groping his way towards a humanist and materialist philosophy'. *The Law of Freedom* in 1651 showed Winstanley as the 'true leveller'—a communist in the widest sense of the word. The Norman Yoke had meant the theft by landlords of the earth that had been and could be again a common treasury. But it was not enough to wait passively for the return of Christ. Action was needed; and action had been taken in the symbolic form of digging up the commons on St George's Hill. Now it was time to show Cromwell how 'true magistracy' could be compatible with liberty and equality. It involved some detailed plans of government that were bound to look like compromise. In a powerfully original appendix to *The World Turned Upside Down* Hill showed how Winstanley and Hobbes, 'two opposite poles', were both determined to 'penetrate the bedrock of politics' and grasped the same problems of authority.[34]

In 1974 appeared *Change and Continuity in Seventeenth-Century England*—'Old hat stuff', said Hill, 'not a proper book'. It was a further selection of essays written in the previous twelve years, including some of the best specimens of his work. Two chapters were on London and the outlying regions, first on Puritans in the north and west and second on an 'endearing' character, Arise Evans—a Welshman in London. Under 'Continuity in Change' there were studies of three groups attacked by radicals—the two universities, the Inns of Court and the medical profession. A section on social attitudes showed the alarm of men of property at the 'many-headed monster'. Each essay, incidentally, had like almost all Hill works, one or two delightfully apt quotations before the title. The book acquired unexpected notoriety, from an implacably hostile review. Professor J. H. Hexter of Yale was later described by a colleague as a 'rough tough wreckster'. His review of *Change and Continuity* was the occasion to attack Hill's whole historical method. After paying tribute to the 'simply astounding achievement', of his output and erudition, Hexter seized on the chapter 'Protestantism and the Rise of Capitalism'. Some arguable reviewer's points led to the fundamental accusations. Hill was a 'lumper' who put the past into boxes. He 'can be sure of arriving at any conclusion he aims at' and of finding evidence to support it. He 'could go on for ever writing about the relationship between Protestantism and capitalism . . . without for a moment feeling impelled to inquire whether any Protestant capitalist expressed any views relevant to

---

[34] 'The Religion of Gerrard Winstanley' is reprinted with additions in Hill, *Collected Essays*, 2 (London, 1986), 185–252. His writings on Winstanley also include 'Gerrard Winstanley and Freedom', in Hill, *A Nation of Change and Novelty* (London, 1990), pp. 114–32 and 'Gerrard Winstanley: The Law of Freedom', in Hill, *Liberty against the Law* (London, 1996), pp. 273–97.

the matter'. He had 'failed his colleagues'. The tone was so offensive that it brought protests from historians of many different opinions as well as a restrained reply from Hill that pointed out some of Hexter's own contradictions.[35] Years later an ageing Hexter was entertained by the Hills in Oxford. 'It was difficult to hate him', wrote Bridget. As it happened *Change and Continuity* contained a review by Hill as devastating as Hexter's. 'A One-class Society' was on a popular book by Peter Laslett, *The World We Have Lost* (1965) based on research by the Cambridge group for the History of Population and Social Structure. But Hill used specified points to destroy Laslett's picture of an ill-defined past and to show his sheer incompetence. One instance was his misuse of Parish Registers, with which Hill, said to neglect manuscript sources, was evidently well acquainted. Laslett had not read his sources 'with any comprehension' and had done a 'disastrous disservice'.[36] There was not much response to that.

Besides the disputes with historians, Hill's devotion to poetry had brought him into conflict with literary critics. The argument is well summarised by Margot Heinemann, a Marxist writer whose work Hill had for years admired. 'One of Hill's most important contributions', she wrote, 'was to free students and teachers from the restrictive view of seventeenth-century literature . . . based on T. S. Eliot and F. R. Leavis.' To study 'the words on the page' without enough investigation of the author, his readers and their social setting ignored the conflict in society that was 'the central context'.[37] One great event forgotten by many critics but stressed by Hill was the collapse of censorship which from 1641 made possible the huge increase in printed works. They could now be written in plain prose addressed to a popular audience. We might have heard more about the sudden appearance of newspapers; but perhaps they lacked the appeal of the introspective individual writer.

One figure above all others seemed ideally made for studies by Hill. Milton was 'the greatest English revolutionary who is also a poet, the greatest English poet who is also a revolutionary'. Hill, according to a typical aside, had been 'thinking about Milton off and on over a long period'. The thoughts had appeared in many of his books. *God's*

---

[35] J. H. Hexter, 'The Burden of Proof' in *Times Literary Supplement*, 24 Oct. 1975, reprinted in Hexter, *On Historians* (London, 1975). Replies by Hill in *TLS*, 7 Nov. 1975 and by others in *TLS*, 14 Nov. and 12 Dec. 1975.

[36] Hill, *Change and Continuity and Seventeenth-Century England* (London, 1975) ch. 9. See also 'Sex, Marriage and Parish Registers', in *Collected Essays*, 3 (London, 1986), 188–209.

[37] Margot Heinemann in Eley and Hunt (eds.), *Reviving the English Revolution*, pp. 74–9.

Englishman had cited the apparent allusions to Cromwell in *Samson Agonistes* as well as the warning, in 1655, that 'a stubborn and intractable despot' could turn his followers into new royalists.[38] Appendix 2 in *The World Turned Upside Down* had shown how Milton's radical intellectual convictions, such as his hatred of 'priests, an established church, forms, ceremonies and tithes', clashed with his 'patrician social prejudices'.[39] In 1977 *Milton and the English Revolution* appeared and brought Hill to the forefront of literary as well as historical controversies. Anyone who took seriously his sardonic claim to be 'only a historian' and that 'such expertise as I have is not literary'[40] would be disillusioned by his demolition here of hostile scholarly critics. Milton had been the subject of passionate literary disputes ever since Leavis in 1936 claimed to have dislodged him 'after two centuries with remarkably little fuss'. Now he had to be 'defended from his defenders'. The 'immensely productive Milton industry', particularly in the United States, had made him 'the poet of scholars and academic critics', though he was really the arch-enemy of academic pedantry.[41] Many of his underestimated qualities are discussed—such as his sense of humour and the romanticism that links him to Blake and Wordsworth. But the major theme is the effect on Milton of the English Revolution and radical ideas.

Hill is cautious in his assessments of Milton's relations with radicalism. He was not a Leveller, Ranter, Fifth Monarchist or Muggletonian but 'lived in a state of permanent dialogue' with radical views. How close he came to radicalism is a question treated here with carefully chosen words. The influences of the Revolution were 'much more radical than has been accepted'. A claim, which critics were quick to pounce on as lacking due evidence, was that Milton got ideas from talking to 'plebeian radical thinkers'.[42] (The 'persistent attempts' to get him into a pub—the Mermaid Tavern was just round the corner from where he grew up—seem a light-hearted extravagance.) Early enthusiasm for popular movements had led to bitter disillusionment in the post-war chaos. Even so in 1651 *The Defence of the People of England* had proved a 'fantastic success' in explaining the republican Commonwealth to the Europeans as well as the English. But the Revolution went wrong, betrayed by leaders who 'turned out to be avaricious and ambiguous, or hypocrites'. After the

---

[38] Hill, *Milton and the English Revolution* (London, 1977), pp. 4, 471; *God's Englishman*, p. 191.
[39] Hill, *The World Turned Upside Down*, pp. 321, 324.
[40] Quoted in Eley and Hunt (eds.) *Reviving the English Revolution*, p. 74
[41] Hill, *Milton*, p. 3.
[42] Hill, *Milton*, p. 4; B. Worden, 'Milton among the Radicals' in *Times Literary Suplement*, 2 Dec. 1977.

Restoration, when the three great poems were completed, the renewal of censorship made it necessary to bury topical comment in allegories. Hints of anti-trinitarianism and materialism were easy to find. Milton, it is constantly admitted, was uncertain and inconsistent and Hill admits that the political analogies might not always have been in the poet's mind.[43] But cumulative evidence upheld the arguments. The noble Cause, which was God's Cause, had failed and like the fall of Adam it was a moral failure. Pride and arrogance were vices of Satan—and of Cromwell. Many allusions were obviously to Milton's personal torments and determination. The biographical content of the book is a convincing demonstration of Hill's insistence that literature can only be understood by relating it to the writer's life. *Samson Agonistes* and *Paradise Regained* escaped from despair. There was hope of Salvation, not as a gift from Christ but from man's own effort. The struggle must go on, but longer, soberer, less exhilarating . . . '.[44] Disentangling analogies did not diminish Hill's appreciation of the style of the poems, liberated from the 'straitjacket of the rhymed couplet'.[45] With its reference to almost all Milton's works and 800 or so other sources the book would have been a lifetime's achievement for many scholars. For Hill it was one activity among many.

During the writing of *Milton* Hill was involved in the establishment of a journal, that brought his dual interests together. *Literature and History* first appeared in 1975. It did not aspire to the status of *Past and Present* but it attracted some eminent contributors. Hill was critical of its 'preoccupation with, and indulgence in, theory'; but in the following years he supplied fifty-four reviews and gave papers at two of its associated conferences.[46] In 1998 an issue on the seventeenth century was dedicated to him. A better-known periodical was *History Workshop Journal*, which first appeared in 1976. History Workshop had been founded at Ruskin College by Hill's former pupil Raphael Samuel in 1967. It persuaded students with little previous training to find and write small histories of ordinary individuals as well as studying popular movements in every period. It naturally had Hill's active approval. Sometimes he was able to join in workshop discussions as, more or less, a normal member of the group. The movement spread from Ruskin to local associations in England and abroad, holding regular conferences. The *Journal* broadened

---

[43] Hill, *Milton*, pp. 285–95, 331, 380.
[44] Hill, *Milton*, p. 390.
[45] Hill, *Milton*, p.404.
[46] *Literature and History* 3rd series, 13 no. 1, R. C. Richardson, 'Complementaries: Christopher and Bridget Hill and Literary History'.

its scope to include worldwide subjects. Three of Hill's contributions suggested its range. In 1980 'Defoe and Robinson Crusoe' showed, predictably, a thorough knowledge of the varied interpretations—including Marx's. In 1984 a reprinted lecture to one of the London workshops had a splendid Hill title: 'God and the English Revolution' and he reviewed a book by Alan Bray on 'Male Homosexuality in Seventeenth-Century England' that opened up 'quite a new subject in English social history'.[47]

Besides all this, Christopher and Bridget had been bringing up a family. There was a daughter, Fanny, from Christopher's first marriage. She died in 1986. The first child of the second marriage had been tragically killed in a road accident; but Andrew (born 1958) and Dinah (1960) were a lively and understanding pair. Each was later thanked for help with a book. An escape from immediate College tasks was the house the Hills acquired near Verteillac in Périgord. It did not have a telephone. It had a meadow, sometimes cut energetically by hand-mower. The popular Dordogne settlement area was well to the south. There in vacations country life, such as walks to the local bistro, with bar-football, or swimming in the River Dronne, was a total change from Oxford. Hospitality could be offered to many visitors. But at a prescribed time in the day or evening the study door would close and the typewriter would begin forthwith. There was no wasted time.

In 1978 Hill retired from the mastership of Balliol. He and Bridget left Oxford for a country home at Sibford Ferris, within easy reach of the Bodleian. Retirement for Hill was not the end of a career but the beginning of a further twenty years of high-powered work. He had been involved with the Open University from before it opened in 1969. Bridget had taught there and had been responsible for much of its development. A university open to all students, teaching by correspondence, radio, television and summer school and offering courses not restricted to a single conventional subject approached Hill's educational ideals. He accepted an appointment for two years as a professor. He led the planning and teaching of an inter-disciplinary course on seventeenth-century England that included science, art, philosophy and music as well as his own specialities. Holding together the experts in so many fields must have needed all his tact and tolerance. The course was an immediate success, with nearly 2,000 students a year. (Balliol had no more than twenty a year

[47] Hill, 'Defoe and Robinson Crusoe', *History Workshop Journal*, 10 (1980), 'God and the English Revolution', *History Workshop Journal*, 17 (1984), 'Male Homosexuality in 17th-Century England', *History Workshop Journal*, 18 (1984) reprinted in Hill, *Collected Essays*, 1. 105–30, 2. 321–42, 3. 226–35.

reading history.) One of the teachers who took part, Anne Laurence, described how he joined the rest of them in commenting on each other's draft material and was happy to rewrite his section on the historiography of the Civil War when it was thought too difficult. At the same time he was 'a consummate politician' well able to deal with committees and administrators. The course remained on the syllabus for eight years—a long time by Open University standards.[48]

The Hills now had more opportunity for overseas visits. North and South America, Australia, New Zealand and Japan were among the places where Christopher's lectures and informal discussions were great occasions. In 1981 he was for three months a visiting professor at the Humanities Research Centre of the Australian National University, Canberra. One lecture there was on Lodowick Muggleton, whose unfortunate name had, Hill admitted, led him to misplace the Muggletonians on the 'lunatic fringe' of seventeenth-century sects. He quickly recognised their place in the 'cultural underworld' and the lecture was reprinted, with other chapters by Barry Reay and William Lamont, in *The World of the Muggletonians* (1983), dedicated to the memory of the last Muggletonian, who died in 1979.

In 1984 there appeared *The Experience of Defeat*. 'Experience' suggested its emphasis on the individual rather than the movement. Hill had long accepted that the 'Puritan Revolution' ('a facile anachronism') had been defeated 'in a superficial sense'. Now he faced outright what the defeat of the radical revolution meant to those who suffered it. His purpose was to 'understand the elation of the fight and the desolation of defeat when it was realised that the world was not after all to be turned upside down'. The defeated were studied in groups—the 'first losers' in 1649–51, the second in 1653–60. William Erbury, William Sedgwick and Isaac Pennington were 'bewildernessed' into changes of allegiance. The two Pordages, Stubbes and Marvell were 'survivors' who adapted their radicalism to post-Restoration conditions. Even Cromwell experienced defeat, after the collapse of Barebones' Parliament. It had been seen in *God's Englishman* as the moment when 'his high hopes had gone and he became a tired, disillusioned old man'. (He was 54.) For nearly all these the defeat was that proclaimed by Milton, the failure of sinful man to uphold

[48] Anne Laurence, 'Christopher Hill at the Open University 1978–80' (typescript kindly supplied by Professor Laurence).

God's Cause. Harrington was silenced by defeat; but his followers modified his ideas into another cause that led to eighteen-century whiggery.[49]

Hill's position at the very height of academic success was now recognised everywhere. In 1985 he was back in Australia for a term at the University of Adelaide. There had also been three months at Rutgers University, New Jersey. In England he was giving generous time to lecturing. The Centre for Seventeenth-century Studies at Durham, the South Place Ethical Society, King Alfred's College, Winchester, and the Lancashire Polytechnic, Preston, had major lectures. Much as he disliked the national honours system, honorary degrees were an acceptable way of extending his academic contacts. He was given ceremonial doctorates by Hull, East Anglia, Glasgow, Exeter, Leicester, Sheffield, Bristol, York, the University of Wales, the Hungarian Academy of Sciences, the Academy of Sciences of the German Democratic Republic and the Sorbonne nouvelle. He had become a Fellow of the British Academy in 1965. He was glad to be made, like his father, a Freeman of York.

The Experience of Defeat might well have been the title of a last Hill work. Happily it was nothing of the kind. *A Turbulent and Seditious People: John Bunyan and his Church 1628–1688* (1988) was derived from another lecture series, the Sir D. Owen Evans Memorial Lectures at Aberystwyth. It won the W. H. Smith Award, for which neither Christopher Hill nor John Bunyan would seem likely candidates. But the book managed more smoothly than Cromwell or Milton to combine straightforward and fascinating biography with continuous discussion of, among other topics, the radical tradition and the moral and practical problems of life after the Restoration. It was also an opportunity to say still more about local history. Bunyan was 'the first major writer who was neither London based nor university educated'. The Bedford congregation of 'such as in those days did bear the name of puritans' has a big part in the story.[50]

One book had been overwhelmingly important to nearly every writer in the seventeenth century. The Bible, it might have been supposed, would be an essential subject of study for historians of the period. It had not been; and somehow *The English Bible and the Seventeenth-Century Revolution* (1993) seemed an unexpected Hill title. 'I have done the best I can', he remarked in the Preface, 'on the basis of many years of desultory

[49] Hill, *The Experience of Defeat* (London, 1984), pp. 48, 321, 323, 326–7.
[50] Hill, *A Turbulent, Seditious, and Factious People: John Bunyan and his Church 1628–1688* (Oxford, 1988), pp. 3, 90, 346.

general reading in and around the subject.'[51] (Was ever a reader less desultory?) Despite the title, the book extends from the Geneva Bible of 1557 to 'the Bible dethroned' after 1660. It does not examine the text but its multiple effects on society, politics and literature. The clergy, so men of power and property assumed, would guide worshippers to the passages in the new Authorised Version demanding obedience to authority. But other verses seemed to justify revolution. It did not matter if no law permitted the execution of the king when Isaiah, Daniel and especially Revelation upheld it. God was less prominent in the next book, *Liberty against the Law: some Seventeenth-Century Controversies*. It had been suggested that as a historian of ideas Hill was less interested in the mental world of 'the less-than-radical majority'.[52] The section here on lawlessness includes some of the 'the class of permanent poor' who rejected wage-labour and the law. Who, he goes on to ask, are the people? Whose law? Whose liberty? There were, as there still are in the welfare state, many who are hardly included as 'the people'. There was room too for one more essay on Winstanley. His 'superb prose gave expression to the half-formed ideas of the inarticulate men and women whose outlook I have been fumbling to recapture'.[53]

Apart from the books a lot of Hill's work was by now becoming almost unobtainable. Collections were out of print; back numbers of periodicals were lost. Then in 1985–6 the Harvester Press reprinted over forty of his essays, chosen from thirty years' writing, in three volumes, *The Collected Essays of Christopher Hill. Volume 1: Writing and Revolution in Seventeenth-Century England* (1985), *Volume 2: Religion and Politics in Seventeenth-Century England* (1985), *Volume 3: People and Ideas in Seventeenth-Century England* (1986). The essence of his output was suddenly available. Some chosen pieces are delightfully easy reading, such as the anecdotal account of Karl Marx in England or the 'footnote' on Marvell 'Till the Conversion of the *Jews*.' Important essays reprinted include those on 'Censorship and English Literature' (originating in seminars held in Switzerland), 'Parliament and People in 17th-Century England' (a Sir John Neale Memorial Lecture), 'The Poor and the People' (from a lecture at Brown University and a festschrift for George Rudé) and 'Science and Magic' (from a lecture at the J. D. Bernal Peace Library and a festschrift for Eric Hobsbawm).

---

[51] Hill, *The English Bible and the Seventeenth-Century Revolution* (London, 1993), p. vii.
[52] e.g. David Underdown in Eley and Hunt (eds.) *Reviving The English Revolution*, p. 327.
[53] Hill, *Liberty against the Law: some Seventeenth-century Controversies* (London, 1996), p. 274

There were two more collections. *A Nation of Change and Novelty* (not everyone will recognise the quotation from Aphra Behn): *Radical Politics, Religion and Literature in Seventeenth-Century England* (1990) has chapters from other festschrifts, from lectures, and conferences, with expansions and additions. *England's Turning Point: Essays in 17th-Century English History* (1998) was a nicely varied assortment of sixty years' writing in chronological order. The samples are selected from so many that Hill himself is occasionally uncertain whether a piece had already been published. One or two certainly had not been. The changes in outlook are shown and discussed; but the sequence illustrates clearly how the essential conclusions remained. So, after some deliberate mellowing, did the style. The clarity, the sometimes shattering wit and the generous appreciation are always evident.

Christopher Hill died on 24 February 2003. In his last years his immensely powerful brain was, with cruel irony, destroyed by Alzheimer's Disease. Bridget, by then an important historian herself, was able to care for him almost to the end, hiding the fact that she was dying of cancer. It had been the most productive life he could have wished. His writing had remained so prolific and confident that it was easy to forget the turmoils he had overcome. One dogma—Methodist Christianity—had been rejected. Another—Marxism—had been drastically changed. A stock reply to the regular question 'Are you still a Marxist?' was, in the familiar sentence: 'It depends what you mean by Marxism.' What mattered was the lasting contribution of Marxism to the development of his thought. 'My position is I suppose a modified Tawneyism', he remarked in a postscript to 'Parliament and People'. 'I have changed my vocabulary', he explained in the 1991 essay 'Premature Obsequies': 'Bourgeois' had been an unproductive term. He had become 'more careful and less strident'. But the main Marxist point remained: the events of 1640 to 1660 were 'aptly described as a revolution'.[54] Without it the later developments could not have happened. Certainly Hill was never an economic determinist: ideas in all their variety became for him the essence of history. From ideas expressed by a minority he was able to reconstruct the beliefs and aspirations of the silent majority. 'History from below' was truer and more important than the old history seen only through the eyes of the powerful. He had studied the revolutionary years through the experience of individuals, from the Lord Protector and the greatest poet to the poor

---

[54] Hill, *Collected Essays*, 3. 65; *History Today*, 41 (April 1991) reprinted in *England's Turning Point* (London, 1998), pp. 291–6.

and unknown. They were all part of Winstanley's 'universal community' of equals. Some day it would not be defeated.

Hill's sympathy for the downtrodden and unsuccessful was an unchanging part of his historical and his practical beliefs. Everyone who knew him will remember the cheerful, communicative and unassuming Christopher whose vast knowledge and thought were borne so lightly. The world-eminent historian who after delivering a major lecture queued for fish and chips with two former pupils and the lucid thinker who seized on whatever was valid in the blundering of others seemed unique. He was often described as 'quizzical' and some remarks were recalled, on reflection, as skilfully ambiguous. He could make unsupported assertions and evade awkward questions; but on fundamental principles he would not be shaken. On everything else he was increasingly ready to admit that he might be wrong. 'Certainties come, certainties go: history alone remains, because history changes with the events it records.'[55] And history meant the interconnection of society, politics, economics, religion and literature. Who else connected them so well?

DONALD PENNINGTON
Balliol College, Oxford

Note. Grateful thanks to all who have helped, including Ursula Aylmer, Vicky Baldwin, Ron Bellamy, Irene Corfield, Penelope Corfield, Gail Cunningham, Matthew Cunningham, John Jones, Anne Laurence, Gordon Leff, Peter Marshall, Gerrard Roots, Ivan Roots, Dorothy Thompson and especially to my wife, Marjorie Pennington, for her help, forbearance and encouragement during the weeks of work.

[55] Hill, *The Century of Revolution*, p. 311; Brian Manning, 'The Legacy of Christopher Hill', *International Socialism Journal*, 99 (2003).

RODNEY HILTON

Rodney Howard Hilton
1916–2002

RODNEY HILTON, born on 17 November 1916, was brought up in Middleton, near Manchester, and throughout his life his speech retained traces of his Lancashire origins. His grandfather had lived in Samuel Bamford's former cottage, and his family believed that their radical heritage went back to Peterloo. His parents, John James Hilton and Anne Howard Hilton, were active in the Independent Labour Party, and their son followed in their path of political dissent. His father had worked as a manager for the local Co-operative Society, but was killed in a road accident when Rodney Hilton was very young; his mother, who took an active part in local civic life, had an especially strong influence on him. Her fondness for her youngest son meant that she much regretted his departure from home, and feared that he would take up 'foreign ideas' in Oxford. He nonetheless excelled at Manchester Grammar School and gained a scholarship to Balliol, Oxford.

As a history undergraduate between 1935 and 1938 he was attracted to the medieval period by the teaching of two outstanding Balliol scholars, Vivian Galbraith and Richard Southern, and he also came into contact with Maurice Powicke. He began a life-long friendship with Christopher Hill, who encouraged his political and intellectual commitment to the Left.[1] His contemporaries as students included Edward Heath, who

---

[1] The information about his early life is based on Rodney Hilton's and Tim Hilton's reminiscences; T. Hilton, *One More Kilometre and We're in the Showers* (London, 2004), pp. 1–5; E. Lemon (ed.), *The Balliol College Register* (Oxford, 1969), p. 237; R. G. C. Levens (ed.), *Merton College Register 1900–1964* (Oxford, 1964), p. 300; *Interviews with Historians* (a recording of an interview with John Hatcher) (Institute of Historical Research, University of London, 1990).

Proceedings of the British Academy, **130**, 53–77. © The British Academy 2005.

recalled in his early days at Oxford making in public an ill-advised historical generalisation. Hilton, overhearing the remark, corrected him forcefully and loudly, and Heath resolved in future to think before speaking.[2] Hilton's circle included Denis Healey, Allan Merson, and Nicholas Myant: all were active in student politics, focused on the Labour Club, coinciding with such exciting events as the Oxford by-election of 1938, and they became caught up in the international anti-fascist campaigns. As a northerner Hilton was acutely aware of the misery of the depression and consequent high levels of unemployment. At Oxford he was indeed influenced by 'foreign ideas' and joined the Communist Party, of which he remained a member for the next two decades. He conceived his future academic life as closely linked to his political convictions, and planned an idealistic programme of research that would begin with a study of late medieval peasants and artisans, and continue with work on the modern working class.

When he came to choose his subject for his D.Phil. thesis, under the supervision of Reginald Lennard, he worked on monastic estates in Leicestershire. The research was based on Charyte's register of the lands of Leicester Abbey which was compiled in 1477, but as well as a detailed rental for that year, the register included earlier documents which allowed changes in the economy, and especially among the peasantry, to be traced back over the previous two centuries. This perfectly suited Hilton's aim of investigating social and economic aspects of the later middle ages which pointed towards the emergence of agrarian capitalism. He researched and wrote the thesis in less than two years: his quick brain, capacity for clear thought, and ability to concentrate on the essential issues enabled him to complete the task, but his mind was also focused by the knowledge that the war would imminently take him away from academic life. When gathering material for his thesis in London he formed a close friendship with a Cambridge research student, then a Marxist, Edward Miller. In this hectic period he was a Senior Scholar at Merton, and found time to write an article for the *English Historical Review* on a late thirteenth-century poem in which a canon of Leicester Abbey gloated over the defeat of the peasants of Stoughton in Leicestershire, after they had brought a law suit

---

[2] E. Heath, *The Autobiography of Edward Heath. The Course of My Life* (London, 1998), pp. 24–5. The incident must have had a great impact on Heath, who was remembering it sixty years later. The intervention was entirely typical of Hilton later in life, and many students and colleagues have been reproved (usually with good humour) for poorly thought-out statements in similar fashion.

disputing their obligations to their lord, the Abbey.[3] In 1939 he married Margaret Palmer, who had been a student at Somerville. She was also a communist academic, who later became a university lecturer in French. Their son, Tim, was born in 1941.

Writing in 1946, in a striking understatement Hilton referred to his 'absence from England, in circumstances uncongenial to academic studies', from 1940 to 1946.[4] These years, mainly in the Royal Tank Regiment, took him to North Africa, Italy, and the Middle East; he participated in the invasion of Sicily and the landings at Anzio, and at the end of the war was posted to Lebanon, Palestine, and Syria, where he attended staff college, and for a time was attached to a unit of the Indian Army. He could not have been a conventional army officer, as he was able to make contacts with local people who were also communists, to the puzzlement of his superiors when they noticed that he 'knew the same songs'. He acquired an enduring taste for salted peanuts from visits to the bar of Shepherd's Hotel in Cairo, and in an officer's mess in the Middle East he helped to invent a new cocktail, consisting of gin and Owbridge's Lung Tonic. He recalled these lighter moments, but never regarded his time in the army with much nostalgia, and was especially scathing about the empty phrase that described someone as having a 'good war'. Nonetheless he did experience a part of the world that would not normally have been visited by a young historian, and on his return to academic life he taught a course on the history of the Near East.[5] He also (setting aside such miseries as Anzio) benefited from his time in Italy, a country for which he retained a great affection. He learned the Italian version of *Lily Marlene* from young women he met there, and his friends in England remember his rendering, sixty years after he first heard it, of the socialist song, *Bandiera Rossa*.

Hilton returned to England in 1946 and took up a lectureship at the University of Birmingham. He was appointed to the post (while he was on leave) after an interview conducted by R. R. Betts, then the Professor of History, in the bar of the Mitre Hotel in Oxford. He returned to his D.Phil. thesis, and prepared it for publication (it appeared in 1947) in the Oxford Historical Series, under the austere title *The Economic Development of*

---

[3] 'A Thirteenth-Century Poem on Disputed Labour Services', *English Historical Review*, 56 (1941), 90–7.
[4] *The Economic Development of Some Leicestershire Estates in the 14th and 15th Centuries* (Oxford, 1947), p. iii.
[5] E. Miller,' Introduction', in T. H. Aston, P. R. Coss, C. Dyer, and J. Thirsk (eds.), *Social Relations and Ideas. Essays in Honour of R. H. Hilton* (Cambridge, 1983), p. ix.

Some Leicestershire Estates in the 14th and 15th Centuries. In this book he showed that a small landlord (Owston Abbey) could fare better in the late medieval economic decline than those with large estates. In the Leicestershire villages under the lordship of Owston and Leicester Abbeys larger peasant tenements emerged in the fifteenth century, and wage labour was vital to the economy both of the lords' home farms and the holdings accumulated by the more prosperous yeomen. Here some of the preconditions of agrarian capitalism could be recognised. The book also briefly explored such themes as urban decline and patterns of consumption, prophetically opening discussions which were not taken up generally by historians for another thirty years.

Meetings of the Communist Party's Historians' Group, which had been foreshadowed by pre-war gatherings at Balliol, began in 1946.[6] The encounters with an older generation of Marxist scholars such as Maurice Dobb and Dona Torr, and regular contacts with his contemporaries Christopher Hill, Eric Hobsbawm, and Victor Kiernan, played an important role in his intellectual development. Later the Group was joined by Dorothy and Edward Thompson. The discussions within the Group included a scheme to update and improve A. L. Morton's *A People's History of England*, and it was as part of that programme of extending public understanding that Hilton contributed chapters on the historical background to the 'Peasants' Revolt' of 1381, to a narrative account of the rebellion which had been written by H. Fagan. The joint work was published in 1950 as *The English Rising of 1381* and, though it is now little known, Hilton's chapters give a remarkably lucid and readable introduction to feudal society.[7] The inspiration of the Group of course came from Marxist theory, but Hilton and others were also concerned to emphasise the continuity of an English radical tradition. They traced their intellectual and political lineage through such figures as William Morris, back to the Diggers and Levellers of the English Revolution, and to their precursors among the Lollards and rebels of the middle ages.

A fruitful offshoot of the Historians' Group was the journal *Past and Present,* which was founded in 1952.[8] It originally carried the subtitle 'A journal of scientific history' which signalled its Marxist leanings, but it

---

[6] E. Hobsbawm, 'The Historians' Group of the Communist Party', in M. Cornforth (ed.), *Rebels and Their Causes* (London, 1978), pp. 21–48; H. J. Kaye, *The British Marxist Historians. An Introductory Analysis* (Cambridge, 1986), pp. 8–17.

[7] (With H. Fagan), *The English Rising of 1381* (London, 1950).

[8] C. Hill, R. H. Hilton, and E. J. Hobsbawm, 'Origins and Early Years', *Past and Present*, 100 (1983), 3–14.

was always intended as a link with historians who were not communists; early issues contained articles by such radical but non-Marxist scholars as W. G. Hoskins, and the editorial board was joined by Geoffrey Barraclough. Hilton supported the journal loyally throughout his life, but made an especially important contribution in its early fragile years, for example by writing for the first number an article which is still widely cited: 'Capitalism—what's in a name?' He was later to be Chairman of the Editorial Board (from 1972), and Vice-President of the Past and Present Society from 1987.[9] Under the editorship of T. H. Aston, who worked closely with Hilton, the journal had become by the mid 1960s the leading historical journal in the English language, enjoying a large readership, and showing the way forward in such fields as social and cultural history, while maintaining the highest scholarly standards. Although the 'scientific history' subtitle was dropped, Marxist history still influenced the journal's approach. *Past and Present* insisted that articles should derive general conclusions from particular studies, and authors were expected to answer well-formulated questions. Contributors were encouraged to write in accessible English for a non-specialist readership. The journal encouraged historical work which was informed by insights from other disciplines, especially the social sciences.

If we survey Hilton's publications in the first ten years after his return to academic work three interrelated themes emerge. First he was researching and writing on the medieval economy in general, and contributing to such conventional subjects as estate management and field systems. His article on Winchcombe Abbey and the manor of Sherborne in Gloucestershire (1949) explored the acquisition of landed wealth by a monastic lord in the Cotswolds, and in particular the methods that it used in the fifteenth century to grow and sell its wool.[10] In his study of the leases issued by Gloucester Abbey he explained that better-off peasants in the thirteenth century took advantage of their lord's need for cash by paying a lump sum for their servile obligations to be converted into money rent.[11] W. G. Hoskins must have encouraged Hilton to write more

[9] P. Coss, 'R. H. Hilton', *Past and Present*, 176 (2002), 7–10.
[10] 'Winchcombe Abbey and the Manor of Sherborne', *University of Birmingham Historical Journal*, 2 (1949), 31–52, repr. in H. P. R. Finberg (ed.), *Gloucestershire Studies* (Leicester, 1957), pp. 89–113, and in *Class Conflict and the Crisis of Feudalism. Essays in Medieval Social History* (London, 1985), pp. 18–35.
[11] 'Gloucester Abbey Leases of the Late Thirteenth Century', *University of Birmingham Historical Journal*, 4 (1953), 1–17, repr. in *The English Peasantry in the Later Middle Ages: the Ford Lectures for 1973 and Related Studies* (Oxford, 1975), pp. 139–60.

about Leicestershire, which bore fruit in an essay about Kibworth Harcourt. Hoskins presumably also commissioned the chapter on medieval agriculture in the *Victoria County History* of Leicestershire, which contained insights, among other things, into the rotation of crops and the network of local markets.[12] This study also revealed the relatively light burden of labour services imposed on the peasantry of the county in the thirteenth century, and the importance of money rent, a generalisation which became a major theme of an incisive Occasional Paper for the Dugdale Society on the social structure of rural Warwickshire.[13] In addition to pursuing his own research, he helped to make available to English-speaking scholars the work of a leading Soviet historian, by editing for publication a translation of E. A. Kosminsky's analysis of the thirteenth-century Hundred Rolls.[14]

Secondly he examined peasant revolts, partly as a means of investigating peasant attitudes and consciousness. More influential than his chapters in the *English Rising* book of 1950 was his 1949 article on 'Peasant movements before 1381', which used local agitations and protests to prove that peasants regularly opposed their feudal lords.[15] Peasants resented the rents and services imposed on them as unfree villeins, and could organise themselves to resist these dues. This article shows that he was conceiving of medieval peasants as a social class. They objected to rents and dues mainly because these payments eroded their incomes, but also because they had a principled objection to the restriction of their freedom. They could be regarded as active participants in a class struggle, and makers of their own history. This was both a contribution to understanding the medieval peasantry, but also shows him acting as an early exponent of the approach later known as 'history from below'.

His third strand of thinking and writing connected with a major concern of the Historians' Group, the periodisation of history and the

---

[12] 'Kibworth Harcourt: a Merton College Manor in the Thirteenth and Fourteenth Centuries', in W. G. Hoskins (ed.), *Studies in Leicestershire Agrarian History* (Leicester, 1949), pp. 17–40, repr. in *Class Conflict*, pp. 1–17; 'Medieval Agrarian History', in *Victoria County History of Leicestershire*, 2 (London, 1954), pp. 145–98.

[13] *Social Structure of Rural Warwickshire in the Middle Ages*, Dugdale Society Occasional Paper, 9 (Stratford-upon-Avon, 1950), repr. in *The English Peasantry*, pp. 113–38.

[14] E. A. Kosminsky, *Studies in the Agrarian History of England in the Thirteenth Century*, trans. R. Kisch (Oxford, 1956).

[15] 'Peasant Movements in England before 1381', *Economic History Review*, 2nd ser., 2 (1949), 117–36, repr. in *The Middle Ages*, Institute of History of the Academy of Sciences of the USSR (Moscow, 1956–7), pp. 92–111, and in E. M. Carus-Wilson (ed.), *Essays in Economic History*, 2 (London, 1962), pp. 73–90, and in *Class Conflict*, pp. 122–38.

transition from feudalism to capitalism (often simply called 'the transition'). His *Past and Present* article in 1952 had proposed a rigorous definition of capitalism, emphasising such characteristics as the investment in enterprises and the use of wage labour, which prevented any claim that late medieval Europe had a capitalist economy.[16] Nevertheless the study of the Leicester estates had revealed how society had changed significantly by the 1470s, with larger units of production in the hands of peasants. But what had propelled economic and social change in this direction? In 1951 he was stimulated to contribute an article to the French journal *Annales ESC* when Edouard Perroy had characterised the late medieval economy as stagnant and mediocre. Hilton's 'Crisis of Feudalism' was an exercise in grand generalisation, typically succinct, in which he argued that feudal society was faced by an economic impasse around 1300, marked particularly by low levels of productivity.[17] The ruling class was extracting too much from the economy, failing to reinvest their profits, and contributing to technological stagnation. Lords turned to war and taxation to keep their revenues flowing, and the demands for money provoked peasant resistance. This ensured that the lords were no longer controlling the economy at the end of the middle ages, and the precursors of capitalist farmers were already active in the countryside. Two years later he contributed to an international debate on 'the transition' in the pages of the American journal *Science and Society*, where one of his purposes was to correct social scientists' misconceptions about the medieval economy.[18] He argued, in a development of his views in the *Annales* article, that the moving force in feudal society was not an external factor such as international trade, but the 'struggle for rent' which lay at the heart of the relationship between lords and peasants, and that the aristocracy suffered a crisis because peasants forced them to scale down their demands.

By 1956 Hilton, in his fortieth year, had established an international reputation as an authority on the medieval economy in general, and in particular had put forward new ideas about social class, conflict, the feudal crisis, and the origins of capitalism which commanded respect,

---

[16] 'Capitalism—What's in a Name?', *Past and Present*, 1 (1952), 32–43, repr. in R. H. Hilton (ed.), *The Transition from Feudalism to Capitalism* (London, 1976), pp. 145–58, and in *Class Conflict*, pp. 268–77.

[17] 'Y eût-il une crise général de la féodalité?', *Annales, Économies, Sociétés, Civilisations*, 6 (1951), 23–30, repr. as 'Was There a General Crisis of Feudalism?', in *Class Conflict*, pp. 239–45.

[18] 'A Comment', *Science and Society* (Fall, 1953), repr. in *The Transition from Feudalism to Capitalism: a Symposium* (London, 1954), pp. 65–72, and in *Transition*, pp. 109–17.

both because they were theoretically informed, and because they were supported by empirical research. He was inspired by the writings of Marx, Lenin, and their more recent disciples, and applied their ideas, such as Marx's discussion of the origins of capitalist ground rent in the third volume of *Capital*, to the experiences of the English countryside between the thirteenth and the fifteenth centuries. A notable feature of his work was that he combined these excursions into theory and debates with the preparation of texts for learned societies. He edited a set of ministers' accounts (records of estate finances) for the Warwickshire manors of the earldom of Warwick for the years 1479–80 for the Dugdale Society.[19] An American scholar had begun to edit for the same society a more complex source, the Stoneleigh Leger Book, and Hilton completed the work and provided an introduction which demonstrated the document's significance for understanding the society of the Forest of Arden in the later middle ages.[20]

Hilton's first marriage had ended in divorce, and in 1953 he married Gwyneth Evans, a secondary school teacher; they moved away from Birmingham into Worcestershire, and in 1956 settled at Phoenix Cottage in the village of Fladbury. They had two children, Owen and Ceinwen.

The year 1956 proved a turning point. Communists for years had felt themselves to be under siege. Their candidates gained little support in elections. They had been subject to constant surveillance and discrimination because they were regarded as the agents of a hostile foreign power. Applications from known communists for academic jobs were often unsuccessful. At the same time academics were liable to be criticised by their own Party, with its obsession with discipline and unity, if they expressed a view that was out of line with the current orthodoxy. They were expected to speak up for the government of the Soviet Union (whatever their private doubts), but that position was strained to breaking point when Khrushchev in a secret speech revealed Stalin's crimes, and loyal communists realised that they had been defending the indefensible. Later in 1956 the new Soviet government behaved in the old ruthless fashion by suppressing revolt in Hungary. Members of the Communist Party of Great Britain agitated for both internal reform of the Party structures, and some appropriate response to the events in eastern Europe, and when

[19] *Ministers' Accounts of the Warwickshire Estates of the Duke of Clarence, 1479–80*, Dugdale Society, 21 (Stratford-upon-Avon, 1952). Introduction repr. in *Class Conflict*, pp. 48–62.
[20] *The Stoneleigh Leger Book*, Dugdale Society, 24 (Stratford-upon-Avon, 1960). Introduction repr. in *Class Conflict*, pp. 63–100.

these demands were refused Hilton and many other academics resigned their membership.

Leaving the Party meant giving up a way of life: the Historians' Group meetings in London ceased, but so also did the busy round of meetings and campaigning at local level, the contacts with friends and allies in Britain and abroad, and the constant engagement with communism by reading the appropriate literature. The gap could not be filled by subsequent involvement in the New Left, and a brief period in the Labour Party proved a very poor substitute. Hilton rejoined the Communist Party shortly before it disbanded.

In the late 1940s and 1950s Hilton was participating actively in the life of the History Department of the University of Birmingham. It included on its staff, as did all universities at that time, those who regarded their role primarily as teachers, but Hilton was by no means alone in his enthusiasm for research. He supported the *University of Birmingham Historical Journal*, contributing to an early issue an article on a fifteenth-century household account jointly written with the Professor of Medieval History, H. A. Cronne, and other articles of his own followed.[21] Cronne's character and outlook differed from Hilton's, but he held him in great respect. Hilton enjoyed the company of Douglas Johnson, a lecturer in modern French history, and another medievalist, Shirley Bridges, and together they led a way of life regarded as bohemian in Easy Row, an offshoot of the history department separate from the main university building (which until 1960 was located in the centre of the city). He collaborated also with a later Easy Row resident, a sharp-minded lecturer specialising in early medieval history, Peter Sawyer, and together they wrote a devastating review of Lynn White's book on the history of technology.[22] Hilton got on well with students, and particularly the post-war intake of ex-servicemen who shared his experiences and attitudes. He joined in student social events, and took groups on field-work expeditions, including a 'Cotswold survey' of timber-framed buildings and deserted village sites in Gloucestershire.

A constant theme running through all his work was his commitment to the study of localities. Grand theories about social and economic change could only be demonstrated by meticulous research on particular regions and even individual villages where lords, peasants, and artisans

---

[21] (With H. A. Cronne), 'The Beauchamp Household Book (an Account of a Journey from London to Warwick in 1432)', *University of Birmingham Historical Journal*, 2 (1950), 208–18.
[22] (With P. H. Sawyer), 'Technical Determinism: the Stirrup and the Plough', *Past and Present*, 14 (1958), 30–44.

lived and worked. He had begun research on Leicestershire, and continued with his interest in that county after his return from the army. But his
lectureship in Birmingham encouraged him to become immersed in the
history of the west midland region. He was encouraged by two lecturers
in the Birmingham department, Philip and Dorothy Styles, and quickly
began publishing with the Dugdale Society. A considerable part of his
time in the 1950s was spent in the local record offices, and in reading
microfilm of monastic cartularies kept in London depositories. He taught
courses on west midland history both in the university and to extra-mural
students, and encouraged a series of research students in the 1950s and
1960s to work on west midland projects for their MA and Ph.D. theses.[23]
When he was living in Worcestershire, as well as reading and analysing its
records, he became aware of the moribund state of the Worcestershire
Historical Society, and together with colleagues, including Peter Sawyer,
revived the organisation in 1960 and began a new series of record publications.[24] From 1959 until 1968, he arranged an annual season of excavations with John Wacher (for one year) and thereafter with Philip Rahtz on
a deserted medieval village site in the Cotswolds at Upton near Blockley.[25]
This venture combined intellectual curiosity about the contribution that
archaeology could make to the understanding of the medieval peasantry,
with his enjoyment of the company of the staff and students who
volunteered to work on the site.

   The culmination of his investigations into the west midland region
came in 1966 with the publication of *A Medieval Society*, though typically this local study had an international dimension. He had long been
an admirer of the school of French social and economic historians which
had been founded by Lucien Febvre and Marc Bloch. Bloch's books on
monarchy, feudal society, and rural history established new approaches,
with their emphasis on geographical context, insights from the social
sciences and especially anthropology, and their use of the comparative
method. Bloch was killed by the Gestapo in 1944, but the tradition continued with the journal that he had founded, *Annales ESC*, and by the

[23] These included Peter Bill, Jean Birrell, Peter Coss, Ralph Evans, R. K. Field, Catherine Hall,
T. H. Lloyd, E. K. Vose, John West, and the author of this memoir. Postgraduates who worked
on west midland theses after 1970 included Trevor John, Richard Holt, Mary Hulton, Simon
Penn, Kyle Rae, and Zvi Razi.
[24] *Miscellany I*, Worcestershire Historical Society (Worcester, 1960) appeared without any
named editor or other bibliographical information, but is now recognised as volume 1 of the
society's new series. It included Hilton's edition of the swanimote rolls of Feckenham Forest.
[25] (With P. A. Rahtz), 'Upton, Gloucestershire, 1959–64', *Transactions of the Bristol and
Gloucestershire Archaeological Society*, 85 (1966), 70–146.

work of such distinguished scholars as Robert Boutruche, Georges Duby, Guy Fourquin, and Robert Fossier. These historians began their careers with formidable doctoral studies about French regions, and they encouraged their students to follow the same course. Hilton read (and often reviewed) the books that came out of these theses and appreciated their combination of historical geography with institutional, social, and economic history to create a rounded picture of a whole functioning society. Through the study of regions, it was possible to construct *histoire totale*.

Hilton's *A Medieval Society* had no intention of matching the exhaustive detail and monumental scale of the regional works that came from France, but instead he produced a readable survey of the main features of society around the end of the thirteenth century.[26] The chosen territory coincided approximately with the diocese of Worcester, and included the three counties of Gloucestershire, Warwickshire, and Worcestershire. The book focused on the social structure of the region, so there were chapters on the landlords, their estates, peasants, villages, towns, markets, and social controls. The evidence included excavations and standing timber buildings, but most of the information derived from an impressive array of documentary sources. His writing was always made more accessible and attractive by specific examples of individual people and incidents, and *A Medieval Society* has a particularly rich vein of lively human material extracted from the archives. For example the criminal career is recounted of Malcolm Musard, a prominent member of the gentry and lord of the manor of Saintbury in Gloucestershire, who in the early years of the fourteenth century poached, robbed, assaulted, raided, and vandalised his way through the region, only to be rewarded with offices by the crown and the Despenser family. The book also benefited from an eye for the telling detail in an unexpected source, such as the reference in a thirteenth-century boundary description of Alvechurch in Worcestershire to a place 'where the *binlaues* (by-laws) are usually held', revealing the existence of rarely documented meetings between the inhabitants of adjoining villages to settle matters of common concern.[27]

The book was originally designed to set the scene for another work, which would follow through the region's development in the fourteenth and fifteenth centuries. Eventually this was at least partly achieved, as we shall see, in a number of publications about west midlands peasants and towns.

---

[26] *A Medieval Society: the West Midlands at the End of the Thirteenth Century* (London, 1966); 2nd edn. (Cambridge, 1983).
[27] Ibid., pp. 152, 255–6.

Hilton was not an enthusiast for university administration, but in the 1960s was able to play an important part in taking history at Birmingham through a transition which paved the way for later success. In the early 1960s the head of department did not devote his full attention to the role, as he was accustomed to visiting the university from his Oxford home only on Thursdays. In 1963 major changes were accomplished by establishing a School of History, which brought together in a federation the departments of Medieval, Modern, and American history. The heads of each department would serve in turn as Chairman of the School. At the same time Hilton was appointed to a personal chair of Medieval Social History. He served his time a little later as a successful Chairman of the School, but in 1969 was happy to hand over administrative tasks to others, and returned again to focus on his research and teaching. When the chair of medieval history became vacant in 1970, he was anxious that the post be filled from outside, and Ralph Davis was appointed.

At Birmingham, as at many universities before the 1970s, there was much communication between the disciplines. Hilton's broad-minded approach to scholarship led him to work with those in other departments. He collaborated closely with R. E. F. Smith in the Russian department, a specialist in Russian urban and peasant history, and had some contact with Harry Thorpe, the historical geographer, and a student of his, J. B. Harley. Relations with archaeology were not so close, which resulted in the engagement of outside specialists in the early days of the Upton excavations, and ultimately in the appointment of a Lecturer in Medieval Archaeology in the School of History, a post initially filled by Philip Rahtz.[28] Hilton's interest in social mentality, together with his own avid reading of modern novels, naturally led him to treat literature as historical source material. In the aftermath of 1956 he developed an interest in the Robin Hood ballads, and wrote an article called 'The origins of Robin Hood' offering an interpretation of the woodland bandit as a peasant hero, who expressed popular grievances by flouting forest law and attacking corrupt officials and members of the higher clergy.[29] These ideas sparked an intense debate, and although the original argument has not survived intact, the article stimulated Robin Hood studies which continue into the twenty-first century. His interest in literature was sustained by

[28] P. Rahtz, *Living Archaeology* (Stroud, 2001), pp. 90–1.
[29] 'The Origins of Robin Hood', *Past and Present*, 14 (1958), 30–44, repr. in R. H. Hilton (ed.), *Peasants, Knights and Heretics: Studies in Medieval English Social History* (Cambridge, 1976), pp. 221–35, and in S. Knight (ed.), *Robin Hood. Anthology of Scholarship and Criticism* (Cambridge, 1999), pp. 197–210.

friendly relations with the medieval specialists in the Birmingham English department, and particularly with Geoffrey Shepherd. For much of the 1960s and 1970s Birmingham medieval history postgraduates and their counterparts in English met regularly with Hilton and Shepherd to discuss matters of common interest, and sometimes to be baffled by the very wide divergences in their approaches.

During the 1960s he was still pursuing alongside his west midland studies the hypothesis about the crisis of feudalism that he had sketched briefly in his 1951 *Annales* article. By this time a dominant voice in interpreting the medieval economy was that of M. M. Postan, who made the crisis of the fourteenth century a central episode in his interpretation of the whole period. Like Hilton he saw the late thirteenth century as a period of growth, followed by a downturn in the first half of the fourteenth century. Postan believed that this reversal of trends, however, was precipitated by ecological problems, when under pressure of population growth poor land was taken in for cultivation. As the pastures were ploughed up, the old established fields, starved of manure, suffered a loss of productivity.[30] For Postan, emphasising the weight of numbers and the fertility of the fields, such factors as feudal lordship and serfdom were of secondary significance. His ideas went back to the classical economists, Malthus and Ricardo, rather than to Marx. Postan and Hilton agreed, however, that the crisis of productivity around 1300 did not lead to technical improvements in agriculture, as happened in the sixteenth and eighteenth centuries, when expansion in population was accompanied by the introduction of new farming methods. Postan wrote of the other-worldly mentality of medieval intellectuals which prevented them from addressing this problem. For Hilton the technical malaise was embedded in the social structure: the lords extracted so much rent from the peasants (especially the serfs) that they were prevented from making improvements, and the lords themselves spent the rent money and estate profits on high living, war and religion.

Hilton defended his interpretation by investigating the origins of the servile peasantry, and in an article published in 1965 showed that serfdom in a clearly defined form, the villeinage of the common lawyers, had developed quite late, at the end of the twelfth and in the early years of the

---

[30] M. M. Postan, 'Medieval Agrarian Society in its Prime: England', in M. Postan (ed.), *Cambridge Economic History of Europe*, 1, 2nd edn. (Cambridge, 1966), pp. 548–632. Hilton and Postan, though differing in their historical interpretations, shared some similarities of outlook, and there was a degree of mutual admiration and affection.

thirteenth century.[31] This coincided with a period of inflation, when lords
were seeking to increase their revenues, and to exploit their control over
the peasants on their estates. This set the origins of this type of serfdom
in an economic and social context, as a means of class domination for
financial gain, and not as an archaic survival, or a by product of new legal
doctrines by the royal lawyers who sought to divide the free and unfree.
Hilton was asked by the Economic History Society to consider the decline
of serfdom in a pamphlet published in 1969.[32] Again he argued that serfdom was a central feature of lord–tenant relations. In the thirteenth
century lords needed, and obtained, profits from serfdom and especially
labour services, and the peasants pressed for freedom and therefore
lighter services and dues. In the late fourteenth century lords clung to
serfdom in spite of the fall in population that in theory strengthened the
bargaining power of now scarce tenants.

It was part of the case for a social crisis of feudalism to show that serfdom was a real burden, and that lords extracted more from the peasantry
in the thirteenth century. The other crucial point concerned investment,
the lack of which prevented technical improvements. In a paper to the
International Economic History Conference in 1962 Hilton calculated
the percentage of lords' estate income that was invested in such assets as
buildings, equipment, livestock, and reclamation or enclosure schemes,
and found that the figures in the late thirteenth and early fourteenth centuries often lay around 5 per cent.[33] Such a small expenditure ensured that
lords made few innovations or major improvements to the efficiency of
farming. Low levels of productivity and technical conservatism among
peasants could be associated with their lack of cash and resources for
investment after they had paid their rents and taxes.

A weakness in the argument that pressure from landlords played an
important part in peasant impoverishment, and therefore precipitated the
fourteenth-century crisis, lay in the number of free tenants, and the
apparently light burdens on the unfree tenants, at least in terms of labour
services, in some regions. Hilton himself had revealed the lack of heavy
obligations in Leicestershire and Warwickshire. He had an opportunity to
address this point when he was invited to give the Earl Lecture on

[31] 'Freedom and Villeinage in England', *Past and Present*, 31 (1965), 3–19, repr. in *Peasants, Knights and Heretics*, pp. 174–91.
[32] *The Decline of Serfdom in Medieval England*, Studies in Economic History (London, 1969); 2nd edn. (London, 1983).
[33] 'Rent and Capital Formation in Feudal Society', in *Second International Conference of Economic History: Aix-en-Provence*, 2 (Paris, 1965), 33–68, repr. in *English Peasantry*, pp. 174–214.

Staffordshire history at Keele in 1969.[34] Staffordshire was famously a county of relatively free peasants, partly because of its woodland landscape in which settlers were encouraged to clear new land with easy conditions of tenure. Hilton gave a rounded picture of the rural society of the county, depicting its hierarchy of lords, and showing that most peasants were freeholders and the customary or servile tenants rarely did much labour service. He discovered, however, that lords were able to compensate themselves by exploiting the revenues gained from 'the exercise of lordship'. Profits of jurisdiction, death duties, and entry fines allowed lords to make more from their tenants than descriptions of their annual money rents and services would suggest. These extra payments ate into the peasants' surplus, and made them more insecure, as they were nervous of irregular and unexpected charges.

A new urgency and excitement came into social history in the late 1960s, as the young rebelled, and the conventions and conservatism of the postwar world were set aside. In particular students protested that they were given no voice in the government of their universities. Birmingham University became one of the centres of this movement; the students claimed that the institution was being controlled by an oligarchic and secretive management, and they campaigned for change with mass meetings and an occupation of the administrative offices.[35] Hilton, then Chairman of the School of History, was caught up in the events. He naturally sympathised with rebellion and demands for more democratic university government, and one of the academic events of the 'sit-in' was his lecture in the Great Hall of the university on the revolt of the Ciompi in Florence in 1378. His communist past made him suspicious of the students' lack of coherence— not all of their ideas came from the left, and those that did were sometimes rather wild. In the aftermath of the 1968 troubles universities were divided for some years by controversy over the role of students (and to some extent the staff) in their government. At Birmingham the appointment of a lecturer in sociology who had played a leading part in the 1968 sit-in was blocked by the university, and the left opposed this manipulation of the usual procedures. Hilton (who at this time was also active in the Association of University Teachers) led a group who supported the rejected candidate, and out of this agitation a national body, the Council for Academic Freedom and Democracy, was formed.

[34] 'Lord and Peasant in Staffordshire in the Middle Ages', *North Staffordshire Journal of Field Studies*, 10 (1970), 1–20, repr. in *English Peasantry*, pp. 215–43.
[35] E. W. Ives, D. Drummond, and L. Schwarz, *The First Civic University: Birmingham 1880–1980* (Birmingham, 2000), pp. 353–74.

   After the 1968 troubles in Britain and other developed countries rebellion did not seem such a remote activity. The much more serious struggles
of colonial peoples for independence, and in particular the war in Vietnam,
included an element of peasant revolt. Popular rebellions were once more
the subject of research, and student interest in them revived.[36] Hilton had
made frequent reference to the subject through the 1950s and 1960s, and
now wrote a book on European medieval peasant unrest in general,
beginning in the ninth century, but with a focus on the English Rising of
1381. *Bond Men Made Free* showed that peasant risings were not an occasional freakish outbreak, concentrated in the fourteenth century, but an
integral feature of medieval social history.[37] If the peasants were a conscious class, with interests opposed to those of their lords, they would
when possible seek to reduce their obligations or win some freedom. They
used the existing channels for pressing their demands, such as the public
courts of law. When these avenues were denied them, as only free men had
full legal rights, they resorted to direct action, such as refusing labour
services, and in some circumstances used violence. To emphasise the
centrality of revolt in medieval society, he could identify the rebels of
1381 as a cross section of non-aristocrats, including artisans, lesser clergy,
and some quite wealthy peasants. Their programmes were coherent and
expressed the ancient aims of the removal of aristocratic privileges and
restrictions; in particular they insisted that they should be free. This was
not just an adjustment in the social balance between one class and
another: if the serfs had been given their freedom, and (following the
demand at Smithfield attributed to Wat Tyler) lordship was to be 'divided
among all men', the aristocracy would have been removed, and the
country would have been ruled by peasant communities under a popular
monarchy. Although rebellions could be readily suppressed, and in the
case of the 1381 revolt collapsed rapidly under pressure, in the early
stages they were quite well organised. Far from being a transient episode,
the revolt of 1381 had long-term effects, which strengthened subsequent

[36] A general book covering European peasant revolts was M. Mollat and P. Wolff, *Ongles Bleus,
Jacques et Ciompi* (Paris, 1970), but it did not offer adequate explanations for them. A very use-
ful stimulus to new work on the 1381 rising was R. B. Dobson, *The Peasants' Revolt of 1381*
(London, 1970). There was of course a growing literature on modern rebellions and discontent.
Hilton contributed to a collective volume on peasantries which sought to use history to improve
understanding of contemporary problems: 'Peasant Society, Peasant Movements and Feudalism
in Medieval Europe', in H. A. Landsberger (ed.), *Rural Protest: Peasant Movements and Social
Change* (London, 1974), pp. 67–94.
[37] *Bond Men Made Free: Medieval Peasant Movements and the English Rising of 1381* (London,
1973).

negotiations between peasants and lords. As the title of his book proclaimed, most bond men were made free within a century of the revolt. Hilton's final conclusion was a message for the modern world: '. . . conflict is part of existence and . . . nothing is gained without struggle'.

In the 1970s he attained a high point in his career as a historian, in an environment conducive to academic creativity. In 1971 he married Jean Birrell, also a medieval historian who had been a lecturer at the University of Sheffield and then took up a post in the West Midlands region of the fledgling Open University. She encouraged and stimulated his work. In the School of History younger scholars were being appointed who held him in some awe, but gave him a local audience on which he could try out his ideas. A body of postgraduate students had also gathered at Birmingham to be supervised by him, including Grenville Astill, Peter Coss, Catherine Hall, Richard Holt and Zvi Razi, all of whom later gained chairs.[38]

While *Bond Men Made Free* was being prepared for the press Hilton was invited to give the Ford Lectures at Oxford, a recognition from his old university. His first reaction was to base the lectures on the poll tax records of 1377–81, which showed how he was attracted to cross-sectional studies at a point in time, as he had been able to do earlier for Leicestershire and Warwickshire. Colleagues (including Ralph Davis) suggested that he take the opportunity to produce the study of the west midlands in the fourteenth and fifteenth centuries that he had promised in 1966. He decided to follow that course, in part, by devoting the lectures to peasant society in the west midlands. He shifted the definition of the region a little to include Staffordshire (the subject of the Earl Lecture), and concentrated on the period 1350–1480.

The lectures were delivered in 1973 and published two years later as *The English Peasantry in the Later Middle Ages*.[39] The general title was justified by the broad themes pursued. The evidence came from west midland sources, but the questions posed were of universal significance. This was most obvious in the first chapter in which the medieval peasantry was identified as a class, based on comparisons with other societies, both in the past and in more recent times, not just in Continental Europe, but

[38] A number of students came from overseas: from Israel (Razi), Argentina (Maria Moisa), Canada (Kyle Rae and Gabriel Scardellato), Greece (Aglaia Kasdagli). After his retirement students came to Birmingham from China and Turkey, to be supervised by younger academics, but attracted by his presence.
[39] *English Peasantry,* see above, n. 11.

throughout the world. He was anxious to show that the medieval peasantry did not belong to some amorphous 'peasant society', but should be
placed in the specific context of west European feudalism, in which they
possessed land, lived in families and villages, and had obligations to lords.
The rest of the book was concerned with a number of paradoxes, in
which Hilton carefully steered the argument between the extremes.
Peasant society was clearly stratified, between those with large holdings
and those with cottages; some villagers hired workers, and some sought
employment. Yet peasant society was still bound together by common
interests, and the really profound gulf in medieval society was still that
which separated peasants from their lords. Peasants often produced their
own food, and depended on family members as their main source of
labour. They were also caught up in the market, and sold produce and
employed labour for wages, but their way of life was not dominated by
commerce.

He devoted his fifth chapter to a novel study of the small towns of the
west midlands, which were functionally separated from the surrounding
villages by their varied occupations, and which had many points of contact
with the local peasants, for example by providing markets where crops and
animals could be sold. The final chapter was also a new venture —under
the stimulus of the recent development of women's history, he examined
the role of peasant women. Again the reader was presented with a paradox:
women in the village suffered from many disadvantages, but can be seen
acting independently and could sometimes gain a good living.[40]

The book, being based closely on the texts of the lectures, had limited
space, but it was typical of his economical style that he could make his
essential points with a few deftly chosen words. In preparation for the fifth
chapter on small towns he spent many days working through the voluminous court rolls of the borough of Pershore, and then distilled the evidence
into three printed pages which summed up the town's government, society
and economy, portraying vividly its 'public street', petty traders, prostitutes,
and wandering pigs.

In the 1970s and 1980s Hilton was enjoying a peak of international
celebrity. His early articles had been translated into Japanese, and his
work in the 1950s was well known in the USSR and eastern Europe, but
now his Marxism was widely accepted as a valid approach, and indeed
had become fashionable in parts of the western academic world. He had

---

[40] This balanced judgement was criticised by some later practitioners of women's history as too
optimistic.

always had close links with French medieval historians, and in particular maintained a friendship with Georges Duby which had begun in the 1950s. For a time he had close contact with Guy Bois. He lectured at the Collège de France in 1981, and was invited to a succession of French conferences—he especially enjoyed the gatherings at Flaran in Gers, where high quality historical discussion was conducted in an idyllic rural setting, in a region with an especially rich gastronomic tradition. A number of books by leading French historians appeared at his instigation in translation in the Cambridge University Press series sponsored by *Past and Present.* He read Italian and addressed conferences there. He was invited to many other countries, including the USA, and in 1974 spent a term as a visiting professor at the Indian university of Aligarh. His work had a particularly strong impact in Spain. After 1975 Spanish historical studies experienced a renaissance, in which left-wing academics were at last free to practise their subject, and to welcome contact with the outside world. Hilton's books were translated, and he was much admired for his combination of political and academic radicalism. One young Spanish academic, asked about Hilton's reputation in his country, compared his status (with no more than a hint of irony) with that of Jesus Christ. Another recalled that for the group of research students to which he belonged it was not enough to read Rodney Hilton, or to write like Rodney Hilton—they aspired to *be* Rodney Hilton. He welcomed Isobel Alfonso from Madrid, who spent a year in Birmingham. He entertained numerous visitors from overseas throughout his life, but particularly at this time, and his generosity to these guests, and willingness to spend time with them, expressed his instinctive internationalism.

Much attention abroad, and in some circles in England, was attracted by the publication in 1976 of a new edition of the *Science and Society* debate on the transition from feudalism to capitalism, which had first appeared in the 1950s, for which Hilton provided a new introduction.[41] This was translated into Spanish and German. The invitations to speak abroad generated a stream of conference papers in which he revisited the themes of earlier writings—peasant revolts and their ideas, feudalism and capitalism, and the medieval social order.[42] Meanwhile the academic

---

[41] *Transition*, see above, n. 16.
[42] e.g. 'Soziale Programme im englischen Aufstand von 1381', in P. Blickle (ed.), *Revolte und Revolution in Europa* (Munich, 1975), pp. 31–46, repr. as 'Social Concepts in the English Rising of 1381', in *Class Conflict*, pp. 216–26; 'Idéologie et Ordre Social', *L'Arc*, 72 (1978) [special issue in honour of Georges Duby], 32–7, repr. as 'Ideology and Social Order in Late Medieval England', in *Class Conflict*, pp. 246–52.

establishment in his native land recognised his achievement, by belatedly electing him to the fellowship of the British Academy in 1977. He was not very active in this body, and regarded himself still as an outsider. He was more enthusiastic about his role on committees of the Social Science Research Council, and he was encouraged by observing other scholars' use of research grants to apply for funds to employ two researchers to list the best series of manorial court rolls, and to enter on to a computer (long before such methods had become commonplace) the early records of two manors.[43]

A great stimulus for him and his approach to history came in the late 1970s when a young American Marxist, Robert Brenner, put forward a challenging new interpretation of the origins of agrarian capitalism, arguing that the English peasants' lack of secure tenure made them vulnerable to the acquisitive gentry around 1500.[44] Hilton joined in the debate with an article which restated his view of a crisis of feudalism, and which forcibly made the point that peasants had the advantage that their holdings and household units of production could exist without lords, while the lords depended on the rents of peasant tenants, and in the long run lords' power was vulnerable to pressure from peasants.

In his research and thinking he was still breaking new ground in the 1970s. He read social science avidly, finding the works of Weber particularly stimulating, and also more recent writers such as Runciman. This enthusiasm can be seen in the opening chapters of *Bond Men Made Free* and the *English Peasantry*, which both demonstrate that he regarded modern sociology and anthropology as supplementing rather than replacing the ideas of Marx. When he was embracing social science he was also developing a new specialism in the history of towns. He had taken an interest in urban society throughout his academic life. He plotted the sources of goods purchased by Leicestershire monasteries in his thesis, included a full chapter on towns in his west midland book, and contributed an essay to Maurice Dobb's festschrift on the property holdings of late medieval merchants.[45] Medieval urban history had struggled to

[43] A important output from this research project was the list of court rolls: (with J. Cripps and J. Williamson), 'Appendix: a Survey of Medieval Manorial Court Rolls in England', in Z. Razi and R. Smith (eds.), *Medieval Society and the Manor Court* (Oxford, 1996), pp. 569–637.

[44] 'A Crisis of Feudalism', *Past and Present*, 80 (1978), 3–19, repr. in T. H. Aston and C. H. E. Philpin (eds.), *The Brenner Debate. Agrarian Class Structure and Economic Development in Pre-Industrial Europe* (Cambridge, 1985), pp. 119–37.

[45] 'Some Problems of Urban Real Property in the Middle Ages', C. H. Feinstein (ed.) *Socialism, Capitalism and Economic Growth: Essays Presented to Maurice Dobb* (Cambridge, 1967), pp. 326–37, repr. in *Class Conflict*, pp. 165–74.

escape from the shadow cast by the constitutional historians in the early twentieth century, who made it seem a very dull subject. Now in the 1970s, with so much stimulating work in modern urban history, and when it was clear that commerce had penetrated into the medieval countryside, it was time to open up the study of medieval towns once more.

He investigated occupational specialisation, and showed in a number of chapters and essays that much could be learned from tax records, especially the returns of the poll taxes in 1379 and 1381.[46] There were numerous craftsmen and traders scattered over the countryside, but towns, including very small towns, stood out because of their concentration of butchers, bakers, shoemakers, tailors, and many other artisans and providers of goods and services. How did towns relate to the rural and feudal society of lords and peasants? One view, still being expressed in the 1970s, regarded the towns as alien and subversive growths, forming islands of capitalism which would eventually take over the economy. Hilton argued the opposite in an article in an obscure American journal published in 1979.[47] Towns were part of the feudal order, as many of them were ruled by lords, and provided lords with rents. The urban traders supplied the aristocratic market with manufactured and imported goods. The social structure of towns resembled in some ways that of the feudal countryside, with the mercantile oligarchy using their power and privilege to exploit the artisans, who like the peasants worked as family units in their own houses. In another paper on popular movements published two years later he pursued the comparison between social structures and rebellion in town and country, and argued that the peasants, not the urban artisans, offered the main threat to the feudal order, as they questioned its very basis, and aimed to remove the aristocracy.[48]

He was following up these ideas with archival research on the small towns which he had first discussed as a special category in the *English Peasantry*. In the early 1980s he pointed the way with a short essay on the urban characteristics of Evesham in Worcestershire, and pursued the subject at more length in three essays, two of which derived much of their

[46] 'Some Social and Economic Evidence in Late Medieval English Tax Returns', in S. Herost (ed.), *Spoleczenstwo, Gospodarka, Kultura: Studies Offered to Marion Malowist* (Warsaw, 1974), pp. 111–28, repr. in *Class Conflict*, pp. 253–67.
[47] 'Towns in English Feudal Society', *Review (Journal of the Fernand Braudel Institute for the Study of Economies, Historical Systems and Civilizations)*, 3 (1979), 3–20, repr. in *Class Conflict*, pp. 175–86.
[48] 'Popular Movements in England at the End of the Fourteenth Century', in *Il Tumulto dei Ciompi: un Momento di Storia Fiorentina ed Europa* (Florence, 1981), pp. 223–40, repr. in *Class Conflict*, pp. 152–64.

substance from the borough records of Halesowen in Worcestershire and Thornbury in Gloucestershire.[49] The detail was as rich as in his earlier west midland work, as he portrayed the people who made up the turbulent society of newly established towns, like the family of Mable Walters of Halesowen between 1280 and 1322, who sold ale (and broke the rules), stole corn, and quarrelled fiercely with their neighbours. These small towns were distinguished from nearby villages by their diversity of occupations and the intensity of their social and economic interactions, yet some similarities between town and country are apparent. For example, the townspeople adopted antagonistic attitudes towards their lords, just like the peasants, and the lords attempted to extract money and services from them, and to control their behaviour and trading practices. They were closely connected with the peasantry, as the urban market encouraged 'simple commodity production' among small-scale cultivators.

Hilton's retirement from his chair at Birmingham came in 1982, and in the following year he was honoured with a festschrift contributed by students and friends, appropriately published in the *Past and Present* series, and presented to him at a *Past and Present* party.[50] He continued his connection with Birmingham University, and he became the first Director of the Institute for Advanced Research in the Humanities, which provided a base for those who had achieved distinction outside regular university employment, and for retired academics who were still active in research. He was still writing about towns at this time, and a book on English and French towns appeared in 1992 which marked a further stage in the development of the ideas that he had advanced over the previous fifteen years.[51] Medieval towns, he reiterated, were a dimension of feudal society, and their internal government and social hierarchy shows that they had much in common with the rural world, with their workshops based on family units and elites anxious to control their subordinates through municipal regulation. The urban rulers used taxes to extract

---

[49] 'The Small Town and Urbanisation—Evesham in the Middle Ages', *Midland History*, 7 (1982), 1–8, repr. in *Class Conflict*, pp. 187–93; 'Lords, Burgesses and Huxters', *Past and Present*, 97 (1982), 3–15, repr. in *Class Conflict*, pp. 194–204; 'Small Town Society in England Before the Black Death', *Past and Present*, 105 (1984), 53–78, repr. in R. Holt and G. Rosser (eds.), *The Medieval Town. A Reader in English Urban History, 1200–1540* (London, 1990), pp. 71–96; 'Medieval Market Towns and Simple Commodity Production', *Past and Present*, 109 (1985), 3–23. A fifth article, probably written in the late 1980s, was not published until a decade later: 'Low-Level Urbanization: the Seigneurial Borough of Thornbury in the Middle Ages', in Razi and Smith (eds.), *Medieval Society*, pp. 482–517.

[50] Aston *et al.* (eds.), *Social Relations and Ideas*, see above, n. 5.

[51] *English and French Towns in Feudal Society. A Comparative Study* (Cambridge, 1992).

money from the townspeople rather as lords took rent from peasants. Urban society was based on classes, and they often came into conflict. A chapter in the book indicates the influence on him of the advance of cultural history, in a survey of the imagery and ceremony of civic life, entitled 'How urban society was imagined'.

This record of scholarship in its historical context gives only the highlights of a life of research and writing. Many essays and papers have been omitted—eleven works by him were published for example between 1985 and 1990, of which only one has been mentioned here. Brief reference can only be made to the dozens of book reviews, or his lectures to student societies, branches of the Historical Association, and many other organisations. He contributed articles to popular journals, and edited collections of essays. He was intensely industrious, reading omnivorously, and while his writing reflects the breadth of his knowledge and understanding, he footnoted only a minimum of the sources that he used.

All of this must give a picture of an earnest and devoted scholar, but for all of the dedication and hard work he also enjoyed life. A memory of the early 1950s recalls him attending gatherings of the unconventional intelligentsia of Birmingham, in the company of surrealist artists and 'freckled young women wearing gypsy dresses'.[52] In later life he was very convivial, and one often encountered him with a group of companions, engaged in bantering, light-hearted conversation. He often visited public houses, and was very fond of wine, warning (ironically) of the danger of drinking water, which might be polluted.[53] He also enjoyed good food, which he often cooked himself, being especially prone to use formidable quantities of garlic. He could break into spontaneous singing.

His most important contribution as a university academic was as a stimulus for more serious and experienced students (in the later phase of his teaching career first-year students found him rather daunting), and above all as a supervisor of postgraduates. He encouraged their research work, and was always aware of the danger of narrow obsession with archival data gathering. When there were enough students to form a seminar, he would organise discussions at which theory and historical literature were discussed, so that no student was unaware of the need to set their discoveries in a broader context. He would encourage reading of books from Continental Europe wherever possible, and when an important new work

---

[52] From a letter to the author of this memoir from Tim Hilton.
[53] The idea was suggested by a notice seen on one of many visits to France: 'L'eau est pollué; buvez du vin'.

appeared, such as Duby's *Guerriers et Paysans*, he would urge students and colleagues to read it. From about 1969 research students prompted by him held informal seminars on Friday evenings in their houses or flats in rotation, at which papers were read and discussed and much wine consumed. The 'Friday night seminars' attracted scholars from other universities, and even from overseas, and continued long after his retirement. When research students wrote their chapters, they were returned promptly, with pages of unusually thin paper covered with annotations, comments, and suggestions for improvements in a small but very legible hand. If a student came up with a good idea or a significant discovery, he recommended its publication. Outsiders spoke of a 'Birmingham School', but the research students were a very heterogeneous group. Perhaps one can see some common traits among those who were supervised by him, such as a concern for generalisation and context, or a tendency to distrust authority, whether that of medieval lords, ecclesiastics, and governments, or of members of the modern historical establishment.

His strong personality—he was among the few academics to whom the word charismatic can be applied—meant that conversations with him were often memorable. He had a particular intonation, and emphasised key phrases, which became lodged in the minds of those engaged with him. What he said was often apposite, or amusing, or thoughtful, or all three. His opinions were forcefully put, in pithy, colloquial language: 'possibly the most boring book ever written' was said of more than one prestigious work. A mention of historical geography provoked the comment: 'The problem with historical geographers is not what they know, but how they know it.'[54] He was irreverent, delighting in pricking the bubble of any hint at self-importance or complacency. He applied this to himself, and anyone who attempted to flatter or praise him incurred his immediate displeasure. He was capable of making life awkward for those in authority, even when they probably meant well. Students and colleagues wished to please him, and even to draw from him some word of approval, but these were not given very freely, as Philip Rahtz complained rather plaintively.[55]

Setting aside his tendency to mischievous conversation, he could at the appropriate time adopt much more responsible attitudes, taking very seriously the decision making on university committees, and on the board of

---

[54] Remembered by Howard Clarke, who while he was not a student of Hilton, was much influenced by Hilton in the 1960s. Sally Harvey was similarly drawn into Hilton's circle at this time.

[55] Personal comment by Philip Rahtz.

Past and Present. Whatever happened in 1956, he did not cease to be a communist. He remained loyal to the ideals which he believed had been betrayed by those in power. He always viewed the world in Marxist terms, emphasising class and struggle in everyday life, and analysing events and situations within that framework of ideas. In his historical thinking he could never accord much significance to growth and decline of population, as he regarded the fashionable emphasis on these trends as detracting from the really vital factors such as class conflict. In university or academic life he was always aware of antagonism, or of some impending threat from the right, and he was conscious of struggling against opposing forces. In Britain any hostility tended to be insidious and difficult to pin down, but there was no doubt about the attacks on historians in Czechoslovakia after 1968, or in India in the 1970s, and he was outspoken in defence of their academic freedom.

In his personal contacts, but more widely through his writing, he had a major role in making the subject of medieval economic and social history a lively field of enquiry and debate, which is a legacy that continues into the new century. After his death on 7 June 2002, his friends and students decided that the most appropriate way in which his memory could be honoured was by holding a conference, called 'Rodney Hilton's Middle Ages', to discuss the themes and ideas that he had pioneered. The aim was not to dwell on the past, but to look forward to future developments. It was fitting that papers were given by younger scholars, as well as those who had known him. Historians from twelve countries were present, and in view of the possible pollution of water supplies, much wine was drunk.

CHRISTOPHER DYER
Fellow of the Academy

Note. I am very grateful to Jean Birrell, Peter Coss, Ceinwen Hilton, Tim Hilton, Eric Hobsbawm and Chris Wickham for comments, improvements and correction of errors.

KEITH HOPKINS

Morris Keith Hopkins
1934–2004[1]

'BE BOLD, BLOODY, AND YOURSELF.' Such was the advice Keith Hopkins offered to a group of his early Cambridge graduate students, and he seemed to be transmitting his own code of scholarly behaviour. It certainly took a considerable amount of audacity to do all that Hopkins did to broaden the study of ancient and in particular Roman history. Yet the rethinking he advocated was not always well understood, and it remains to some extent an open question how deep the effects of his work have been and will be. Whether this is more because of the bloodiness of the reformer, the conservatism of his colleagues, or the utopian nature of the changes he hoped to bring about, could be endlessly debated. Of course anyone can be bloody: Hopkins wanted the sort of bloodiness that would lead to a more imaginative ancient history ('empathy' was a favourite word) and effectively diminish the amount of humbug and triviality perpetrated by his fellow ancient-historians; this was essentially an optimistic mission.

When Hopkins looked back on his tenure of the Cambridge chair that he had long desired and then occupied for sixteen years, he was dissatisfied with himself; but it can easily be argued that no one in his generation did more to keep the subject in vigorous health. He introduced new topics, and demonstrated the importance of topics that had once been marginal. Having learned historical sociology (from Elias, Giddens, and others), he was able to conduct a series of structural analyses of Roman society such as had rarely if ever been attempted by previous historians. He arguably

[1] I am profoundly indebted to Rachel Hopkins for letting me see a videotaped interview that she conducted with her father on 25 January 2004.

Proceedings of the British Academy, **130**, 81–105. © The British Academy 2005.

did as much as anyone in this field has ever done to make his colleagues reflect about historical method. And over a long period, because of the breadth of his interests and the accessibility of his writing, he shared with his mentor Moses Finley much of the privilege and responsibility of telling British scholars in other specialities what the ancient world had really been like. As much as anyone since Momigliano, he suggested to a wide variety of them not only that Roman history was an intrinsically important field but that some of its practitioners were sometimes worth reading. And it may be added that although the sales of Hopkins's book *A World Full of Gods* did not rival those of say *The World of Odysseus* (the book which gained Finley a non-specialist following), he spoke to a larger public—often, in recent years, on television—than most other scholars reach. What that public heard, whether it knew it or not, was a deeply original voice.

What scholars encountered, when they listened to Hopkins or read his works, was a sharp intelligence and a person who derived deep satisfaction as well as frequent amusement from applying that intelligence to history and historians. What saved him from excessive bloodiness, in the eyes of those who knew him well, was that he criticised himself as searchingly as he criticised anyone else. He constantly wanted to improve his practice of the historian's art. In his later career, therefore, he tried hard to fashion a new kind of ancient history appropriate to the 1990s, an effort that was in the end partially frustrated. But his colleagues also encountered a personality that was sometimes too aggressive to be capable of persuasion. With people he liked, Hopkins was charming to the point of seductiveness, and he judged with fine precision just how much self-revelation conduced to solid friendship. As an ancient historian he deserves to be remembered as one of the most original, perhaps the most original, of his generation, notwithstanding many flaws in his work and one large scholarly argosy that did not return to port.

Morris Keith Hopkins was born at Sutton in Surrey on 20 June 1934, and died in Cambridge shortly after twelve on the night of 8–9 March 2004. His father Albert was a successful trader in textiles, his paternal grandfather was a Kentish stone-mason. For the first seven years of Hopkins's life, his father worked for a London firm in what is now Ghana, and visited England and his two children at rare intervals. His mother Hélène was the daughter of an Austrian Jewish lady ('Austrian' in the pre-1918 sense), Helen Wagschal or Wagschall, who was born in Isfahan. She was the daughter of a Russian dentist who was naturalised as an American but practised in court circles in Iran, a world that is vivaciously described by the dentist's sister under the pseudonym 'Khush-Amed' in a volume entitled *Memoirs of a Lady Dentist and her Experiences in the East* (London: H. J. Drane, 1907).

Helen Wagschal eventually moved to England, in circumstances which cannot now be known, and survived long enough for her beauty and her 'outrageous' behaviour to make strong impressions on her young grandson. Hélène was sent to a Catholic school but remained Jewish in some sense, later getting baptised in order to be married. While she was a young mother she mostly resided in the Gold Coast too, so that the two Hopkins children, Keith and his older sister April, did not live with both parents until Keith had been some years in boarding schools. He first went away to school before his fourth birthday, and entered Brentwood School at the age of seven, leaving in 1952.

Legend has it that the six-year-old Hopkins wrote a precocious letter from school asking for books by Gibbon and Macaulay so that he could get down to writing the history of ancient Rome. The letter in question, which is undated but clearly belongs to that period of the boy's life, does not mention Gibbon, Macaulay or any other author, but asks for books so that the writer can become 'a great man'. Meanwhile there were war-time hazards for anyone in the vicinity of London. His sister recalls an occasion when, while they were staying in Hampstead, an explosion, which must have been a V-1 or a V-2 rocket, blew out the French windows in the room where the children lay in bed. Their mother reacted fatalistically, far too much so in April's opinion.

Hopkins did not send any of his five children to a boarding school. He was inclined to puncture the pretensions of Brentwood. But this ambitious youth did very well there, and not only as a pupil; he was also part of the establishment—senior NCO of the cadet force, captain of the chess team (an unusual combination), yet also editor of the school magazine, a member of the rugby XV, head of his house, and finally senior prefect of the whole school. Photographs show a good-looking young man sitting next to the headmaster, wearing a gown and also a proper expression of entitlement. Classics were still at that time regarded in such schools as almost the only proper intellectual activity for the most able pupils: in short, Hopkins conformed and excelled, and in December 1952 he was elected to an Exhibition in Classics at King's College, Cambridge (later he became a Scholar). He knew how to accept responsibilities, more than most males of his age, and he had a thorough knowledge of Greek and Latin.

If this upbringing had any lasting ill effects, they were invisible in the later decades of his life. Those who knew him when he was young are inclined to suppose that his early life made for a level of irascibility that diminished only in the 1960s and 1970s. As his bloodiness gradually confined itself to specialised academic channels, a sense of his own imperfections came more into view; this was indeed one of his most attractive characteristics.

Early in 1953, the eighteen-year-old visited the United States for the first time, as Britain's representative to a 'world high school forum', which meant many weeks of seeing the sights in different parts of the country. Enthusiastic letters home still survive. The other surviving record is a photograph of the international delegation of students in the company of a quite bemused-looking President Eisenhower.

National service followed. Hopkins had no special affinity for the sea, but he did have an affinity for Russian and entered the Royal Navy's language programme. After basic training, Midshipman M. K. Hopkins completed a year of Russian at London University (School of Slavonic Studies), and then six months of further training at the Joint Services School at Bodmin, qualifying as a 'Service Interpreter' in February 1955. He was not displeased to recall later that out of 300 or 400 who began the course, only twenty-five were commissioned at the end of it. Besides Russian, he also learned that a high proportion of naval officers continued to come from prominent public schools.

At King's too, as an undergraduate, Hopkins seems to have been especially aware of the peculiarities of the British class system, all the more so because during several vacations—and this was a most unusual thing to do—he taught in a secondary modern school where his best pupils were, in his opinion, excluded from Oxbridge precisely by class and not by lack of ability. At the same time he could see the social mobility in his own family: his father, he used to say, was a cockney, though well-to-do and an aggressive Tory.

Hopkins was taught classics at King's by L. P. Wilkinson and Donald Lucas, but as an undergraduate he probably did not at first see himself as a future scholar. His Part I Tripos result was a II.1, which makes it very difficult to suppose that he was deeply engaged by the classics. Sir Nicholas Goodison recalls 'play[ing] bridge in each other's rooms in Bodley's Court, usually with a bottle of something good chosen by him from the College's wine list—then extraordinarily good value because the College never raised the price'. In or about 1957, however, Hopkins attended a seminar taught jointly by Cambridge's two most prominent ancient historians, A. H. M. Jones and Moses Finley,[2] and in his third year Finley was his

---

[2] Finley must still have seemed very American: he had only had a regular position at Cambridge since 1955.

supervisor; it can be conjectured that Hopkins now quickly saw that ancient history could be a real intellectual challenge. And Finley, he said, made him work as he had never worked before.

Not that his progression into academia was unhesitating, and there was some thought of following a career similar to his father's. He also took and passed the Civil Service exam. A year in America was in fashion, however, and before the Tripos results were known he was accepted by the History Department at the University of Illinois in Urbana, where he spent a year acquiring a wider historical education than Cambridge offered to its classicists.

Hopkins's first in Part II of the Classical Tripos in 1958 must have helped to convince Jones, who was Professor of Ancient History, to encourage his academic inclinations: in 1959 he took up a State Studentship and was awarded the university's Henry Arthur Thomas Studentship. Jones was writing his encyclopaedic *The Later Roman Empire*, and it must have been with his help that Hopkins saw that late antiquity was at that time practically a historian's Eldorado; this was to be Hopkins's scholarly focus for four or five years (but not thereafter, one can only guess why). The crucial influence right at the beginning was, however, Finley, who was beginning to work a scholarly revolution in those years, helped by a wide historical education, a magnetic personality, and considerable ambition. Finley, like Arnaldo Momigliano, saw and deplored the intellectual insularity of ancient history in Britain, and most of all the feebleness of a view of antiquity that paid no attention to such fundamental facts of ancient life as slavery.

From Urbana, then, it was back to Cambridge (with stays in Tübingen and Geneva), where Hopkins started a never-to-be-completed Ph.D. dissertation with Jones as his supervisor; its intended subject is no longer clear, but from a phrase Hopkins wrote some six years later it appears that contraception under the Roman Empire was at least part of the object of his research.[3] Another early line of inquiry produced his first scholarly article, 'Social Mobility in the Later Roman Empire: the Evidence of Ausonius',[4] a well-written essay in which a single family is used as a lever to overturn the then-popular notion that late-Roman society was highly immobile. Nowadays one might carp about this argument, but in 1961 Jones and Finley—and Hopkins—were the only ancient historians

---

[3] 'Contraception in the Roman Empire', *Comparative Studies in Society and History*, 8 (1965–6), 124 n*.

[4] *Classical Quarterly*, 11 (1961), 239–49.

who were capable of formulating a sustained argument about social mobility at all—and Hopkins was the one who did it. Meanwhile Finley was determined that Hopkins should overcome what he saw (not without some envy, in my view) as the defects of a British classical education: he needed to learn some social science, and for Finley that meant above all sociology or economics.

In those days young British academics moved quite quickly into teaching positions, and when the lectureship or teaching fellowship came, you took it. In 1961 the Sociology Department at the University of Leicester, which was headed by the distinguished Ilya Neustadt,[5] and also contained the equally distinguished though not yet famous Norbert Elias, needed assistant lecturers. The appointments committee presumably had little difficulty in selecting Anthony Giddens, a fresh Ph.D. in Sociology and the future director of the London School of Economics. The simultaneous appointment of Hopkins was more daring, since he had no serious sociological credentials whatsoever, and it was engineered by Moses Finley, as Hopkins later recounted; Neustadt, however, was the person who had to take his courage into his hands. Later on, Hopkins more or less seriously credited Giddens with having taught him sociology; and both of them used to attend the lectures of Elias. The latter 'emphasized', in Giddens's words, 'a comparative and developmental approach to sociology, which clearly resonated with Keith's approach to ancient history'. Giddens also recalls the great scandal young Hopkins caused by entering the Leicester University senior common room not wearing a tie. But he was not staying for long: he learned sociology so rapidly that two years later he was given a position at Britain's social-science power-house, LSE.

He was teaching sociology but his work continued to have Roman history as its object: he began writing a fellowship dissertation for King's called *The Later Roman Aristocracy: a Demographic Profile*. In this first large-scale work (never published as such), he argued that under the emperors Rome's senatorial order suffered from serious infertility, and then explored in detail various possible explanations.[6] King's was impressed and awarded Hopkins a fellowship, which he held from 1963 until 1967. Not even Finley had written about ancient demography, and the truly modern bibliography of the subject consisted of a single article

[5] See T. H. Marshall's account of him in A. Giddens and G. Mackenzie (eds.), *Social Class and the Division of Labour: Essays in Honour of Ilya Neustadt* (Cambridge, 1982), pp. xi–xvi.
[6] See 'Elite Mobility in the Roman Empire', *Past and Present*, 32 (1965), 12–26: 24–26, repr. in M. I. Finley (ed.), *Studies in Ancient Society* (London, 1974), pp. 103–20: 117–19.

in the *American Journal of Sociology*.[7] Another remarkable piece of work in this period was the article 'Eunuchs in Politics in the Later Roman Empire',[8] which gave quite magisterially a structural explanation of the rise and continuation of the eunuchs' power in the late imperial court, showing how even their nasty reputation ('lizards and toads' are the words of Basil of Caesarea) had a definite function.

* * *

In 1963 Keith Hopkins met and married Juliet Phelps Brown, a child-therapist in the making and a powerful intellect who was to have a large influence on his personality (it can be presumed that she was in part responsible for her husband's undergoing a year of psychoanalysis in the mid-1960s) and on his work as well (throughout their married life she read most of his work in time to offer useful criticism). They had three children together, Rachel, Edmund and Ben, all of them great sources of parental pride.

Hopkins was now the son-in-law of the labour economist Sir Henry Phelps Brown, who also became a scholarly adviser and helped him mature as a social scientist. Phelps Brown, he wrote in 1978, had given him 'repeated tutorials in economics', and the lessons were highly visible.

The student was now on a par with his Cambridge teachers, and both Jones and Finley recognised his extraordinary ability; a quiet remark in the preface of *The Later Roman Empire* reveals that the only scholar to whom Jones had entrusted a reading of the whole of Part II, the ambitious analytic part of the book, had been 'Mr. Keith Hopkins of London University'.

The move to LSE (assistant lecturer in Sociology 1963, lecturer 1964) was brought about by the professor of demography there, D. V. Glass. He had been asked by King's to assess Hopkins's fellowship thesis; having read it, he 'telephoned and offered me a job', pointing out that if Hopkins really wanted to learn demography, LSE not Cambridge was the place to be. King's most obligingly allowed him to retain his fellowship. The move in the direction of sociology seemed more pronounced now, and it must have been in the next year or so that Hopkins showed for the first time the strong interest in quantification that was to mark most of his career. This

[7] Some had asked the questions (see for instance R. Meiggs, *Roman Ostia* (Oxford, 1960), p. 243), but had not found good ways to answer them.
[8] *Proceedings of the Cambridge Philological Society*, 189 (1963), 62–80, later revised as ch. 4 of *Conquerors and Slaves*.

can be seen in 'The Age of Roman Girls at Marriage' and even more in 'On the Probable Age-Structure of the Roman Population'.[9] These two articles can be said without exaggeration to be the beginning of serious study of the historical demography of the ancient world. In both cases Hopkins essentially set the terms of the debate that has unrolled ever since. 'Contraception in the Roman Empire' was another wonderfully original paper;[10] as with demography, the subject was not utterly new, but it had not previously received informed or thoughtful treatment, and it certainly was not part of mainstream ancient history. Three papers in three years changed the basis of Roman social history, not simply by putting new topics on the agenda but by showing which techniques would produce the most plausible results. All of these papers are buttressed by the traditional philological and bibliographical prowess of the ancient historian, but their aim was to make an impression on sociologists and social historians: the choice of the journals to publish in (see above, notes 3 and 9) was not casual. And though the majority of the problems addressed were quite technical, one of the most impressive qualities of these contributions is the author's concern with wider issues, including family and emotions: Hopkins was already thinking about empathy, a central theme in his later work.

The degree to which Hopkins now carried conviction as a sociologist was indicated in 1964 when he was appointed review editor of the *British Journal of Sociology* (a position he held until he left Britain in 1967). And he enjoyed himself greatly at LSE: one graduate student of that time, John Cooke, has recalled how in a weekly seminar 'Keith opened our eyes each week both to the classics of sociology and anthropology and to the relevance of applying them to comparative history.'[11] The extraordinary degree to which Hopkins managed to live a double intellectual life in this period is illustrated by another sociology paper based on extensive research, 'Civil-Military Relations in Developing Countries',[12] which reflects contemporary concern, ostensibly non-ideological, with 'development' in poor countries and with the effects on this process of military coups. In the same year there came out another enormously wide-ranging

[9] *Population Studies*, 18 (1964–5), 309–27, and 20 (1966–7), 245–64.

[10] *Comparative Studies in Society and History*, 8 (1965–6), 124–51. Cf. also the sure-footed little paper 'A Textual Emendation in a Fragment of Musonius Rufus: a Note on Contraception', *Classical Quarterly*, 15 (1965), 72–4.

[11] *The Times*, 13 April 2004.

[12] *British Journal of Sociology*, 17 (1966), 165–82.

paper, 'Slavery in Classical Antiquity'.[13] This and 'Structural Differentia-
tion in Rome (200–31 BC): the Genesis of an Historical Bureaucratic
Society',[14] were leading towards the kind of structural analysis of Roman
society and Roman imperialism that finally came together in *Conquerors
and Slaves* (1978). It hardly mattered if he did not quite get the vectors of
Roman expansion right: he was far ahead of anyone else.

All this could have led to a chair in sociology in Britain, but the first
interesting chair that was open was in Hong Kong, with the double
advantage that it could be done on secondment from LSE and that it
looked like a clear break with classics. Hopkins's closest relatives were
somewhat dismayed that he intended to transplant himself to Hong
Kong, but once the opportunity arose acceptance was overdetermined:
Hopkins took his family with him, and he found out for himself what the
British colonial world was like, and how to run a sociology department.
The appointment (which was for three years) seemed to mean giving up
ancient history—sociology written in Hong Kong could hardly be about
the Romans. Yet that seems not to have been Hopkins's long-term intention: he was already at the centre of the debate about ancient history (in
so far as such a sprawling subject can ever be said to be concentrated in a
single debate), and he knew it, and there was a powerful need to finish the
structural and sociological book about the Roman Empire that eventually
became *Conquerors and Slaves*. Hopkins indubitably saw that Finley was
likely to succeed to the Cambridge chair (as he did in 1970), and that he
would have to retire by 1979. There was a grand solution to the sociology-
or-ancient-history dilemma, only available to a person of great mental
energy: do both.

The new professor of sociology threw himself energetically into
studying Hong Kong's massive housing problem. Research teams from
the Sociology Department set about documenting the colony's intense
over-crowding, in conditions which were made more difficult by the
Cultural Revolution (the inhabitants had four hours of water every four
days in the summer of 1967). Hopkins took a lesson in Cantonese every
day, measured rooms without number, and wrote four papers on Hong
Kong housing, one of which, 'Housing the Poor', appeared in a book he
edited under the title *Hong Kong: the Industrial Colony. A Political,
Social and Economic Survey* (Hong Kong: Oxford University Press, 1971),

[13] In A. de Reuck and J. Knight (eds.), *Caste and Race: Comparative Approaches* (London, 1966), pp. 166–77.
[14] In I. M. Lewis (ed.), *History and Social Anthropology* (London, 1968), pp. 63–79.

pp. 271–335.[15] The essay begins 'Hong Kong is a cruel society in which very little assistance is given to the poor', and proceeds to document the assertion: 'in 1956 . . ., in the most overcrowded district, the average living space was only 12 sq. ft. . . . per person'. 'It is amazing that [the] overt paternalism [of the Hong Kong government] has survived . . .'; what rendered such conditions tolerable for many was the colony's almost unparalleled economic growth since the Second World War. He remembered the colonial officials years later ('arrogant, self-centred, narrow-minded'), but also asserted, typically, that he, not they, had been mistaken about housing policy (it appears[16] that he had recommended that the government should divert resources from building high-rise blocks of flats into improving physical conditions in Hong Kong's large areas of improvised squatter housing). At all events, he departed rich in memories of Hong Kong sounds and smells. And the Roman historian had seen something of what he thought ancient poverty might have looked like. The 'cruel society' most in his mind was Rome.

There was also another sense in which Hopkins became a real sociologist in Hong Kong: he was able to think of research projects being carried out by groups, a largely alien mode of operation for British historians and classicists at that time. This was to continue: all three of Hopkins's ancient history books were in one way or another the results of collaboration.

After two years, at all events, Hopkins decided that he had had enough of Hong Kong. Having won an invitation to the Institute for Advanced Study at Princeton as a social scientist (though the School of Social Sciences, soon to be headed by Clifford Geertz, had not yet formally come into being),[17] he resigned from his Hong Kong chair. His parting comment to the *Hong Kong Standard* complained about the 'slow development' of his department, and about the unrest of the university's lecturers he said that it would be 'strange if lecturers do not take a critical view of the university they are teaching in'.

In retrospect what seems most anomalous about this sequence of events is not that Hopkins went to Hong Kong and investigated housing—

---

[15] Phelps Brown was among the contributors. Hopkins also published his inaugural lecture *Public Housing Policy in Hong Kong* (in the University of Hong Kong *Gazette*, Supplement of 21 May 1969), and 'Public and Private Housing in Hong Kong', in D. J. Dwyer (ed.), *The City as a Centre of Change in Asia* (Hong Kong, 1971), pp. 200–15.

[16] See Hopkins's article in *UNICEF News* no. 77 (1973), 16–19. But there is some unclarity on this point.

[17] Given the way the Institute functioned in those days, it seems likely that J. F. Gilliam played an important role in arranging this invitation: he was certainly an admirer of Hopkins's work.

that was a brilliant educational idea; what surprises is that during the rest of his career, which included fifteen years as a sociologist in London— fifteen years that saw the beginning of the Thatcher period—he never spoke out on any question of public policy. Hopkins was indeed politically moderate even when young (though he never, he said, voted Conservative); he would explain that he did not believe that any political party or movement was likely to produce a net decrease in social injustice. 'Right and Left are not the terms in which I think', he was once quoted as saying in an academic context,[18] and there was some truth in that; at all events, he always seems to have avoided a markedly left or right identity. Meanwhile there was a vast amount of work to do, both in ancient history and, after 1972, in building up the social sciences at Brunel.

After the Institute for Advanced Study, Hopkins returned to LSE for two years, as a senior lecturer in sociology. A squib in the *TLS* (March 31, 1972) entitled 'Classicists and Sociologists' accused the ancient historians of living in a hermetic world and of being indifferent to generalisation; the author sensibly remarked that matters might improve 'if ancient historians spent one paragraph in each article explaining the significance of their problem'. Several ancient historians are accused, but three are praised, Peter Brunt, Finley of course—and, less predictably perhaps, Momigliano. The same year provided two enormous opportunities: he joined the editorial board of the young and innovative Trevor Aston-led *Past and Present* (in a sense replacing A. H. M. Jones, who had died in 1970), and he was appointed Professor of Sociology and Social Anthropology at the also still young Brunel University (created in 1966)—with the great advantage of staying in London. For a number of years he did much to shape *Past and Present*'s ancient-historical side (eventually he grew less interested, but did not resign until 1999); this work is the subject of a memoir by his Cambridge successor, Robin Osborne.[19]

The Brunel appointment meanwhile took up a great deal of energy, and Hopkins's colleague Peter Seglow recalls how everyone in the department shared in such tasks as interviewing the undergraduate applicants. The ideological wars of the 1970s sometimes made themselves felt, and for a time Hopkins was quite unpopular with the left-wing staff. But his reputation as a departmental administrator grew (which is worth mentioning, since he never had such a reputation later on in the Classics Faculty at Cambridge), and that was what led to his being appointed

[18] *Sunday Times*, 16 May 1976.
[19] *Past and Present*, 185 (2004), 3–7.

Dean of the Faculty of Social Sciences (1981–5). It was a difficult era of Thatcherian cuts and their after-effects.

The subject of his inaugural lecture at Brunel was nicely selected to connect social anthropology and antiquity: brother–sister marriage in Roman Egypt, an anomalous but well-attested phenomenon—familiar to scholars but still mysterious. Hopkins's study of the problem was so detailed that in many countries the author would have thought that it was a book.[20] He was probably better equipped to explain this custom and its long persistence than anyone had ever been, yet it was a sign of things to come in his intellectual life that instead of arguing for any single explanation he left the issue open and made a prolonged effort to understand the feelings as well as the life-situations of those involved.

The years spent at Brunel allowed a long series of debates with other ancient historians in various settings in the University of London which are invariably remembered with nostalgia by those who took part in them, or at least by those who lived to tell the tale (for it was here that Hopkins delivered his technique of lethal intervention). Deep disagreements were no obstacle, and one of the main reasons was Hopkins, his energy and originality.

This period also saw him quite often in North America, as a visiting professor at the University of Pennsylvania (1974), a member of the Institute for Advanced Study again in 1974–5,[21] and as a visiting professor for one quarter at UCLA (1979). During the second of these visits I invited him to lecture at Columbia, which was our first meeting. At the start of his lecture, the speaker came out from behind the lectern, sat cheerfully on the small table in front of it, and looking as well as sounding like something completely new explained the Romans to us for sixty extraordinarily stimulating minutes. A long and festive but also intellectually strenuous evening at my apartment followed, and the beginning of strong affection.

Two major schemes occupied Hopkins's scholarly energies during the 1970s: one was to put together the structural and sociological account of the Roman Empire which he had already been working on at intervals for several years—this was eventually to become both *Conquerors and Slaves* (Cambridge, 1978) and *Death and Renewal* (Cambridge, 1983). When he was invited to give the Gray Lectures at Cambridge in 1977, at a relatively early age (Moses Finley at work again), he delivered a preliminary version

---

[20] The lecture was published in expanded form in *Comparative Studies in Society and History*, 22 (1980), 303–54.

[21] He was a member of the Institute for a third time, a rare privilege, in 1983.

of the the two central chapters of *Death and Renewal*—the part that is recognisable as traditional sociology. The other notion was to build a model of the Roman economy, or at least of a very important part of the Roman economy—this became 'Taxes and Trade in the Roman Empire' (1980),[22] the culmination of work going back a decade.

Conquerors and Slaves and *Death and Renewal* were presented as a single project, 'Sociological Studies in Roman History', volumes 1 and 2, and they served as an aggressive manifesto. The introduction to the first volume says that it is

> an attempt to analyse a changing social structure and to evoke a lost world. It is also an attempt to apply some modern sociological concepts and techniques to Roman history. . . .The achievements of the Roman world need to be interpreted with *empathetic understanding* [my italics] of what the Romans themselves thought and with concepts which we ourselves use.

A less lucid paragraph proclaims the importance of 'enter[ing] the thought-world of the Romans', and accuses other ancient historians of having failed to do this because they attributed too much modern rationality to the ancients. The charge was not completely unfair, but such sweeping claims grated even on those who were willing to learn. When the author wrote ironically about those who were interested in facts and evidence, it was all too clear that in practice he relied on them as much as most historians and indeed more than some others. He let it be known that he was against the established methods, while in the preface he acknowledged the help of several of those who practised them; the debt to Brunt was particularly clear. The provocation was very effective in a sense, if not always productive: the book was widely reviewed by ancient historians and led many of them to serious reflection.[23] Others, however, ignored what was really new about his approach, and they must have made the author think that the classicists had changed little since he wrote his *TLS* essay of 1972.

The book is not unified by a single topic, although slavery is at the centre of three of its five chapters. It is, however, unified in a different way: precisely as it claimed, it exemplified some of the ways in which a sociologist might approach Roman history. The first chapter remains unsurpassed as an account of the complex effects on the republican

[22] *Journal of Roman Studies*, 70 (1980), 101–25.
[23] Thus the mixed review by E. Badian (*Journal of Roman Studies*, 72 (1982), 164–9) included the most extended methodological reflections to be found anywhere in that author's works, as far as I know.

Romans of seven linked phenomena, 'continuous war, the influx of booty, its investment in land, the formation of large estates, the impoverishment of peasants, their emigration to towns and the provinces, the growth of urban markets'. What was distinctive about his approach was not so much, as the author claimed, the description of macrohistorical developments which the Romans themselves could not possibly have understood—for those Romans who looked around them certainly noticed the phenomena just mentioned and had some understanding of them. What mattered most was rather his ability to link all these large trends together.[24] Not surprisingly, however, the section of the book that seems to have won most assent was more traditional in appearance: it analysed some little known ancient evidence, the 1200 or so manumission inscriptions from Delphi (a study in which Hopkins has P. J. Roscoe as his collaborator). Another chapter concerned Rome's divine emperors, arguing that they provided the empire with 'symbolic unity'. Nowadays this argument may or may not carry conviction, but it effectively restarted a discussion which had long been stalled.

Some complained that *Conquerors and Slaves* exaggerated the extent of the author's departure from traditional methods, and it can be said that he did not have the traditionalists quite in focus. But few will now doubt that the onslaught was needed.[25] Nineteen seventy-eight was indeed the year of provocation. The astute review editor of the *Journal of Roman Studies* was inspired to invite Hopkins to review Fergus Millar's elaborate volume *The Emperor in the Roman World*, the preface of which read as an open challenge to all that was distinctive about the work of Finley and Hopkins. The challenge needed an answer, and the result was a lengthy assault entitled 'Rules of Evidence',[26] which, however, criticised the author quite briefly for failing to consider what social scientists had had to say about kingship and at greater length for the more commonplace sin of generalising on the basis of insufficient evidence; also for leaving out 'the sympathetic understanding of feelings and fears, of ambiguities and ambivalence'.

There is hardly any economic history in any strict sense in *Conquerors and Slaves*, but in the years just before and after the publication of Finley's influential book *The Ancient Economy* (1973) the economic history of the

---

[24] The most serious lacuna in this work may have been its failure to choose between a status model of Roman society and a class model (not that that exhausts the options): cf. the comments by B. D. Shaw, *Helios*, 9, 2 (1982), 17–57 at 31–6.

[25] This book seems to have been translated more than any of Hopkins's other works: it was put into Spanish, Italian, Chinese, and Korean.

[26] *Journal of Roman Studies*, 68 (1978), 178–86.

Roman world became one of the chief objects of Hopkins's reflection. He detached himself from Finley's substantivist view of the Roman economy (perhaps he had not been much attached to it in the first place), according to which genuine growth was always an impossibility. In a series of papers published between 1978 and 1983 Hopkins debated this. A long article called 'Economic Growth and Towns in Classical Antiquity'[27] proposed that contrary to Finley's view, teasingly referred to as 'the current orthodoxy', the Roman Empire brought into being 'a significant volume of inter-regional trade', without directly confronting the issue whether this was accompanied by *per capita* growth across the whole population of the Roman Empire.

Meanwhile (1978–9) the Cambridge chair fell vacant but the election was won by a more seasoned scholar, J. A. Crook.

'Taxes and Trade in the Roman Empire' (1980),[28] possibly the Hopkins production that has been most cited in the scholarly literature, represents, together with the revised version written fifteen years later, the culmination of his published thinking about the Roman economy. The argument was that the Romans' extraction of cash taxes from the provinces acted as a powerful stimulus to long-distance trade, and—once again without facing the question of overall growth—Hopkins cautiously distanced himself from what he later called the 'static minimalist' model of the Roman economy that was so dear to Finley. The attractiveness of the argument was not simply that it provided an explanation for the apparent relative prosperity of the Roman Empire, but that it linked so many different phenomena together, in particular the money supply, long-distance trade, government expenditure and levels of taxation. The vulnerability of the model, perhaps not a grave one, is that it assumes a system in equilibrium.

Finally, for the time being, came his introduction to the collective work *Trade in the Ancient Economy.*[29] This set out with considerable elegance two competing models of the economy of the high Roman Empire: the Finley model, which is said to be 'by far the best model available', and something else. But what was that something else? The alternatives were to agree with Finley or to be 'in marginal dispute' with him. The following pages, however, seem to be in far more than marginal disagreement, and the conclusion that 'the Finley model of the ancient economy is

---

[27] In P. Abrams and E. A. Wrigley (eds.), *Towns in Societies* (Cambridge, 1978), pp. 35–77.
[28] See above, n. 22.
[29] In P. Garnsey, K. Hopkins and C. R. Whittaker (eds.), *Trade in the Ancient Economy* (London, 1983), pp. ix–xxv.

sufficiently flexible to incorporate this modest dynamic, without undermining its basic primitivism' must count as one of the most diplomatic
sentences Hopkins ever wrote. As Hopkins, and indeed Finley, might
have said, the Oedipal blow remained undelivered.[30] And there the matter
rested, as far as Hopkins's published views were concerned, until another
article of thirteen years later.

Death and Renewal might give the impression of being a collection of
essays by various hands, but its central section at least is a unity: this consists of 170 pages of lively but down to-earth argumentation about the
Roman aristocracy, co-authored by the younger scholar Graham Burton.[31]
This centerpiece is framed by essays about gladiatorial games and Roman
funerary practices (the latter co-authored by Melinda Letts),[32] which are
not sociological in any easily recognised sense but look forward to
Hopkins's own more impressionistic and more 'empathetic' later style.
The effect of this book on some of us was to make us wish for more, all
the way through: chapter 2, for instance, argued in effect that the replacement rate of the republican aristocracy was by aristocratic standards not
especially high—though what was original here was not the conclusion
itself but its formulation in statistical terms. Few would doubt now that
Hopkins and Burton were broadly correct about this, but they could have
strengthened their case with a clearer definition of 'aristocracy' and also
by some discussion of contemporary perceptions of aristocratic domin-
ance. Chapter 3 is Hopkins at his best, establishing and explaining the still
more rapid turnover in the senatorial order of imperial times; he thus
brought the emperors' system of government into abruptly sharper focus.
Even the most captious critics found this part of the book difficult to
fault, and its results remain fundamentally important for the history of
Roman government.

Death and Renewal seemed to solidify Hopkins's reputation. He was
elected a Fellow of the British Academy in 1984, and in the following year
he was named to the chair of Ancient History at Cambridge in succession
to John Crook. Yet the old sociological mission seemed to be running out
of passion, and the projected third volume of the series, which was apparently called *The Price of Peace* when it was in effect abandoned, seems not
to have received much attention after 1989 or 1990. The on the whole
somewhat negative reviews of *Death and Renewal* provoked no published

---

[30] For Finley's awareness of the psychological relationship see his review of *Death and Renewal*
in the *London Review of Books*, 22 Dec. 1983.

[31] The author of an insightful obituary published in *The Guardian*, 29 March 2004.

[32] Now Melinda Letts, OBE, Chairwoman of the Long-term Medical Condition Alliance.

response, and no more than two of his later articles were obviously sociological.[33]

The new professor returned to Cambridge, and also to King's, with enthusiasm. The death of Moses Finley in June 1986 must have been a serious blow, but Hopkins now had research students of his own for the first time, and the institutionalised opportunity to lead ancient historians in novel directions. There was also a fair amount of agreement at that time, though no unanimity, that the undergraduate ancient history curriculum needed to be redesigned, and Hopkins naturally favoured the move away from text-centred ancient history to a more thematic structure. And Cambridge seemed to have declared that Hopkins's kind of ancient history was to be preferred to other kinds.

The good was very good indeed. A considerable cohort of extraordinary graduate students frequented Cambridge in those years, and many of them found Hopkins the most challenging academic presence they had ever encountered; this was as true of specialists in Greek archaeology, for instance, as it was of Roman historians (Hopkins himself was growing more aware of visual evidence). Many learned permanent lessons from him. A tiro scholar who encountered him in that period, Jas Elsner, said that 'he was wonderful . . . in encouraging stones to be thrown in every glass house of the academy, and in urging the young to break all the rules. It was invigorating and exciting.' The word 'invigorating' occurs again and again in such assessments, and he was the only leader in the field who provided, in the words of Greg Woolf, 'the really savage root-and-branch criticism that a bright undergraduate or beginning graduate needs to stop complacency setting in'. And 'he was perfectly happy to be treated the same way by us when he gave papers'.

But in several ways the Cambridge professorial role did not in the end suit Hopkins very well, or such at least was what many thought. He treated some graduate students with what was perceived as unwarranted harshness. Incidents of the latter kind he usually regretted, I believe, for he was far from being an unkind person; but he did not always carry out his professional role as a restrained mentor. And being easily bored by institutional procedures, he paid little attention to the British Academy just as he neglected the Cambridge History Faculty—which harmed the

---

[33] 'Graveyards for Historians', in F. Hinard (ed.), *La mort, les morts et l'au-delà dans le monde romain* (Caen, 1987), pp. 113–26 (in which he argues that the 43,000 inscriptions of the western Roman Empire that give of the age of the deceased are demographically useless), and an article of 1998 referred to below.

cause of ancient history; in the eyes of some, he also short-shrifted the Classics Faculty.

The Cambridge chair did not of course mean that Hopkins would subside into being a more normal and conventional scholar. *The Price of Peace* continued for a time, but it no longer had the shock value of the first two volumes; and it may be that the disappointing reception of *Death and Renewal* had somewhat undermined the larger project. Egypt exercised more and more fascination (Hopkins, typically, was not to be frightened off by the papyrological mafia), but the project he often called *Crocodile Mummy*, an attempt to enter the social and religious life of Roman Egypt via the use of writing there,[34] took shape slowly and was ultimately absorbed in part into *A World Full of Gods*.

The move towards religious history, and particularly what was exotic and fantastic in ancient religion, was substantially a new interest discovered after the return to Cambridge, notwithstanding some earlier work on emperor-worship. 'From Violence to Blessing', in part a discussion of the strikingly long survival of the archaic feast of the Lupercalia, showed how difficult a task Hopkins had set himself. He attempts to strike a balance between an analytic approach and an empathetic one. The analysis is as trenchant as anything in *Conquerors and Slaves*; but the empathy was more elusive. The sources are entirely arid about what it felt like to be a Lupercal, or to be beaten by the Lupercals, at any date; yet 'we need', so wrote Hopkins, 'to think and feel ourselves back into how different Romans themselves experienced rituals', as an antidote to the elitism of historians both ancient and modern. The aim was a worthy one, but how could the fellow of King's feel like a man or woman in the ancient Roman street? The question continued to echo through Hopkins's work down to the end. Some of his friends wanted him to address it via the lengthy historiographical debates of the past, going back to Febvre and even to Vico, but he preferred to preach by doing; *A World Full of Gods* was the result.

The old sociological Hopkins and his younger brother the economist Hopkins were still at work in the early and middle nineties. 'Conquest by Book' made use of his new work on Egypt to set some context and highly pertinent question marks around some of the contentions in my book *Ancient Literacy*.[35] 'Novel Evidence for Roman Slavery' attempted to

---

[34] Something of the scope of this plan is indicated in 'Conquest by Book', in M. Beard *et al.*, *Literacy in the Roman World* (*Journal of Roman Archaeology*, Supplement 3) (Ann Arbor, 1991), p. 140 n. 17.

[35] See the volume mentioned in the previous note, pp. 133–58.

evoke the experience of Roman domestic slaves by putting under the microscope the fictitious ancient lives of the slave Aesop.[36] The author tried to show 'how a master and a slave, and by implication how many masters and many slaves, struggled to negotiate their competing interests'. This paper has been contested and it probably underestimates—oddly enough—the distorting effects of story-telling, but it is nonetheless remarkable, for it shows the historian thinking his way into the life of a Roman slave—which was a very considerable achievement.

In 'Christian Number and its Implications'[37] the sociologist put together a most extraordinary synthetic history of Christianity in the first four centuries. Here Hopkins seems to decoy the reader into thinking that the main subject is going to be that old problem, the numbers of the primitive Christians,[38] while in fact he intends to go much further and draw some startling conclusions about the spread of Christianity (for example, that there were perhaps forty-two literate Christians in all about 100 AD, and that there is a good structural explanation for the amazing passion of the Christians for dogmatic exclusivism); thus the reader who does not like the conclusions but cannot reject Hopkins's very plausible numerical reasoning finds him/herself faced with an impossible dilemma—to the great enjoyment of the author. This paper may be judged to be the high point of all Hopkins's later work.

His last important economic-history paper was a detailed reprise of and revision of 'Taxes and Trade', occasioned by a lecturing visit to Japan.[39] More polemical but at the same time more moderate than its predecessor ('the model-builder . . . has to know much of what the sources tell us'), this essay makes two large statements. The first is a reiteration of the importance for the study of ancient economic history of thinking with models. But the conclusion is more intriguing, for it marks a further departure from the Finley model of the Roman economy (in fact Finley scarcely appears):

---

[36] *Past and Present*, 138 (1993), 3–27, reprinted in R. Osborne (ed.), *Studies in Ancient Greek and Roman Society* (Cambridge, 2004), pp. 206–25. The reader will realise by now that the claim at the beginning that the author was not aiming at 'the discovery of truths' was something of a Hopkinsian ritual, rather like the Maori haka. The main aim was to investigate 'the seamier side of slavery' (6), and that meant a search for facts, facts about what the Romans regarded as normal behaviour (8).

[37] *Journal of Early Christian Studies*, 6 (1998), 185–226.

[38] Here he drew on R. Stark, *The Rise of Christianity: a Sociologist Reconsiders History* (Princeton, 1996), pp. 7–13.

[39] 'Rome, Taxes, Rents and Trade', *Kodai*, 6/7 (1995/96), 41–75, reprinted in W. Scheidel and S. von Reden (eds.), *The Ancient Economy* (Edinburgh, 2002), pp. 190–230.

> . . . the political integration of the Roman Empire brought in its train a grad-
> ual integration of the economy. . . . The Mediterranean Sea made transport of
> a trade surplus between coastal provinces relatively cheap and easy. In my view,
> therefore, the balance of probability is that the economy was integrated in [a]
> limited sense. . .

The Roman Empire experienced in consequence 'limited economic growth'. At the same time, this integrated economy 'sat on top of' a huge 'basic natural economy'. None of this was an abrupt break with the Hopkins of 1980 or 1983, yet it seemed to remove an essential foundation stone from the Finleyan edifice. Many questions remained, as the author of course knew.

The genesis of *A World Full of Gods* was unusually complicated. Recognising his own limitations as a historian of the spread of Christianity, Hopkins made use of King's new Research Centre to gather around him, beginning in 1992, four postdoctoral fellows with diverse expertise, Catherine Hezser, Wolfram Kinzig, Seth Schwartz and Markus Vinzent. It was a high-stakes experiment, all the more so because the original plan was that the five should write a collaborative work—notwithstanding differences of style and belief (or disbelief). Expertise about Judaism was to hand, expertise about patristics too. In retrospect it became clear that the project required that all the participants should share a broad similarity of approach; they probably also needed to be of similar academic standing. In one sense, however, the project was an undoubted success: to say that all five learned a great deal would be an under-statement—for some of the collaborators, all of whom have become important figures in their own fields, the time in Cambridge with Hopkins was an intellectually transforming experience.

The collaborative project eventually collapsed, and Hopkins in the end was probably not its main beneficiary, for it is doubtful whether *A World Full of Gods* works even on its own terms. Here was a historian who wanted to represent rather than convince (the book does not argue a case, though it certainly puts large obstacles in the way of some other views of the subject), who wanted more than ever to avoid the traditional monographic form, to get away from what he revealingly called 'the deadly scholasticism of most Roman historical monographs' (*TLS*, 23 April 1993). Above all, the book set out to show the subjectivity and one-sidedness of all accounts of ancient Christianity and its context, not, however with the aim of replacing these accounts with a single verity, but rather, as he once said, with a 'multi-centred view'. And once again, wanting to overturn the view that the religions of the Roman Empire were 'dull, unemotional and colorless', he attempted 'empathetic understanding', of Christians, Jews and pagans alike.

And further still, the author wanted to *épater*, and also to sell many copies. Hence time-travel (the means by which, long ago, the BBC used to teach prehistory), the script of an imaginary television documentary, and a description of a fictional dinner-encounter between pagans, a Jew and a Christian. (None of this, truth to tell, suggested to connoisseurs of historical fiction that Hopkins had missed his calling by opting for academic history.) Another bright idea—back to the scholarly audience again— was to compose imaginary critiques of the book from disguised friends of the author.[40] This was very cleverly done, and may have been the high point of his empathising mode. But what the book may most have needed was in fact real critiques and an author who would listen to them. The stakes go up when you have Finley's chair and hardly any of your friends wants to be your harsh critic any more; besides, Hopkins had in any case usually anticipated their objections. In the end, since the identity of the imagined reader oscillates so much, we may think that no one could be satisfied (in fact the broadsheets liked the book more than scholars did).[41]

Some may be tempted to fit *A World Full of Gods* into a decline-and-fall narrative, but that would be a serious mistake: Hopkins' best work in the 1990s was as inventive, disturbing and thought-provoking as ever. *A World Full of Gods* is in fact rather rich in interesting ideas (for example, the notion that martyr acts were a substitute for, rather than an incitement to, flesh-and-blood martyrdom), and it is not at all short of erudition (though for a self-reflexive book it keeps specific scholarly debates at a surprisingly considerable distance). The book has the old Hopkins verve and energy, and any reader who succeeds in getting past the juvenilia and in jokes is likely to see that it raises fundamental questions both about historical knowledge and about history writing.

'What would an objective account of early Christianity look like?' he asks. Yet for long stretches the author expounds in a conventional objectivist fashion. He makes conventional critical use of 'the sources' while accusing them of being 'arbitrary' (that cannot be quite the right word).[42]

---

[40] The letters from 'Hartmut', 'Avi', 'Josh', 'Mary' and 'Andrea' were done so convincingly that some have thought they were genuine. There is ample evidence that they were KH's own work.

[41] But the reviewer in *Der Gnomon*, H. Leppin, concluded by saying (74 (2002), 157) that the book was 'ein höchst anregendes Lesevergnügen'.

[42] He speaks of the 'impossibility and undesirability of writing an objective history of a religious movement' (60), yet he quite often corrects the misconceptions of others on the assumption that we will recognise that he is unprejudiced.

The trouble for the historical reader is that while he/she may well agree that objectivity on this subject is impossible, we still think that understanding it requires us to leave aside patently unhistorical views of the matter, and such questions as whether Christianity as it is now practised is good for the human race (as maintained by one of Hopkins's fictive critics). As for empathy, one of Hopkins's time-travellers remarks that being there did not help with the understanding of Roman emotions, and *A World Full of Gods* makes only a very limited amount of progress towards recreating them: Hopkins saw the problem without being able to invent a way around it, as he wrote on another occasion. The author would have had to strip away more of his British academic personality, and answer the still unanswered question 'With what emotions did the diverse inhabitants of the Roman Empire react to the world and the people around them?'

A final verdict on the scholarly parts of this book might be that certain intuitions, to the effect (most notably) that the Christians' obsessive desire to control sex was, paradoxically, part of Christianity's appeal, are extremely rich in possibilities. On the other hand, some central themes are not in the end explored in adequate detail. At one point for example the author proposes a rather dated contrast between older Roman religion as a set of practices and Christianity as a set of beliefs, but at the end of the book he leads us, cleverly it must be said, to a directly opposite view of Christianity: 'for most, *being* a Christian may have mattered more than believing'.

A future biographer would be well-advised, I think, to consider carefully what *A World Full of Gods* reveals and conceals about the author's personality. It is obviously a playful book. It resolutely keeps psychoanalytic considerations at bay—which may weaken its handling of emotions. It hints at some points, so it seems to me, that its atheistic author is not fully indifferent to religion after all ('Andrea''s letter). And in an intriguing passage, one reader at least sensed that the author felt strong sympathy for a position he attributes to 'Avi'. Quoting a passage from the Talmud, Avi says 'what I like particularly is its wry humor and implicit self-questioning. . . . It is as though the rabbis collectively knew that no religious interpretation is, or can be, final.' Yet this means only what it means, not that the real author was identifying himself with the rabbis.

Hopkins would probably not have welcomed any such conventional marker of old age as a Festschrift, but two of those who had worked with him, Catharine Edwards and Greg Woolf, were ingenious enough to devise an equivalent gift, a collection of papers by nine former students and protégés entitled *Rome the Cosmopolis*.[43] Its variety, sophistication and readability speak extraordinarily well both of Hopkins and more generally of Cambridge in his time.

The main project that was cut off by Hopkins's death was a short book about the Colosseum, commissioned by Profile Books for a series edited by Mary Beard. He drafted quite long sections, but almost nothing was ready for the press. Professor Beard took the manuscript in hand, and effectively wrote a book of her own,[44] with Hopkinsian elements, notably a very characteristic speculation about the number of gladiators who are likely to have died on the job every year, empire-wide, and its demographic significance. One new article is in the press,[45] but in the judgement of Hopkins's literary executor, Dr Christopher Kelly, there is little if anything in his surviving papers that was ready for publication. We can, however, hope for a collection of the most notable at least of his published essays.

In 1999 Hopkins once again undertook administration, becoming Vice-Provost of King's. He enjoyed this so much that he effectively silenced the voices of those who would have preferred him to stick to the life of a scholar. Whether the fellows of King's got quite what they expected it is beyond the scope of this memoir to inquire. It can be assumed that they had never before Hopkins's time received a memo from the college grass (requesting them not to walk on it in the winter). There were strains on old friendships over various issues, but at least it may be said both that Hopkins presided successfully over the election of a new Provost and that he was deeply devoted to what he saw as the college's best interests. It was appropriate that the inveterate sceptic, having been buried in the churchyard of Finchingfield in Essex, in sight of his own house, was commemorated with a memorial service and fine music in King's chapel.

Keith and Juliet Hopkins were divorced in 1989, and in 1991 Hopkins married his long-standing companion Jennifer Simmons. Two daughters, Charlotte and Sarah prevented the aging professor from becoming too professorial ('we had to stop playing Monopoly because Dad used to sulk for hours if he lost'). The last period of this family's life together was spent in a house at Finchingfield. Its garden became one of the chief

---

[43] Cambridge, 2003.

[44] K. Hopkins and M. Beard, *The Colosseum* (London, 2005).

[45] 'The Political Economy of the Roman Empire', due to be published in I. Morris and W. Scheidel (eds.), *The Dynamics of Ancient Empires*.

objects of Hopkins's care and one of his chief pleasures. He derived intense enjoyment from deploying arguments, but at least as much from creating harmonies and contrasts in his flower beds. This was an authentic passion, always to be shared.

Keith Hopkins's public persona was the unembarrassed hedonist, who sought pleasure with fine wines, at table (he was an outstanding cook), in gardens, in far-off places, and in the company of women. These pleasures were, obviously, quite genuine, and it was an added pleasure that they sometimes scandalised his staider colleagues. He unstintingly gave great pleasure to others too, and was a profoundly sociable being. His numerous friends found him endlessly delightful company—to an extraordinary degree he could make people feel more themselves, more alive.

Arguably, and perhaps paradoxically, hedonism made him a better historian. He undoubtedly had more ability to empathise with his historical subjects than most historians, and was vastly better qualified to understand members of the Roman elite than drier members of our fraternity (and that means effectively all of us). But the Petronian façade should not be allowed to conceal the very industrious scholar (he rejected much of his own work, otherwise there would have been more publications), constantly curious and constantly wanting to do better.

He had an exceptional talent for the quick comprehension of an argument and its weaknesses (Hopkins QC would have been a fearsome courtroom presence), and he could be a very hard critic. Those who had a ready arsenal of replies could be enormously invigorated, but not everyone was able to benefit, and a modern style of teaching is normally held to require a more patient approach. It has to be admitted that there was a touch of cruelty sometimes. And in criticising the work of others, he allowed himself too many purely subjective judgements, dismissing as 'boring' work by historians, sometimes very good ones, who happened to have interests different from his own (which is not to deny that he was commonly right). Towards the end of his life he was still speaking of 'the conservatism of my fellow professionals'. He regularly 'tr[ied] to upset fellow scholars by non-conformity' (1998), and indeed there is never any shortage of conformists of all ages who need upsetting. He sometimes reminded me of Brigadier Ben Ritchie-Hook, a character in some of Evelyn Waugh's novels who was 'barely one part bully. What he liked was to surprise people', preferably with explosives.

Yet the overall effect of Hopkins's critical and teaching activities was immensely positive for Roman history in general as for many individuals. It is enough to imagine what the field would be like if Hopkins had chosen to become a civil servant. He loved the brilliant young, and drove them on, realising that they would all be different from him—except in one respect, namely that they would reflect about how they worked and wrote.

For most of his scholarly life, Hopkins returned constantly to problems of evidence and epistemology. They were not really his forte. His use of evidence was usually very sophisticated—though sometimes it is possible to find fault. But by the 1980s and 1990s it was not a revolutionary stance among historians of any kind to assert that all history is subjective. And the theoretical debates ignited by Hayden White and others did not in fact interest Hopkins much if at all (I remember no reference to the linguistic turn anywhere in his work). The theory also needed to correspond better with the practice, which had a good deal of factuality about it.

But the defence arguments crowd in. While many ancient historians nowadays realise that their calling requires a very agile imagination, most of the field's old 'grandees' (another favourite Hopkins word) would have tended to deny it, and very few of us have discussed in print what the implications might be; Hopkins, above all people, put this matter on our agenda. At the beginning of his career, as stated earlier, he increased the range of ancient history to a degree very rarely achieved by an individual scholar. It is very important too that he seldom if ever deployed his efforts on the side of orthodox verities: sometimes it was full frontal revisionism, sometimes what he practised was a sort of insidious undermining—but in any case he wanted a better solution, or a more empathetic description. While he exaggerated the sins of the 'conventional' historians, it was a healthy instinct to search for unconventional answers. And while he was a harsh critic, this predatory behaviour, as Greg Woolf has remarked, 'improved the fitness of the herd'.

Throughout his career as a scholar Hopkins strove to solve fundamental and very difficult historical problems, and to do this in an exciting and immediate fashion. Just as he refused to lead an entirely routine academic existence, so he refused to conduct routine research—almost every paper has something daring about it. And he never deluded himself into thinking that he had written the final and definitive word about any historical subject. Richard Saller has written perceptively that 'he was a restless intellect, unwilling to stick with what he did best'. I would put it rather differently: his intellectual energy was such that he could never sink into complacency. And that is the scholarly attribute that most deserves to be remembered.

W. V. HARRIS
Columbia University

PETER LASLETT

Thomas Peter Ruffell Laslett
1915–2001

PETER LASLETT was born in Bedford on 18 December 1915 and died on 8 November 2001 in his eighty-sixth year. He was one of seven children of George Henry Ruffell Laslett, a Baptist minister, and his wife Eveline Elizabeth, née Alden. Much of his childhood was spent in Oxford but his secondary education took place in the Grammar School at Watford, where his father had become minister. Both his paternal grandparents belonged to the Plymouth Brethren, while his mother's family, the Aldens, were closely connected with the Alden Press. Peter himself saw his upbringing as puritanical (no dancing, no cinema), and retained through-out his life a stern critical distance from the English establishment, along with a keen (and sometimes gleeful) interest in its workings: an instinctive nonconformist, if no sectarian. At school he showed early promise as an historian, but much regretted in later life that he was obliged to give up mathematics before learning the calculus, 'leaving me at a permanent disadvantage'.[1]

In 1935 he went up to St John's College, Cambridge to read history, graduating with a double first in 1938. Despite some irritation at the con-descension of wealthier public school contemporaries, he played an active part in college life, rowing at Henley for the Lady Margaret boat club. After graduation he spent eighteen months in research in the History Faculty before joining the Fleet Air Arm in 1940. Of the men who appeared in his degree photograph, Peter subsequently noted, seven did

---

[1] English transcript of an interview with the Italian journal *Passato e Presente* (1989).

Proceedings of the British Academy, **130**, 109–129. © The British Academy 2005.

not survive the war. He himself had little confidence in doing so after the horrors of a Murmansk convoy. But later he was taken out of active service to learn Japanese for naval intelligence, working at Bletchley Park and afterwards in Washington as an expert on Japan.

On his return to Cambridge after the war Peter spent a brief period in Peterhouse, where Herbert Butterfield sought to further his career. The London School of Economics had been evacuated to Peterhouse during the war, giving him the opportunity to meet luminaries like Tawney and Laski. He was, however, somewhat ill at ease in a college setting and greatly welcomed the opportunities which opened up when he left Cambridge to join the BBC Third Programme.

In 1947 he married Janet Crockett Clark, who provided the secure and happy foundation for all his other activities over the next half century. Janet was a charming hostess who made their home the scene of innumerable agreeable dinner parties, and helped him endlessly in his many ventures, academic and otherwise. Undaunted by the legendary illegibility of Peter's handwriting, she converted it imperturbably into elegant typewritten prose. With their two sons, George and Robert, Peter and Janet took great pride in their elegant Clarkson Road home. Peter, a keen student of contemporary architecture, had commissioned Trevor Dannatt to design the house and found much pleasure in showing off its carefully conceived attractions to their many visitors. As an enthusiastic gardener he also spent a great deal of time for the rest of his life enhancing its immediate surroundings.

From his childhood, well before showing any special aptitude for formal historical study, Peter was intensely fascinated by the past inhabitants of England. His interest set out from the visible traces which they left behind them—landscapes, churches, streets—but it reached out insistently towards the figures who had created these settings and lived their lives among them. 'I wanted to see those long lost individuals, to talk to them, understand their society, their aims and their experiences.'[2] What was most characteristic in that interest was the force of his passion to communicate what he discovered about them, and the acuteness with which he felt their continuing presence. In his subsequent career as a professional historian, the passion was duly tempered by the disciplines of research, but it was never absent and seldom seriously camouflaged. It found a natural expression both in his years as a talks producer for the BBC Third Programme before he entered academic employment, and in

[2] English transcript of an interview with the Italian journal *Passato e Presente* (1989).

his two great public campaigns in later decades to launch the Open University and the University of the Third Age.

The enthusiasm to establish contact with people in the past was evident in the research which he undertook as a graduate student in Cambridge before the outbreak of the Second World War and which later, in 1948, won him a Research Fellowship at St John's College in Cambridge. This centred on the life, milieu and thought of Sir Robert Filmer, John Locke's principal butt in the *Two Treatises of Government*, and the best known and most systematic of all exponents of patriarchalism as a theory of politics (or why there should be no such thing as politics). In his prewar inquiries, through the good offices of G. M. Trevelyan, Peter had had the good fortune to identify, and explore seriously for the first time, a large archive of Filmer's life and thought, still in the possession of his last surviving descendant, in the rambling Kentish manor house of East Sutton, in the parish in which Filmer had been born, and of which in due course he became the patriarchal head. The most striking single item in this collection was Filmer's own finely bound manuscript copy of his magnum opus *Patriarcha*, unpublished in his lifetime and in this form perhaps intended for presentation to Charles I himself, a volume since relocated in Cambridge University Library.

From these materials, Peter set himself to rectify, as he saw it, a set of injustices, to evoke a lost milieu of great historical importance and impressive cultural vitality, to pin down not merely how Filmer himself thought, but why he thought as he did, and to capture just why that thinking seemed to Locke to require such sustained criticism. The grouping he evoked was the community of Kentish gentry, linked by kinship and a common quest to preserve their family lands and fortunes, within the county itself in a shared burden of political and administrative tasks, and beyond it in continuing dialogue with the royal government, the Inns of Court, and the city merchants of London. There was nothing introverted or insulated about this community, as Peter was at pains to insist. It was at the centre of the intellectual and cultural life of the country, and the interests of its members stretched well beyond the metropolis to the most prosperous and dynamic of the new American colonies. What made them a community was less their common tasks or shared predicament than the vigour, assiduity and energy with which they discussed the challenges and opportunities they faced. Most of Filmer's works (including *Patriarcha* itself) were intended not for publication but as personal contributions to the ongoing conversation of this very practical community. Kent, for this reason, as Peter conceived it, was not a purely spatial category. Its gentry formed an unmythical and dynamic grouping, a community in and for themselves, contributing critically, at some points by their actions and at others through their disorganisation or relative inactivity to shaping the politics of the nation, as England moved towards civil war. (The intended contrast, later made quite explicit, was with what he took to be the essentially mythic character of a national class defined by its position within the relations of production.)

All the concerns which arose from this research were set out with some bravura in two articles in 1948.[3] A year later those which centred more narrowly on Filmer himself were presented at greater length and more systematically in an impressive edition of Filmer's writings.[4] Each of Peter's major characteristics as a historian of political thought figure prominently in the brilliant and wide-ranging 'Introduction' to the texts, though the texts themselves perforce appeared without the bibliographical apparatus or depth of annotation on which he later insisted in his edition of Locke's *Two Treatises.*

The 'Introduction' immediately struck an unmistakable note:

> For over two hundred years the name of Sir Robert Filmer has been a byword —
> a byword for obscurity. None, or almost none, of the thinkers or historians who
> have examined Filmerism, refuted it, anatomized it or simply dismissed it as
> stupidity have known exactly who Sir Robert Filmer was, when he lived, what
> he did and what he wrote. It so happens that all the important evidence about
> his life and his writings was preserved by the line of English baronets which
> descended from him and which persisted until 1916. It is set out here with two
> objectives. First, to fix him in his historical context and to make it easier to
> understand why he wrote as he did. Second, to correct the inaccuracies and
> misconceptions caused by this lengthy story of contemptuous neglect.[5]

The immediate purpose of recovering the context in which Filmer wrote was explanatory — to understand his reasons for writing and what it was about his thinking which gave it such resonance. But beyond this plainly professional task it linked historian and subject in a bond of solidarity, as much against the sting of contempt as against the stolid indifference of neglect. Here, as so often, Peter was every inch a partisan.

Few of the many who followed in his footsteps felt this impulse in quite the same way, let alone with comparable urgency. But the explana-

---

[3] 'The gentry of Kent in 1640', *Cambridge Historical Journal*, 2nd ser., 9 (1948), 148–64; 'Sir Robert Filmer: the man versus the Whig myth', *William and Mary Quarterly*, 3rd ser., 5 (1948), 523–46.
[4] Sir Robert Filmer, *Patriarcha and other Political Writings*, ed. P. Laslett (Oxford, 1949).
[5] Ibid., p. 1.

tory gain which his approach opened up is now very widely recognised, and the breadth of that recognition may owe as much to Peter's missionary eloquence as to the strictly cognitive merits of the line of thought that he sought to trace out. It certainly helped Peter to see clearly how much the impact of Filmer's patriarchal writings came from his combination of resolutely conventional assumptions with sharp critical intelligence unleashed on the presumptions of others.

In his own day Filmer had been a figure of limited political consequence, admired by some of his closer acquaintance for that critical ability, and no doubt reassuring to others because so many of his assumptions were widely shared in the circles in which he moved. He became of some political importance largely posthumously, at the time of the Exclusion controversy, when England's monarchy was once again under pressing political attack. In this new context the combined appeal of imaginative solidarity with the Royalist gentry and corrosive scorn for the intellectual coherence of the beliefs of their Whig assailants and for their personal sincerity proved potent enough to prompt at least three systematic and urgent attempts to demolish Filmer's intellectual credentials.

It was the most enduring and decisive of these antagonists, John Locke, who furnished Peter with the main theme of his researches for at least the next decade and conferred on his life many of its principal entanglements and preoccupations over this period. During the year which he spent in St John's College on leave from the BBC he once again had the good fortune to locate and explore a very large body of books and manuscripts left behind by a writer of great historical importance: in this case the half of Locke's library and papers which he left at his death to his young cousin Peter King. It was principally this discovery which prompted the decisive shift in Peter's interests and in due course earned him a reputation which was unmistakably international. It also put him in touch with some remarkable contemporaries, notably the great American philanthropist Paul Mellon, subsequently an Honorary Fellow of the Academy, and responsible, with Peter's enthusiastic prompting, for donating many of Locke's manuscripts along with a large proportion of his surviving library to the Bodleian. By the time that Mellon had completed his benefactions, the result, in Peter's boast, was 'the most complete collection of the literary possessions of a great British intellectual which has ever come into existence.'[6]

---

[6] P. Laslett, 'The recovery of Locke's library' in G. A. J. Rogers and S. Tomaselli (eds.), *The Philosophical Canon in the 17th and 18th Centuries: Essays in Honour of John W. Yolton* (Rochester, 1996), p. 81.

The discovery brought Peter both a lectureship in the History Faculty in Cambridge and also a Fellowship at Trinity College which he was to hold until his death. In this setting he settled down to a new and, as it proved, exceptionally rewarding line of work. At the Third Programme he had revelled in the opportunity to draw into public hearing the most stimulating voices he could find among his contemporaries. The BBC at the time, as he noted, enjoyed such prestige that even as a young man 'you could ring up anybody in Britain or Europe from Jean-Paul Sartre, to Jan Masaryk, to Bertrand Russell or Arnold Toynbee and request a broadcast at short notice'.[7] In his work on Locke he devoted the same ready social initiative (and comparable social assurance) to building a personal network of intellectual relations with philosophers, intellectual historians, sociologists, librarians and political theorists across North America and western Europe.

His initial discovery of the residue of Locke's library in the damp Highland shooting lodge of Ben Damph Forest was the prelude to years of strenuous scholarship. It was also a prelude to years of spirited improvisation and painstaking negotiation between the Lovelace family, who owned the library and by this stage little else of comparable value, the Bodleian Library, the British Treasury and Paul Mellon himself. It made a story, often retold by Peter himself with characteristic breathlessness, as one of high adventure, eked out by plenty of low comedy.

His work on Locke produced two enduring achievements, each of immense value to any future scholar of Locke: an edition of the *Two Treatises of Government* which set new standards of editorial precision for a modern text of political theory, and a catalogue of Locke's library, edited in close collaboration with the librarian John Harrison, based on Locke's own library catalogue and incorporating much of the rich information which Paul Mellon's generosity and interest had helped to assemble.[8] Peter himself consciously intended the edition of the *Two Treatises* as exemplary in deploying the highest standards of textual presentation and bibliographical analysis to a major work of political philosophy, and in combining with it an exhilarating demonstration of the transformative insight into the work itself which close attention to historical context could provide.

---

[7] See above, n. 1.
[8] John Locke, *Two Treatises of Government*, ed. P. Laslett (Cambridge, 1960); P. Laslett and J. R. Harrison, *The Library of John Locke*, Oxford Bibliographical Society, NS, 13 (1965) and 2nd edn. (Oxford, 1971).

Applied to the *Two Treatises* the two together enabled Peter to make his best known and most widely acknowledged historical discovery. This great retrospective apologia for England's Glorious Revolution, he showed beyond reasonable doubt, had been written by Locke almost in its entirety under the very different circumstances of almost a decade earlier when his great Whig patron and friend the first Earl of Shaftesbury had pressed his cause by threatening Charles II with revolution. In itself this was a striking historical insight. But Peter himself was confident that it carried much wider implications about the relations between political experience and political thinking at even the very highest level. Most subsequent scholars have accepted the discovery with little demur, although the precise dating of different sections of the text remains subject to considerable dispute. Peter's sense of its implications for any wider vision of the impact of political and social experience upon the most powerful of political thinking was greeted with less warmth, and was not only less widely shared but also probably less clearly understood.

In retrospect it seems plain that this aspect of Peter's agenda was not merely a little beyond him but also appreciably beyond any one else before or since. It had most in common with the approach of the distinguished émigré sociologist, Karl Mannheim, author of *Ideology and Utopia*, with whom Peter worked for a time in the months before he entered the navy and whom he greatly admired.[9] From Peter's point of view his work on Filmer and Locke was far more than a picaresque adventure in the quest for sources and a demonstration of the potential contribution of techniques which his fellow historians had not previously taken the trouble to employ. It was also a conscious exercise in the sociology of knowledge, applied to the most focused and sophisticated interpretation of political experience. Viewed in this light Filmer and Locke offered a stimulating contrast, with Filmer the exponent of an unrelenting naturalism grounded on assumptions which were already so widely shared as to seem self-evident, and Locke the classic exponent of a vision of political society constituted and enacted through conscious reasoning and personal choice. Peter kept his critical distance from both viewpoints; but he responded keenly to the power of each; and much of his vivid sense of the drama of political thinking came from his awareness of the sharp tension between them.

[9] P. Laslett, 'Karl Mannheim in 1939: a student's recollection', *Revue Européenne des Sciences Sociales et Cahiers Vilfredo Pareto*, 17 (1979), 223–6.

In the case of Filmer most subsequent historians shared many of Peter's preoccupations and most of his interpretative assumptions, and virtually none disputed the force and quality of his work. The range of scholars who had a serious stake in understanding and assessing Locke's political thinking was far wider: philosophers and political theorists every bit as much as historians. This led to a far more diverse response, sometimes prompted by contrasting initial interests, but often reflecting very different intellectual habits, tastes and commitments. It was clearly important to Peter that the historical discovery itself should be accepted as such, and that its excitement should carry to the audience it won him. It is less clear that he was either surprised or especially dismayed by the variety of responses to his own interpretation of its implications. He remained confidently didactic about the superiority of his technical innovations as an editor. He continued to follow closely subsequent academic writing about Locke as a political thinker, and to incorporate his judgement of its cumulative achievements in successive editions of the text itself. He also continued to militate strenuously for the standards he had tried to set as a member of the board of the Clarendon edition of Locke's *Collected Works*, and to do his utmost to hold its often tardy editors to the challenge set by Paul Mellon's generosity and imagination.

Peter also exerted a wider influence upon political theory by his editorship of a series of collections of essays devoted to the changing status and vitality of political thinking. The first volume of *Philosophy, Politics and Society* set a characteristically histrionic agenda with its opening claim that political philosophy, a tradition of some grandeur and considerable antiquity, was now dead, whilst displaying some indecision on who or what was to blame for its extinction.[10] The second, published six years later, with Garry Runciman as co-editor, opened with a lengthy riposte by Isaiah Berlin disputing this verdict, and reprinted John Rawls's classic 'Justice as fairness', which did as much as anything to refute it.[11] Successive volumes, with a changing cast of fellow editors, presented most leading anglophone political philosophers of the last half century, along with contributions from various sociologists and historians of ideas.[12]

[10] P. Laslett (ed.), *Philosophy, Politics and Society*, First Series (Oxford, 1956).

[11] P. Laslett and W. G. Runciman (eds.), *Philosophy, Politics and Society*, Second Series (Oxford, 1962).

[12] P. Laslett and W. G. Runciman (eds.), *Philosophy, Politics and Society*, Third Series (Oxford, 1967); P. Laslett, W. G. Runciman and Q. Skinner (eds.), *Philosophy, Politics and Society*, Fourth Series (Oxford, 1972); P. Laslett and J. Fishkin (eds.), *Philosophy, Politics and Society*, Fifth Series (Oxford, 1979).

The later, more thematic volumes focused on some of the larger themes of Peter's intellectual life, notably the twin issues of communication across, and justice between, succeeding generations. His individual contributions addressed these issues explicitly from 'The face to face society' in 1956 to 'Is there a generational contract?' in 1992.[13] The arc from Filmer to the University of the Third Age spanned a huge space and brought him back in the last two decades of his life very close to where he began. History and political theory, for him, were just two ways of attempting to trace out the contours of community, and to sustain and enhance it by doing so. It was quite a conservative vision, and consciously at odds with many of his left wing contemporaries; but it was also sensitive, egalitarian and challenging, and fired by singular passion.

Trinity and the History Faculty remained at the centre of his career; but his relation to the first was warmer and more fulfilling. He revelled in the range, distinction and independence of its Fellowship, and the beauty of its buildings, but retained a degree of cultivated ambivalence in the face of its imperturbable privilege. He made it an exciting setting for the pupils and younger scholars he assembled around him, many of whom, increasingly, had come to Cambridge to work with him. In the Faculty, where he could be a disconcerting colleague (not least as a fellow examiner), he was appointed in 1966 Reader in Politics and Social Structure but never offered a Chair, a very odd judgement which distressed him considerably. His conception of the scope of historical research had always been sharply (and openly) at variance with some of the Faculty's more eminent and powerful figures; and it responded by preferring scholars who may have been less distinguished but were certainly less controversial. In a less parochial context he was elected a Fellow of the British Academy in 1979 and given a CBE for his services to historical demography in 1997.

Whilst firmly ensconced in Cambridge from the 1950s onwards, Peter travelled tirelessly, spending periods as a Fellow or Visiting Professor at the Institute for Advanced Study in Princeton, Johns Hopkins, the Collège de France, Yale, and Nihon University in Tokyo. He continued to travel extensively deep into his retirement, always returning from a trip which most would have found thoroughly exhausting bursting with enthusiasm, energy, and new ideas. His international reputation was the

---

[13] 'The face to face society' in Laslett (ed.), *Philosophy, Politics and Society*, First Series, pp. 157–84; 'The conversation between the generations' in Laslett (ed.), *Philosophy, Politics and Society*. Fifth Series, pp. 36–56; 'Is there a generational contract?' in P. Laslett and J. Fishkin (ed.), *Justice between Age Groups and Generations* (Oxford, 1977), pp. 24–47.

envy of his contemporaries; and he maintained close and highly productive links with scholars throughout the world, especially in France, the United States and Japan.

Peter was never entirely sure that he had made a wise decision in choosing a conventional academic career. He had been deeply disappointed when the BBC decided to reduce and eventually to end Third Programme broadcasts but continued to try to ensure that the Corporation remained true to its Reithian heritage.[14] In 1962 he became the chairman of the Viewers and Listeners Association of Great Britain. He had greatly enjoyed his work for the Third Programme and remained certain that education should benefit the whole population rather than a minority, and that it should be a life-long process rather than being confined to youth and early adulthood. He devoted much of his time and energy throughout his Cambridge career to initiating and furthering attempts to fulfil these ambitious aims. Soon after his permanent establishment in Cambridge, he had published an article in the BBC journal, *The Listener*, in which he advocated the creation of a new university structure for Britain in which the staff of all universities would also be treated as members of Oxford and Cambridge which would become purely postgraduate research institutions. It need occasion no surprise that the proposal found only limited support but it was shortly followed by a new proposal which arose from his close links with Michael Young who had arrived in Cambridge as a lecturer in sociology in 1958. This initiative was to have a very different fate. Young and Laslett were central figures in the drafting of a proposal to create an institution which was to become the Open University. Harold Wilson was persuaded to adopt it as a Labour Party initiative. The combination of radio, television, and correspondence contact between teacher and student, which was a distinguishing mark of the Open University system, proved highly effective and has been much copied elsewhere. Peter served on the government committee which oversaw the creation of the Open University in the 1960s. He and Michael Young later collaborated in another venture with a similar aim two decades later when they were active and effective in the founding of the University of the Third Age. Here their intention was to ensure that people in later life should have an opportunity to develop and extend their interests across as broad a range of subjects as possible. They were determined to show that those of retire-

---

[14] Humphrey Carpenter gives a range of striking vignettes of Peter in action in this struggle in his elegy to the Third Programme, *The Envy of the World: Fifty Years of the BBC Third Programme and Radio 3* (London, 1996), taking both his title and his epigraph from Peter's 1957 *Cambridge Review* accolade: 'a service which is literally the envy of the world'.

ment age could benefit as much as the young from exposure to new ideas and that it was mistaken to suppose that mental activity must atrophy in the third age.

Filmer and Locke had claimed most of Peter's attention in the first two post-war decades, but in the 1960s he turned to social structural history rather than the history of political thought, and in so doing again brought about a profound change in the received wisdom about a question of fundamental importance to the understanding of social and economic change in the past. This second area in which he made his mark had developed indirectly from his work on Filmer. How far, he wondered, were Filmer's prescriptive views about the patriarchal family mirrored by local practice in seventeenth-century England. The *Rector's Book* of Clayworth in Nottinghamshire provided him with answers which were to transform the prevailing view of pre-industrial family life and social structure. The rector, William Sampson, had made two detailed listings of the inhabitants of Clayworth in 1676 and 1688 in a form which enabled the composition of each family and co-resident group to be defined. His discovery, shortly thereafter, of comparable listings for the Northamptonshire village of Cogenhoe, where family and household characteristics were very similar, suggested that patterns found at Clayworth were likely to prove widely typical. Peter first published his findings about the two settlements and his reflections on their significance in 1963.[15] His determination to follow through the implications of his preliminary findings gave rise to some striking achievements in the next two decades and absorbed most of his time and energy over the this period.

Peter published 'Clayworth and Cogenhoe' at a time when sociology in North America was riding high. It was widely assumed by American sociologists that the family forms characteristic of communities in western countries were of recent origin and were closely associated with the decay of agrarian, rural society and its replacement by the strongly urbanised communities which arose in the wake of the industrial revolution. The writings of scholars such as William Goode were taken as authoritative not only by his fellow sociologists but in other disciplines including history, either directly or at one remove.[16] In the modern world families were small and the co-resident group rarely included members other than the nuclear family. Before the industrial revolution, in contrast,

---

[15] 'Clayworth and Cogenhoe' (written in collaboration with John Harrison), in H. E. Bell and R. L. Ollard (eds.), *Historical Essays, 1600–1750, presented to David Ogg* (London, 1963), pp. 157–84.
[16] W. J. Goode, *World Revolution and Family Patterns* (New York, 1963).

extended families were common and the co-resident group was frequently complex. Peter's work showed conclusively that in much of western Europe, and notably in England, 'modern' family characteristics were of long standing. Far from industrialisation having produced the modern family, it was possible that among the pre-existing features which helped to bring about the industrial revolution in England were its familial and demographic characteristics, an issue which Peter explored in several essays.[17]

It may be helpful to summarise the picture which emerged from Peter's work and that of John Hajnal (the two were in close contact throughout the period in which Peter worked on these questions; Hajnal's pathbreaking essay on European marriage patterns, comparable in its impact to 'Clayworth and Cogenhoe', was published in 1965).[18] One might characterise a society at the opposite pole to that of early modern England as one in which marriage, at least for women, was early, universal, and closely linked to the attainment of sexual maturity; where newly married couples joined an existing household rather than establishing a new household of their own; and where, in consequence, household structures were frequently complex from either vertical or lateral extension, and the co-resident group was relatively large. How closely any given society conformed to this model became a matter for investigation wherever possible. Subsequent work has shown the danger of assuming that it was universal. Demographic constraints ensured that many households must be relatively simple even if complex households were formed readily where possible. To consider the opposite extreme was, however, useful at least in establishing the scale of the possible contrast between early modern England and most other societies. In early modern England, rather than marriage age for women being determined by their changing physiology, it was principally governed by the ability of the couple to acquire the resources necessary to establish a separate household since convention frowned on two or more married couples sharing the same household. This rule implied an economic barrier to entry into marriage high enough in practice to prevent a proportion of each rising generation of young men and women from marrying at all and to affect the average age at marriage of those who did marry. It proved possible to show that secular

---

[17] For example, 'The European family and early industrialization' in J. Baechler, J. A. Hall, and M. Mann (eds.), *Europe and the Rise of Capitalism* (Oxford, 1988), pp. 234–41.

[18] J. Hajnal, 'European marriage patterns in persepective', in D. V. Glass and D. E. C. Eversley (eds.), *Population in History: Essays in Historical Demography* (London, 1965), pp. 101–43.

changes in real incomes exerted a marked influence on long-term trends in nuptiality for both sexes.[19]

In general the pre-industrial English household was notably similar to the English household after the industrial revolution, consisting principally of one married couple and their children, if any. There was, however, one major difference. A large proportion of pre-industrial households included resident servants. Typically, adolescents left the household of their parents in their middle or later teens and spent most of the time before their marriage as servants in other households, usually staying for a year in any one household before being hired out for a further year at an annual hiring fair, often held at Michaelmas. Leaving the family home to spend years in service was as common for girls as for boys, and the practice was so widespread that probably more than half of each new generation spent time in service. The ending of life as a servant and the beginning of married life were closely associated. Hence the widespread surge in marriages in the late autumn when the service year ended and there was a new round of hiring fairs.

The prevalence of small and simple households containing a single nuclear family implied vulnerability to demographic accident, a topic which Peter explored when discussing what he termed the nuclear hardship hypothesis.[20] Where households were large, the extended family was common, and kinship links were strong and dependable, widows and orphans, the sick and the maimed, were, arguably, in a better position to secure help and support than where simple, nuclear families predominated. One of the most interesting and distinctive features of early modern England was the development by the central government of a system of support for those unable to help themselves, using the proceeds of local taxation based on statute. The poor law provided pensions for widows, apprenticeships for orphaned children, support for parents burdened by many offspring, even medical attention for the impoverished sick. Poor law provision varied widely from parish to parish and between the south and east on the one hand and the north and west on the other,

[19] Evidence of the link between trends in real wages and a discussion of the possible causal connection between the two series may be found in E. A. Wrigley and R. S. Schofield, *The Population History of England 1541–1871* (Cambridge, 1989), pp. xx–xxx, and a review of more recent developments in E. A. Wrigley, 'British population during the "long" eighteenth century, 1680–1840', in R. Floud and P. Johnson (eds.), *The Cambridge Economic History of Modern Britain*, vol. 1, *Industrialisation 1700–1860* (Cambridge, 2004), 73–9.

[20] See, for example, 'Family, kinship and collectivity as systems of support in pre-industrial Europe: a consideration of the "nuclear-hardship" hypothesis', *Continuity and Change*, 3 (1988), 153–75.

but its existence and progressive development from Tudor times onwards was an important element in the growth of a distinctive structure of welfare provision in England independent of family and kin. Peter's work was a major factor in bringing about a fuller recognition of its significance.

Peter realised from a very early stage of his work on family and household that to draw out the significance of their features in England depended critically on the existence of parallel information about family structures in other places and periods. He was indefatigable in assembling comparative data, in organising conferences, and in editing joint publications to facilitate this process. All three activities are especially well exemplified in the background to the publication of *Household and Family in Past Time*.[21] The work contained both methodological and substantive essays and involved scholars from several different European countries, North America, and Japan. Those who participated remained in touch with one another for many years thereafter and the network of scholars with similar interests extended considerably, always with Peter as a key link and inspirer. One of the contributors, Eugene Hammel, later collaborated with Peter in devising a standard system for describing and analysing family and household characteristics. The system was not without its critics, but its high value and utility is made clear by the fact that it has been very widely employed by scholars interested in family systems in many different countries and periods.[22]

The importance of assembling comparative data on a large scale meant that research was best conducted by a research group rather than a lone scholar. Peter played the leading role in the creation of the Cambridge Group for the History of Population and Social Structure. The Group began life on a very small grant from the Cambridge History Faculty but soon became the recipient of a substantial funding from the Gulbenkian Foundation and when this grant expired was for many years a research unit of the Social Science Research Council (later to become the ESRC). Peter was one of its directors from the beginning and remained very active in its affairs for the rest of his life. His ability to arouse the interest and enthusiasm of others, especially young research students, in social structural history while at the same time drawing stimulus and inspiration from them himself was never better exemplified than

---

[21] P. Laslett and R. Wall (eds.), *Household and Family in Past Time* (Cambridge, 1972).

[22] E. A. Hammel and P. Laslett, 'Comparing household structure over time and between cultures', *Comparative Studies in Society and History*, 16 (1974), 73–110.

at the daily coffee breaks which were such a prominent feature of life at the Cambridge Group. Although he could be occasionally didactic, Peter greatly valued the exchange of ideas in an informal setting: he was invariably approachable and frequently approached, not only by his fellow academics and by research students but by a host of amateur historians who became associated with the work of the Group and provided much of the research material analysed by the Group.

Peter's work, and that of his colleagues in the Cambridge Group, exemplified the importance of establishing a constant dialectical interchange between empirical work and the construction of explanatory models. He was vividly aware both of the necessity of assembling quantitative data which were free from bias and on a sufficient scale to permit significance testing and equally of the futility of doing so unless their assemblage made it possible to test an important hypothesis effectively. Success in securing research funding enabled him to employ research assistance to undertake the sifting and analysis of the very large data sets involved. He was particularly fortunate to enjoy the close collaboration of Richard Wall in this work.[23]

One example of this aspect of his work was his interest in the history of bastardy in the past. He identified a number of features about the history of illegitimacy which were both of interest in themselves and whose significance in a broader context he discussed. For example, the demonstration that unmarried women had their first child at much the same age as married women served as a basis for the discussion of the notion of the procreative career and the range of possible explanations for the observed patterns. Or again, the fact that illegitimacy was least common when marriage was late and many women never married and most common c.1800 when marriage was much earlier and more universal suggested interesting conclusions about the regulation of sexual activity outside marriage.[24] The finding was especially intriguing in that this pattern was reversed in eighteenth-century France where illegitimacy increased as the average age at marriage rose.

Peter himself had only a comparatively limited knowledge of statistical techniques, yet he was very quick to recognise the opportunities which more advanced techniques might offer in work on family structures and

---

[23] Wall collaborated with Laslett in the editing of *Household and Family in Past Time* and, together with Jean Robin, they edited *Family Forms in Historic Europe* (1983). Laslett had supplied the introductory essay for the earlier volume; their roles were reversed in the later one.
[24] See *Family Life and Illicit Love in Earlier Generations: Essays in Historical Sociology* (Cambridge, 1977).

related questions. He became particularly interested in the possibility of simulating the implications of different demographic regimes for the availability of different types of kin at each stage of the life cycle, and in related issues, such as the probabilities of extension or extinction of a patriline. He collaborated with Hammel and Wachter in pursuing these possibilities in the 1970s,[25] and, with the massive increase in the capacity of electronic computing, the use of simulation to further the understanding of dynamic processes in family formation has advanced greatly in more recent decades. Simulation has proved a very effective way in which to secure a better understanding of how, for example, any given improvement in mortality will affect the probability that a child will have all four grandparents alive on his or her tenth birthday, *ceteris paribus*. It is particularly valuable in pursuing topics of this kind when several of the relevant parameters change simultaneously. For example, what if the improvement in mortality is accompanied by a rise in the mean age at maternity? And so on.

Peter communicated his empirical findings on the family, household structure, co-residential groups, and the functioning of community support systems for those unable to fend for themselves and without family support in a long series of papers and edited volumes. He also explored with striking originality and intellectual vigour the implications of his findings for the understanding of the functioning of social systems in the past. But his best known and most controversial book, *The World We Have Lost*, published first in 1965, was still more ambitious in scope than his later writings, and dealt with many topics unconnected with his work on the family and household. It proved both highly successful, continuously in print and selling prolifically for a quarter of a century, and highly controversial.

A first draft of the book had been sketched before the analysis of the Clayworth and Cogenhoe listings revealed the extent of the clash between Filmer's view of appropriate family structures and contemporary English practice. Some of this new information was incorporated in the later drafts of the book and therefore in the published version and he was also able to include some of the early findings about the early modern demography of England. It was already possible to claim with confidence, for example, that young men and women married relatively late in life and that a significant number never married. He was very conscious of the difficulty of deciding when best to call a halt to the constant revisions,

---

[25] P. Laslett, K. W. Wachter, and E. A. Hammel, *et al.*, *Statistical Studies in Historical Social Structure* (New York and London, 1978).

noting in the introduction that it was 'almost impossible to decide when the time had come to pause and write down a summary of the knowledge acquired to date'.[26] It was not, however, primarily these new findings which made the book so influential and controversial. It was rather his development of the argument that seventeenth-century England was what he termed a one-class society and that the then prevailing explanations of the tensions which gave rise to the Civil War were untenable. To scholars whose models of social change and conflict were Marxist, such as Edward Thompson or Christopher Hill, such a view was anathema, and they were trenchant and unsparing in their criticisms.

The World We Have Lost was as much a series of essays as a conventional monograph, including, for example, a chapter on the transformation of English society in the twentieth century which was only loosely connected with the main themes developed elsewhere in the book. The final chapter was entitled 'Understanding ourselves in time'. In it Peter set out his vision of the proper scope and nature of historical scholarship. It was one of several essays in which he argued for the merits of what he termed 'sociological history'. He did not regard this as an ideal title, though adequate for his purpose.[27] The study of social structure, functioning, and change were, or should be, fundamental to every aspect of historical investigation yet such issues were treated by historians as capable of resolution merely by the exercise of common sense plus some elementary economic theory. He was determined to make clear the extent of his dissatisfaction with past practice. 'We have glanced back over our history books and found them full of the crudest sociological generalisation, of highly unconvincing speculation on the nature of social development'[28] Yet he was also anxious not to exaggerate the extent of the differences between his model of best practice and much that had been written in the established modes of historical narrative, showing himself to be especially conscious of the danger of supposing that quantification, however desirable in itself, was intrinsically more authoritative than traditional forms of description. Further, he was apprehensive about being thought to be interested only in the collectivity rather than individual men and women. 'Certainly', he wrote, 'the imaginative reconstruction of a former society can only foster an interest in its people as people. The shortcomings we have mentioned have been called failures in sympathy as

---

[26] *The World We Have Lost* (Cambridge, 1965), p. vii.
[27] Ibid., p. 230.
[28] Ibid., p. 232.

well as of method, and if the future is to see the historian in partnership with the other social scientists, it is important that he should never lose sight of his humanity.'[29] Here, as in so many other contexts, he emphasised the importance of the comparative method and argued that instructive comparisons were possible no less with non-European than with European societies.[30]

Perhaps the most telling indication of Peter's commitment to sociological history as the encompassing underpinning of all historical writing is to be found in the acknowledgements in the introduction to *The World We Have Lost*. He mentions relatively few historians (and most of them North American) but many sociologists and social anthropologists — David Glass, Tom Marshall, Max Gluckman, Meyer Fortes, Jack Goody, Audrey Richards, David Lockwood, John Goldthorpe, Edmund Leach, Edward Shils, Michael Young, Garry Runciman. Social science, and perhaps especially social anthropology, could not only afford invaluable insights into the functioning of all aspects of life in past communities but could provide incontrovertible demonstrations that work on one small community could be as important and instructive as comparable work on larger units. Such work need not be microscopic but could be microcosmic.[31] Peter was antipathetic to what might be termed grand narrative schools of history which privileged, for example, political history seen largely as the activity of small élites. If it were demonstrable that a careful analysis of the rector's listing of the inhabitants of the obscure parish of Clayworth in 1676 and 1688 could lead to a revolutionary reassessment of the socio-economic structure of England in the pre-industrial period, it was also clear that a dialectic between model-building and empirical work could be built up as effectively for a small village as for a nation state, and the potential implications of work on all scales were similar. Peter returned to the advocacy of sociological history on many occasions, sometimes as an aside when discussing the implications of a new piece of research, sometimes making it the central theme of an article.[32]

---

[29] *The World We Have Lost*, p. 239.

[30] Ibid., p. 231.

[31] To make use of a distinction which Munia Postan deployed to excellent effect.

[32] See, for example, 'Social structural time: an attempt at classifying types of social change by their characteristic paces', in M. Young and T. Schuller (eds.), *The Rhythms of Society* (London, 1988), pp. 17–36; 'The wrong way through the telescope: a note on literary evidence in sociology and in historical sociology', *British Journal of Sociology*, 27 (1976), 319–42; or 'Introduction: the necessity of a historical sociology' in P. Laslett, *Family Life and Illicit Love in Earlier Generations*, pp. 1–11.

At about the time of his own retirement, Peter's centre of intellectual gravity shifted once more. He became deeply interested in the history of ageing and the position of the elderly in society. He was also among the first to appreciate the immense significance of the very rapid change in the age structure of contemporary western societies which must follow from the striking fall in fertility which had occurred from the early 1970s onwards. In many countries the net reproduction rate was far below unity, and each successive generation, in the absence of substantial net in-migration, could be expected to be no more than two-thirds the size of its predecessor. He stressed the importance of distinguishing between what he termed the third and fourth ages. The unexpectedly sharp improvement in mortality rates in the age range above the conventional age of retirement meant that a rapidly growing number of people could confidently expect perhaps a couple of decades of continued activity and sound health after retirement (the third age) before the restrictions and debilities of the final period of life (the fourth age). He was a passionate advocate of the importance of recognising the difference between these two phases of post-retirement life and of the immense contribution which those in the third age could and should make to every aspect of life in the communities in which they lived. In 1989 he published *A Fresh Map of Life*, setting out both the statistical background to the unprecedented rise in the proportion of elderly people within the population and at the same time advancing with great vigour his views on the part which they should play in the new situation which had arisen.[33] He was an implacable and effective denunciator of those conventions inherited from the past which might be invoked to limit the freedom of action of those in the third age. He was deeply involved in the promotion of the University of the Third Age. In some ways it came closer to embodying his educational ideals than any other venture. It was to be open to anyone who wished to remain mentally active and alert; it was to be free from the hierarchies which direct and constrain so much of the activities of universities (not excluding the Open University); and it was to encourage as many members as possible to be both learners and teachers.

Peter was a most effective communicator, especially perhaps when face-to-face in a small group. He could galvanise those who were initially only mildly interested by the urgency and clarity with which he put forward a hypothesis and outlined its significance, and would evoke from them a committed response. He served to stimulate and provoke in equal

---

[33] P. Laslett, *A Fresh Map of Life: the Emergence of the Third Age* (London, 1989).

measure. He was also a dynamic lecturer. Whereas attendance at a lecture for most undergraduates might be useful but was seldom electrifying, attendance at one of Peter's lectures was often anticipated with pleasure and frequently afforded stimulus unobtainable elsewhere. Several of his most distinguished research students were drawn into his orbit first in this fashion. His gift for finding a telling phrase stood him in equally good stead when communicating through the written word. He took great care, where possible, to find striking titles for his books. His prose style was often direct, simple, and persuasive but he was not uniformly successful in this regard. At times there were clumsy lapses.[34] Some of his literary devices could be distracting. For example, he used the pronoun 'we' very frequently, perhaps especially when he was less than sure of his ground. At times it was a royal 'we' but more often it appears rather as a device to associate the reader with the view of the author. He was also occasionally apt to bypass a major difficulty in the argument he was developing by remarking that space prevented him from dealing with it on that occasion.

Peter belonged to the very select group of scholars who can transform a subject by providing a new paradigm for its understanding; achieving this not once but twice in the course of his scholarly life. The world of early modern England appears very differently now from a generation ago and for this much of the credit rests with him. Yet any assessment of Peter's life and work should recognise that he was never simply an academic scholar; but also and primarily an advocate. A Cambridge colleague once remarked that he was a man who had made a conscious decision to be original. The remark was not intended kindly, though it could as easily be taken as a compliment. However interpreted, it captured something of his approach to his writing. He was a man not of the secluded study, but of the forum. Influenced perhaps by his period as a producer on the Third Programme, he wished to reach a wide audience and confront them with striking and thought-provoking ideas. A man who had spent the bulk of his life as an organiser in the Workers' Educational Association once said that no other book which he had recommended as reading to his classes had been so universally welcomed and admired as *The World We Have Lost*. This was the type of recognition which meant

---

[34] Some survived several revisions of an original text. For example in *The World We Have Lost Further Explored*, 3rd edn. (London, 1983), there are many awkward phrases such as: 'We shall find ourselves arguing in something like this way from time to time in this essay' (p. 74), or 'of the kind we found ourselves discussing' (p. 169).

most to Peter because it showed that he had bridged the gulf which so often separates the scholarly world from the general public. Much of his life was spent in opening passageways between them.

JOHN DUNN
Fellow of the Academy

TONY WRIGLEY
Fellow of the Academy

Note. We wish to express our deep gratitude to Janet Laslett for her help and advice over many months, and for her generosity in making available Peter's bibliographical notes.

GEOFFREY MARSHALL

Geoffrey Marshall
1929–2003

I

GEOFFREY MARSHALL was regarded by many as the greatest constitutional theorist this country has seen since Dicey. He brought to the study of politics and the law the tools of analytical philosophy and jurisprudence developed at Oxford, and showed that they could yield insights of permanent value in the analysis of the British Constitution.

He was born on 22 April 1929 in Chesterfield, the only child of Leonard and Kate Marshall (née Turner), just before the advent to power of Ramsay MacDonald's second Labour government. The family moved to Blackpool, in 1931, to avoid, so Geoffrey insisted, the consequences of Ramsay MacDonald's National Government. His mother kept a boarding house at Blackpool. Geoffrey won a local authority place at Arnold's School in 1940, where his Latin master, Mr Haythornthwaite, sparked his lifelong interest in language and precise expression. Geoffrey excelled both academically and on the sporting field, conceiving a particular admiration for Stanley Matthews and becoming a lifelong fan of Blackpool. Indeed, Geoffrey was on the 'books' of Blackpool Football Club for a while as an amateur, and played, on occasion, on the same field as such giants as Stanley Matthews and Stanley Mortensen. He was always strongly athletic, and remained a powerful squash player until nearly the end of his life, being held responsible for the degenerate vertebrae of three of the Fellows of Queen's, as well as several Schoolteacher Fellows and other visitors who made the mistake of agreeing to play

Proceedings of the British Academy, **130**, 133–154. © The British Academy 2005.

against him. He retained also, from his early days in Blackpool, a love of ballroom dancing at which he was highly skilled. Indeed, it was said that Geoffrey's proficiency at this activity was remembered with reverence, if not awe, at the Winter Gardens Ballroom long after he had left Blackpool.

In 1947, Geoffrey was interviewed at Balliol by the Master, Lord Lindsay, whose pomposity and self-importance he disliked.

'I see that you come from Lancashire,' Lindsay inquired.

'Yes, sir,' replied Geoffrey.

'And that you are studying economics.'

'Yes, sir.'

'How many spindles are there in the average Lancashire factory?'

'Around 10,000,' Geoffrey guessed.

'That seems a very large number of spindles.'

'We have some very large factories in Lancashire,' retorted Geoffrey.

Despite this interview, Geoffrey was offered a deferred place at Balliol. Not understanding what 'deferred' meant, he decided to reject it and to take up a place at Manchester University to study Politics and Economics, gaining his BA degree in 1950. This was a fortunate choice, for Geoffrey was to come under the influence of Professor W. J. M. Mackenzie, doyen of the political science profession in Britain in the early postwar years, and Mackenzie urged him to undertake graduate work.

In his final year, Geoffrey heard Harold Laski give the lectures which were published posthumously as *Reflections on the Constitution*.[1] Geoffrey was asked to correct Laski's lecture notes for publication, and this no doubt stimulated his interest in constitutional problems. Geoffrey retained, perhaps surprisingly, a lifelong admiration for Laski. The Laski he admired, was not the socialist propagandist, but the early Laski, the author of *Studies in the Problem of Sovereignty,* and of the essays collected in *The Foundations of Sovereignty,* the pluralist Laski, the critic of state sovereignty.[2] What Geoffrey admired was Laski's attack on the metaphysics of the state, his insistence on looking at the state realistically, and his exposure of the confusion between legal and moral sovereignty.

But while Geoffrey was fascinated by the themes of the early Laski, he never fell under Laski's *intellectual* influence. That perhaps was fortunate. Sir Frederick Pollock, after reading *Studies in the Problem of Sovereignty*, told Oliver Wendell Holmes that Laski's thought was confused, his mind

---

[1] Harold Laski, *Reflections on the Constitution* (Manchester, 1951).
[2] Harold Laski, *Studies in the Problem of Sovereignty* (New Haven, CT, 1917); id., *The Foundations of Sovereignty* (London, 1922).

'often loose and sometimes erroneous', and moreover 'un-legal'.[3] Geoffrey, in discussing Laski's essay on 'The Sovereignty of the State', which was one of the *Studies,* declared that: 'Here and in other essays there is conviction and eloquence wedded to a lack of precision from which on these points Laski never really seems free.' Geoffrey then goes on to consider various different meanings of sovereignty which Laski fails to distinguish—unlimited legal authority, absolute power, undivided allegiance, and the immunity of the Crown and its agents from legal proceedings.[4] Unlike Laski, Geoffrey could never be accused of lack of precision. Indeed, Laski's allusive and slapdash style was as far removed as it is possible to imagine from Geoffrey's approach, which was cool and analytical where Laski was loose, and sceptical where Laski was committed.

After taking his BA, Geoffrey spent a further year as a graduate research scholar at Manchester, completing an MA thesis on the political philosophy of David Hume. Then, in 1951, he became an Assistant Lecturer in the Department of Political Science at Glasgow, where he remained until 1954 and where he wrote his doctoral thesis. The subject of the thesis was parliamentary sovereignty and the constitutional crisis in South Africa over the abolition of the entrenched sections in the South African Constitution. This thesis formed the basis for Geoffrey's first book, *Parliamentary Sovereignty and the Commonwealth,*[5] a work which immediately established him as one of the leading constitutional scholars in the country and which remains, nearly fifty years later, a classic in the field. The book was, Geoffrey wrote, the culmination 'of a long-standing fascination by the idea of sovereignty,' which could 'be traced'

> to a first undergraduate reading of the passage in which Sir Ivor Jennings explains that De Lolme was mistaken in thinking that Parliament could do anything except make a man into a woman and a woman into a man; since if Parliament enacted that all men should be women, they would be women as far as the law is concerned. The intellectual neatness of this arrangement impressed and convinced me at the time, but I have wondered ever since why there is (so far as I know) no full-length study of so curious a constitutional principle.[6]

In 1954 Geoffrey moved to Oxford, becoming a Junior Research Fellow at Nuffield College. At around this time he began to eat dinners at the Middle Temple to prepare for admission to the Bar. He never, however,

---

[3] Mark DeWolfe Howe (ed.), *Holmes-Pollock Letters* (Cambridge, MA, 1946), p. 248.
[4] Geoffrey Marshall, 'Pluralist Principles and Judicial Policies', *Political Studies*, 8 (1960), 4.
[5] Geoffrey Marshall, *Parliamentary Sovereignty and the Commonwealth* (Oxford, 1957).
[6] Ibid., p. v. The passage referred to in Jennings is in *The Law and the Constitution*, 5th edn. (London, 1959), p. 170.

sat the bar examination, and in later years he used to say that he was the oldest unqualified lawyer in the country. In 1957 he married Patricia Woodcock, a student of miliary history; they were to have two sons. In 1957 also, Geoffrey was elected a Fellow and Tutor in Politics at The Queen's College, Oxford, where he remained until his retirement in 1999, becoming Provost of the College in 1993. His pupils have included the political theorist Brian Barry, the political scientist Vernon Bogdanor, the philosopher Peter Hacker, and the Canadian legal scholar Stephen Scott.

Geoffrey's eminence was widely recognised. He was elected a Fellow of the British Academy in 1971 at the remarkably early age of 42. In 1995 he was elected President of the Study of Parliament Group, a body comprising academics and parliamentary clerks meeting from time to time to discuss problems of parliamentary government. He was an assistant editor of the journal *Public Law* for forty-five years. He was also an active member of the Bielefelder Kreis, an international research group, comprising scholars from ten countries, which meets annually to discuss problems of legal theory. In Canada, he served as visiting professor at McGill University and acted as a consultant to the Canadian government on constitutional issues. In 1985 he was appointed Andrew Dixon White Professor at Large by Cornell University. He was asked to become a candidate for the Gladstone Chair of Government and Public Administration, as it then was, at All Souls College, but declined to be considered. His reasons were characteristic. All Souls, he declared, lacked a car park and squash courts. Moreover, the terms of the Chair required its holders to deliver thirty-six lectures a year. Unfortunately, so Geoffrey declared, he possessed only three.

Geoffrey never allowed his scholarly activities to overcome his sense of humour. He once said that he preferred Bentham to John Stuart Mill because there were no jokes in Mill. His interest in the nuances of language and his dry wit were reflected in his book reviews, in letters to *The Times*, and in limericks and other occasional verses, a volume of which would certainly merit publication. One of his poetic efforts is called 'The Rape of Sabine—A Quick History of Political Thought'.[7] Here are three of the twelve stanzas.

> Descartes could take his head apart
> To see what made it go
> Then—oh dear me—he couldn't see
> And stubbed his Cogito.

[7] 'Sabine', of course, refers to G. H. Sabine, author of the standard textbook *A History of Political Theory*, 4th edn. (New York, 1973).

> Montesquieu would hum and hue
> When girls sat on his knee
> But Jacques Rousseau was full of go
> And forced them to be free.
>
> Language, Truth and Logic
> God Almighty much resented
> Unlike Voltaire, he thought that Ayer
> Should not have been invented.

Geoffrey's characteristic air of self-deprecation and fundamental modesty led many to underestimate his scholarly achievement. He made, however, fundamental contributions to the study of the British Constitution, contributions unequalled in his generation.

II

British political science derives, fundamentally, from two basic influences. The first is that of Dicey, who sought to display the conceptual logic of the British Constitution, to discover what it was that distinguished the British Constitution, both from the American Constitution and from the codified constitutions of the Continent. The second basic influence is that of Bagehot, who, with Ostrogorski, sought to understand political 'forms' by analysing the political 'forces' which lay behind them. Both approaches have in common an aversion to grand theory, to approaches to political science derived form the natural sciences, and to ideology.[8]

The bulk of post-war British political science owes more to Bagehot than it does to Dicey. This is particularly true of political science in Oxford, which has been primarily concerned with the empirical observation of government and the analysis of elections. Indeed, the dominant school in the social sciences in post-war Oxford has been severely empirical, whether it be David Butler's work in psephology, the work of Harrod in the Economists Research Group, of Flanders, Clegg, and McCarthy, founders of the Oxford School of Industrial Relations, or the sociological investigations of Halsey, Goldthorpe, and Heath. The concerns of Oxford social scientists have not only been practical; they have also often been reformist. Vernon Bogdanor has sought to influence the debate on constitutional reform;

---

[8] This paragraph is derived from Vernon Bogdanor, 'Comparative Politics', in Brian Barry, Archie Brown, and Jack Hayward (eds.), *The Study of Politics: The Twentieth-Century British Contribution* (Oxford, 1999), p. 175.

Harrod, Donald MacDougall, and Robert Hall were pioneers of Keynesianism; while Halsey sought to remind governments of the demands of common citizenship and of equality in education.

From all this activity, Geoffrey held back. He concerned himself little with the empirical observation of government. Once when asked why he did not do that sort of work, he replied, jocularly, that he was far too old to begin research at his time of life. Moreover, although a university councillor on Oxford City Council in the years 1967–74, and sheriff from 1971 to 1972, Geoffrey did not involve himself in public life or controversy. His work has, however, in an almost subterranean way, affected public attitudes to the control of discretionary power. If there is more scepticism today than there was forty years ago towards the idea that ministerial responsibility to parliament constitutes an effective control of discretionary power, and if support for a Bill of Rights is now widespread, the credit is due, in no small measure to him.

Geoffrey owed much more to Dicey than to Bagehot. He stood apart from most Oxford political scientists, in that his intellectual influences lay not in the social sciences, but in philosophy and jurisprudence.

Of his first book, *Parliamentary Sovereignty and the Commonwealth*, Geoffrey said that it was 'an attempt to look at some of the traditional implications of the sovereignty doctrine in the light of certain ideas about the function and description of legal rules in theoretical writing about law, and also of recent constitutional developments outside the United Kingdom'. Parliamentary sovereignty, he went on to say, in a comment that perhaps forms the *leitmotif* of all his work, 'is an institutional arrangement resting upon an idea, and the idea is one which has philosophical (and even theological) connexions'.[9] Similarly, ministerial responsibility, the theme of *Some Problems of the Constitution* (written jointly with Graeme C. Moodie), and the constitutional independence of the constable, the theme of *Police and Government*, were also institutional arrangements resting upon ideas.[10] To understand the institutional arrangement, Geoffrey believed, one had to understand the idea underlying it, the conceptual foundation. *Parliamentary Sovereignty and the Commonwealth* was thus an attempt 'to indicate the influence of theory upon political and judicial practice'. For, 'Wherever the sovereign capacity

---

[9] Marshall, *Parliamentary Sovereignty and the Commonwealth*, pp. v, 2.
[10] Geoffrey Marshall, and Graeme C. Moodie, *Some Problems of the Constitution* (London, 1959, 5th edn., 1971); id., *Police and Government* (London, 1965).

of legislatures is debated, theoretical issues lie very close to the surface, and political philosophy keeps breaking in.'

But, in order to understand 'the influence of theory upon political and judicial practice', the tools of jurisprudence and of modern analytical philosophy are indispensable. 'The analysis of language,' Geoffrey declared in *Parliamentary Sovereignty and the Commonwealth*, 'which has proved so fruitful in general philosophical inquiries ought to prove no less useful here.'[11] Geoffrey's work owes much to the linguistic analysis pioneered, first by the British empirical philosophers, Hume and Bentham, and in the twentieth century by Wittgenstein and Austin, and adapted to jurisprudence by H. L. A. Hart, Bentham's heir and critic. It is they, rather than the social scientists, who can be considered his intellectual mentors.

Wittgenstein, Austin, and Hart spent much time on analysing the concept of a rule which they saw as fundamental in social and legal life. Indeed, the analysis of different types of rules was an important topic in Austin's famous Saturday mornings. In *Parliamentary Sovereignty and the Commonwealth*, Geoffrey uses a quotation from Wittgenstein's *Philosophical Investigations* as the epigraph to one of his chapters: 'When one shows someone the King in chess and says "this is the King", this does not tell him the use of this piece unless he already knows the rules of the game.'[12]

In his inaugural lecture as Professor of Jurisprudence at Oxford, H. L. A. Hart had argued that progress could be made in the subject if one transformed questions such as 'What is law' and 'What is the state' into questions of the form 'Under what conditions is it appropriate to use the term "law" or "state"?'[13] This was in line with Wittgenstein's celebrated aphorism, 'Don't ask for the meaning, ask for the use.' Similarly, in *Parliamentary Sovereignty and the Commonwealth*, Geoffrey urges us to substitute for the metaphysical question, 'what is sovereignty', the questions, 'what rules govern and define the legislative process,' and 'under what conditions may rules of this kind be revised'.[14]

Geoffrey's answer, then, to the metaphysical puzzles associated with sovereignty is to say that sovereignty is a legal doctrine defining the rules regulating Parliament. The sovereign in Britain is 'a body of persons acting

---

[11] Marshall, *Parliamentary Sovereignty and the Commonwealth*, p. 2.

[12] Ibid. p. 4.

[13] H. L. A. Hart, 'Definition and Theory in Jurisprudence', inaugural lecture at Oxford University, repr., in *Law Quarterly Review*, 70 (1954), 37 ff.

[14] Marshall, *Parliamentary Sovereignty and the Commonwealth*, p. 39.

in a certain capacity and following a certain procedure'.[15] Yet one can determine what that capacity is and what that procedure is only if one has the concept of a rule, for both 'capacity' and 'procedure' are rule-governed notions. Thus the designation of any purported sovereign, even of a Hobbesian Leviathan, must include a statement of the rules for ascertaining, at the very least, how that sovereign is to be recognised and what is to count as a valid command of the sovereign. These rules are logically prior to the sovereign. Thus to say that a legal sovereign exists is to say that a certain sort of rule about the nature of legal authority exists. Sovereignty, then, is a legal doctrine which Parliament is perfectly competent to alter, as it was perhaps to do in 1972 when it passed the European Communities Act.[16] Seen in this light, legislative sovereignty 'becomes a special sort of constitutional rule rather than a signal indicating the non-existence of constitutional rules'.[17]

Parliamentary Sovereignty and the Commonwealth is a fundamental work for anyone interested not only in the British and Commonwealth constitutions, but also in wider issues of jurisprudence. It may well have influenced H. L. A. Hart's *The Concept of Law*, published in 1961, which revived the study of jurisprudence as an independent discipline. The conceptual power and analytical rigour which the book displayed were to remain the hallmarks of Geoffrey's approach. *Parliamentary Sovereignty and the Commonwealth* was, in its deflation of grandiose, highfalutin theories of sovereignty, like so much of his work, and indeed like the man himself, subtly subversive.

III

Geoffrey's second book, written in collaboration with Graeme C. Moodie, was *Some Problems of the Constitution*, first published in 1959. The book's modest title concealed yet more subversive material.

In his *Introduction to the Study of the Law of the Constitution*, first published in 1885, Dicey had drawn attention to two principles which he believed underpinned the British Constitution. They were the sovereignty of Parliament and the supremacy of the ordinary law of the land. He had

[15] Marshall, *Parliamentary Sovereignty and the Commonwealth*, p. 11.
[16] Hart, 'Definition and Theory in Jurisprudence', 44 ff. See also Geoffrey Marshall, 'What is Parliament? The Changing Concept of Parliamentary Sovereignty', *Political Studies*, 2 (1954), 193–209.
[17] Marshall, *Parliamentary Sovereignty and the Commonwealth*, pp. 208–9.

given hardly any attention at all to a third important principle, ministerial responsibility to Parliament. Yet, Geoffrey declared, 'In one sense much of the constitutional history of the present century might be represented as a conflict between this and the two former principles.'[18] *Some Problems of the Constitution* seeks to analyse the problems raised by ministerial responsibility in terms of relationships between ministers and 'the Crown, Parliament, the courts, the administration and the public'.[19]

The central theme of *Some Problems* is the inadequacy of the doctrine of ministerial responsibility as a form of control upon government. The doctrine was, of course, adumbrated long before the tightening of party discipline and the development of modern, highly organised, political parties; and *Some Problems* can in one sense be seen as concerned with the consequences of party government for the constitution. It underlines the point that many of our constitutional conventions reflect the conditions of pre-twentieth-century experience before a two-party system came into being.

Traditionally, in Britain, there were two ways in which power could be controlled—first through the courts, and secondly through the 'High Court of Parliament'. However, the courts had not been particularly successful in controlling the administration. 'It must be conceded', Geoffrey declared '. . . that a fair generalisation about the history in this country of individual efforts to attack the exercise of administrative powers in the courts would be that it is a record of comparative failure.'[20] Part of the reason for this failure was that the doctrine of ministerial responsibility to Parliament had been used to prevent the courts or indeed any other external body from holding power accountable. It was a constitutional fiction, but a fiction useful to the executive, that the courts ought not to intervene on matters of administration of direct concern to the citizen, since the citizen already enjoyed a remedy in Parliament for any abuse he or she may have suffered. The consequence was, as Sir Matthew Hale had noticed as early as the seventeenth century, that if Parliament, perhaps through the exigencies of party politics, was unwilling to grant redress to an individual grievance, the citizen was powerless. For, as Hale said of Parliament: 'This being the highest and greatest court . . . if by any means

---

[18] Marshall and Moodie, *Some Problems of the Constitution*, p. 11.
[19] Ibid., p. 11.
[20] Ibid., p. 94.

a misgovernment should any way fall upon it, the subjects of this kingdom are left without all manner of remedy.'[21]

Thus, so Geoffrey believed, 'A major component of post-war disquiet about governmental discretion has been the growing awareness (in all political parties) that a potential absence of control might lurk behind an artificial phraseology about parliamentary redress and an allocation to the legislature of a role which it does not and could not play.'[22] Parliament, then, in Geoffrey's view, 'must take the major share of credit or blame' for this state of affairs, 'and the doctrine of ministerial responsibility to Parliament may be cast for the role of either hero or villain according to the importance attached to administrative freedom'.[23]

Part of the reason, however, why we had not been more successful in controlling ministers' powers was that we lacked a theory of the state, and so had no theoretical basis on which the consequences to individuals of official action might be elaborated. 'There is', Maitland had declared, in his essay 'The Crown as Corporation', 'wonderfully little of the State in Blackstone's *Commentaries.*'[24] In Britain, the sovereignty of Parliament had been used as a substitute for a theory of the state. There is thus a link between Geoffrey's first book, in which he sought to unravel and demystify the essentially metaphysical notion of the sovereignty of Parliament, and his second, in which he shows that this essentially metaphysical notion gave rise to such absurd fictions as that the king can do no wrong as well as inhibiting the development of new remedies for citizens' grievances.

Marshall believed that there was a gap between the jurisdiction of the courts and that of Parliament, a gap within which the powers of ministers had grown unchecked, as had a host of administrative bodies created by statute. This gap, he believed, should be filled by the creation of an Ombudsman and the development of administrative law.

Today, the whole climate in which we discuss problems of the citizen and the administration has altered out of all recognition since the first edition of *Some Problems of the Constitution* was published in 1959. In 1967 the Parliamentary Commissioner Act was passed creating the Parliamentary Commissioner for Administration, familiarly known as the Ombudsman, while one of the most striking features of the debate on

---

[21] Cited in S. E. Finer's review of *Some Problems of the Constitution*, in *Political Studies*, 8 (1960), 201.

[22] Marshall and Moodie, *Some Problems of the Constitution*, p. 89.

[23] Ibid., p. 94.

[24] Ibid., p. 92.

ministers' powers since the 1960s has been the revolution in administrative law. It is, of course, notoriously difficult to attribute developments in the law and administrative procedure to the influence of any particular individual; nevertheless, it would be surprising if, when the history of the growth of administrative law is written, Geoffrey Marshall is not accorded his place as one of those who, through his writings, altered the climate of discussion of the relationship between the individual and the state.

Geoffrey was also a strong supporter of a Bill of Rights for Britain, Parliament being unable effectively to protect the rights of the citizen, but he was severely disappointed by the Human Rights Act of 1998, believing that its provisions were too weak to be effective. Amongst his last publications are a number of papers criticising various aspects of the Act as inadequate. Recent experience has done little to disprove his fears.

IV

Geoffrey's next book, published in 1965, seemed at first sight to be on an entirely different theme. He had always been interested in the constitutional position of local government, and had, for several years, lectured to police cadets at the now defunct Police College at Eynsham on their powers and duties under the law. In *Police and Government: The Status and Accountability of the English Constable*, he sought to undermine the doctrine that the constable answered to no one but the law and that the police were servants neither of central government nor of local authorities. This doctrine, Geoffrey believed, 'has almost taken on the character of a new principle of the constitution whilst nobody was looking'. He claimed, however, that the doctrine 'implies a rationally indefensible relationship between the functions of police and government'.[25]

The doctrine had, nevertheless, been supported by a series of opinions of various legal and political authorities, which stood 'upon a kind of inverted pyramid'. 'The legal apex of the pyramid' was 'the opinion of Mr. Justice McCardie in *Fisher v. Oldham Corporation* decided in 1930.'[26] The core of the book accordingly comprises an attack on Mr Justice McCardie's decision in this case, [1930] 2 KB 364, that the borough of Oldham was not liable for the actions of the Oldham police because the

[25] Marshall, *Police and Government*, p. 120.
[26] Ibid., p. 34.

police officer was 'a servant of the state . . . a ministerial officer of the central power'.[27]

Geoffrey showed convincingly that the doctrine that the constable enjoyed 'original' authority which guaranteed him from subordination to central or local government, had no historical warrant. The anonymous reviewer of *Police and Government* in the *Times Literary Supplement* thought that the historical analysis of the growth of police powers in the book was 'surely the best treatment of the subject that has been attempted'.[28] But the soundness of Geoffrey's argument, as he himself recognised, was not dependent upon the historical analysis. Whether or not the historical analysis were correct, the fact that powers had originated in a certain way said nothing about the degree of independence which a constable today ought to enjoy in exercising his powers.

Against the doctrine adumbrated in *Fisher v. Oldham Corporation*, Geoffrey pointed out that local authorities were statutorily responsible for the efficient policing of their areas, while the Home Secretary was responsible for law and order in the country as a whole. How could this be so if policing was entirely independent and the police were responsible to the law alone? If the doctrine adumbrated in *Fisher* were correct, then, so Geoffrey claimed, police officers would enjoy 'an independence and freedom from control unique amongst officials exercising executive functions'.[29] Geoffrey concluded in *Police and Government* that the freedom of the police from outside interference applied only to the judicial functions of the police not to their executive ones; and law enforcement was at least as much of an executive as a judicial function.

There is more similarity between the central theme of *Police and Government* and *Some Problems of the Constitution* than might at first sight appear, for both books offer a critique of the existing machinery of accountability. In each case, Geoffrey argues that more controls on executive powers, more avenues of complaint, and more remedies for the grievances of the citizen were needed. One of the reasons, however, why so many were concerned to emphasise the responsibility of the police to the law alone was that they were fearful of the dangers of partisan political interferences in police activities. The legal doctrine about the office of constable that Geoffrey was concerned to undermine had 'been affected by fears about the dangers of party political contamination of the

[27] [1930] 2 KB 371.
[28] *Times Literary Supplement*, 2 Dec. 1965, p. 1107.
[29] Marshall, *Police and Government*, p. 16.

machinery of justice, and a distrust of the competence and capacity of local representative bodies'. 'How,' Geoffrey asked, 'can police be impartial and yet be subject to control by persons not required to be impartial?'[30] He did not, it has to be confessed, offer a really convincing answer to this question.

Geoffrey had been concerned to combat the erroneous view that the sphere of law and order was in some sense 'non-political'. 'This, in some ways peculiar, belief', Geoffrey maintained, 'rests upon the existence of a settled constitution and a stable society, and it most obviously tends to break down when the law is put into operation to enforce policies which are the subject of strong moral or political disagreements within society. The suffragette movement, fascist public meetings, and nuclear disarmament demonstrations provide examples.'[31] The trouble was, however, that the breakdown of the assumption of 'a settled constitution and a stable society', which was beginning to occur in the 1960s, cast more doubt on the political impartiality of central government and local authorities than it did on the probity of the police. During the miners' strike of 1984–5, the Home Secretary was accused of unconstitutionally centralising control of the police, while the South Yorkshire police authority sought to reduce expenditure on the police by discontinuing the use of police horses and eliminating the force's mounted section, an attempt to use the authority's financial powers to affect the manner in which police operations were carried out. With the activities of the police becoming politically controversial, political majorities, whether in central or local government, sought to ensure that the police acted as they, the politicians, wished rather than in an impartial manner. There was, in addition, the danger that political majorities, whether at central or local level, would seek to appoint senior police officers who would be sympathetic to their approach, so producing something resembling a spoils system in the working of this highly sensitive public service. It is hardly surprising that Geoffrey came to modify his approach. In a later book on *Constitutional Conventions*, first published in 1984, Geoffrey quoted with approval the comments of Sir Robert Mark, a former Metropolitan Police Commissioner, from his autobiography, *In the Office of Constable*, published in 1979, that 'the greatest challenge for the police of tomorrow is the threat of change in their constitutional position . . . As political and industrial

[30] Ibid., pp. 19, 75.
[31] Ibid., pp. 112–13.

tensions rise the police will inevitably become the focus of political controversy centred upon their constitutional accountability.'[32]

'That seemed at the time,' Geoffrey remarked, 'too dramatic a judgement. But questions that were once academic now figure in party manifestos.' Geoffrey's final position was that accountability of the police is best secured not through an 'extension of political control but in more effective complaints and consultation machinery and in the acknowledgement of a wider scope for questioning and debating the exercise of police powers'.[33] As in *Some Problems of the Constitution*, he seeks accountability not through the political machinery of Parliament, nor through local government, but through the development of new machinery not controlled by politicians. It is an approach which the Nolan Committee on Standards in Public Life was to find congenial. For the Committee, like Geoffrey, believed that parliamentary self-regulation needed to be supplemented by the introduction of codes, monitored by independent outside figures.[34] The Committee pointed the way, not to a fully codified constitution, policed by a Supreme Court on the American model, but to a halfway house. 'The British,' one member of the Nolan Committee declared, 'like to live in a series of halfway houses.'[35] Geoffrey too had been advocating a reformed constitution based on halfway houses. Perhaps it was the cogency and force of Geoffrey's arguments which had helped to create the intellectual climate within which reforms of the type recommended by Nolan would become acceptable. Once again, he may well, in his quiet way, have succeeded in winning converts amongst those called upon to reform the constitution.

V

In 1971 Geoffrey published his next book, *Constitutional Theory*. This opened up a new and hitherto unfashionable area of investigation for political science. A constitution, the American scholar Edward Corwin had declared, in a judgement which Geoffrey quoted in the epigraph to the book, could be conceived

---

[32] Geoffrey Marshall, *Constitutional Conventions: The Rules and Forms of Political Accountability* (Oxford, 1984; rev. edn., 1986), p. 153.

[33] Ibid., p. 153.

[34] Committee on Standards in Public Life, First Report, *Standards in Public Life*, vol. I. *Report*, Cm. 2850-1 (London, 1995).

[35] Peter Hennessy, *The Hidden Wiring: Unearthing the British Constitution* (London, 1995), p.184.

in the formal sense as the nucleus of a set of ideas. Surrounding this and over-lapping it to a greater or less extent is constitutional law . . . Outside this finally, but interpenetrating it and underlying it is constitutional theory, which may be defined as the sum total of ideas of some historical understanding as to what the constitution is or ought to be. Some of these ideas do actually appear more or less clearly in the written instrument itself . . . others tend towards solidifi-cation in the less fluid mass of constitutional law; and still others remain in a more or less rarefied or gaseous state, the raw materials, nevertheless, from which national policy is wrought.[36]

During the 1930s Sir Ivor Jennings had spoken of the need for 'a five-volume treatise on constitutional law, which would set out in the first thousand pages the general principles of public law and which would dis-cuss and analyse at length the ideas expressed in the similar works of the great continental authorities and in the books on political science in English'. Not surprisingly, perhaps, this five-volume treatise was never written, but the 'general principles of public law' mentioned by Jennings were, for Geoffrey, the essence of constitutional theory, 'a collection of general ideas about the legislative, executive and judicial branches of gov-ernment.'[37] *Constitutional Theory* deals with conceptual or comparative questions about the basic ideas underlying the British and American systems of constitutional government—ideas both about the structure and working of government, such as sovereignty and the separation of powers, and also about ideals such as civil rights, equality under the law, and freedom of speech and assembly. Thus *Constitutional Theory* com-bines topics usually considered the responsibility of the political scientist with topics normally considered to lie in the province of the political theorist.

In 1984 Geoffrey published a book on *Constitutional Conventions*, returning to a topic on which he had written a chapter in *Some Problems of the Constitution*. The analysis of constitutional conventions, more-over, formed a natural complement to the analysis of sovereignty in *Parliamentary Sovereignty and the Commonwealth*. 'Both sovereignty and convention', Geoffrey argued,

> are similar in that, besides having a tangled history, they are difficult ideas whose general character has been, and still is, in dispute. Oddly they are also similar in that in recent times questions about their character have been pro-voked largely by constitutional developments occurring in Commonwealth

---

[36] Edward S. Corwin, *American Constitutional History*, cited in epigraph to Geoffrey Marshall, *Constitutional Theory* (Oxford, 1971).

[37] Ibid., p. 1.

countries as much as in Britain. In the 1950s a crisis in South Africa caused a
revision of ideas about sovereignty. Thirty years later events in Canada have
stirred up new questions about conventions.[38]

Thus while the third and final part of *Parliamentary Sovereignty* consists
of a rigorous analysis of the key South African case of *Harris v. Dönges*
(1952) I TLR 1245, an important chapter in *Constitutional Conventions*
analyses the problem of patriating the Canadian Constitution in 1980–2,
and the solution to the problem laid down by the Canadian Supreme
Court's decision in *Reference Re Amendment of the Constitution of
Canada* (Nos. 1, 2, and 3) [1982], 125 DLR (3d) I. The two books together
provide what remains the best analysis that we have of what has happened
to Dicey's central concepts since the *Introduction to the Study of the Law
of the Constitution.*

    Constitutional Conventions, like *Constitutional Theory*, considers a wide
range of topics—for example, the role of the sovereign, the power of dissolution, hung parliaments, ministerial responsibility, and Ombudsmanship.
But perhaps the core of the book consists of the analysis of the concept
of convention itself in the first and last chapters of the book.

    Geoffrey's analysis turns out to be strikingly Diceyan. He endorsed
both Dicey's distinction between law and convention and his view of the
purpose of convention. The distinction between law and convention was,
Geoffrey thought, 'clear enough and worth maintaining. The evidence for
the existence of law and convention is in standard cases characteristically
different, whether the evidence is assessed by judges or by politicians.'[39]

    Secondly,

> Dicey's instinct was also right about the purpose of convention. Although con-
> ventions cover a wider area than Dicey imagined, and although they do not
> always modify legal powers, the major purpose of the domestic conventions is
> to give effect to the principles of governmental accountability that constitute
> the structure of responsible government. The main external conventions have
> the comparable purpose of seeing that responsible government is shared equally
> by all the member states of the Commonwealth, and that accountability is
> allocated in accordance with political reality rather than legal form.[40]

Where Dicey went wrong, Geoffrey believed, was in underestimating
the variety of constitutional conventions. This led him to offer a wrong
explanation of the reasons why conventions were obeyed; or, rather, to

---

[38] Marshall, *Constitutional Conventions*, p. vii.
[39] Ibid., p. 17.
[40] Ibid., p. 18.

provide an explanation where no explanation was needed. Geoffrey himself had changed his mind on this point since, in *Some Problems of the Constitution*, he had argued that conventions were obeyed, not only, as Dicey had suggested, because disregard of convention would lead to a consequential change in the law, but also because it might lead to a consequential change in the structure of government. Conventions, Geoffrey had argued, 'describe the way in which certain legal powers must be exercised if the powers are to be tolerated by those affected'.[41]

In *Constitutional Conventions* Geoffrey criticised this position on two grounds, first because supposed conventions are not in fact always obeyed; and, secondly, because a breach of a convention may lead to the convention itself being altered. He now tended to the view that it was probably unnecessary to ask why conventions were obeyed, 'since we pick out and identify as conventions precisely those rules that are generally obeyed and generally thought to be obligatory'.[42] On this view, just as treason never prospers—for if it did none would call it treason—so conventions are never breached—for it they were none would call them conventions. Conventions were part of the critical, as opposed to the positive, morality of the constitution and it followed, therefore, that 'we do not need any special or characteristic explanation for obedience to the rules of governmental morality. Whatever we know about compliance with moral rules generally, will suffice.'[43]

VI

It is characteristic, however, of the conclusion of *Constitutional Conventions* that Geoffrey, unlike, say, Dicey or H. L. A. Hart, provided no theory of his own to supplement or replace those which he criticised. He had no doctrine of his own to propound. In this, he resembled perhaps J. L. Austin, the linguistic philosopher, or his hero, David Hume, 'the greatest of the British empirical philosophers'.[44] Plamenatz, in discussing Hume, wrote of a Dutch admiral who tied a broom to his flagship 'as a boast or a warning to his enemies'. Boastfulness was, however, as far from Hume's character as it was from Geoffrey's. Hume, Plamenatz went on to say,

---

[41] Marshall and Moodie, *Some Problems of the Constitution*, p. 35.
[42] Marshall, *Constitutional Conventions*, p. 6.
[43] Ibid., pp. 6–7.
[44] Entry on 'Hume' in A. W. B. Simpson (ed.), *Biographical Dictionary of the Common Law* (London, 1984), p. 263.

'used his broom deftly and quietly, raising little dust, but he used it vigorously'.[45] The same could be said of Geoffrey.

Geoffrey was a critic rather than an originator of new theories. His scepticism reflected his personality, witty, wise, and immune to changes in fashion. Intellectually self-sufficient, his kindly nature was roused to anger only by the arrogant and the pretentious whose pomposity he always delighted in pricking with his witty asides. The most self-effacing of men, he was entirely lacking in self-importance. He probably never realised how much he was loved and admired by his pupils, his friends, and his colleagues.

On his seventieth birthday, he was presented with a collection of essays, entitled *The Law, Politics, and the Constitution*, published by Oxford University Press, and edited by Vernon Bogdanor, a former pupil, David Butler, and Robert Summers, a long-standing colleague and friend.

VII

We may sum up Geoffrey's intellectual contribution in the following way. He was one of a tiny handful of political theorists in the Western world who also wrote extensively on topics in legal theory and jurisprudence, including that vital branch of the general subject of the rule of law relating to standards and procedures for holding police legally accountable for how they conduct their activities. In various essays, and especially in his book *Police and Government*, he focused in general terms on what is to be done when, for example, police assault accused persons for the purpose of inducing confessions, conduct improper searches of persons and private property, fabricate evidence, and the like.

Geoffrey was aware, too, that police 'are extremely exposed to accusations and complaints many of which are virtually certain to be unjust, insubstantial or malicious'.[46] He was also conscious that some police who are themselves subjected to law in the conduct of their activities might become demoralised and perhaps even deterred from vigorous fulfilment of duty. He knew, too, that police could be subject to the danger of 'partisan political contamination'.

Yet in various writings Geoffrey favoured versions of a Police Disciplinary Code, and advocated a more effective complaints procedure

---

[45] John Plamenatz, *Man and Society*, 2 vols. (London, 1963), I. 299.
[46] Marshall, *Police and Government*, pp. 106–7.

for holding police accountable. This especially important branch of the general subject of the rule of law became a lifelong interest. He saw the special importance, symbolic and other, of subjecting the police to the rule of law. His views became well known, and influential. By the time of his death in 2003, many of the ideas for reform that he had originated or supported had become law or established practice, though he would have been loath to claim he had been the sole factor or even a major force in this process. However, it is certain that he contributed key ideas either of his own or by way of examples derived from other systems (including the American).[47]

From the publication of *Some Problems of the Constitution* with Graeme C. Moodie in 1959 onward, Geoffrey also became a leading advocate of more effective accountability of governmental administrators generally, especially for abuses of power contrary to law. This subject, too, is a further major branch of that staple of jurisprudence and legal theory known as the rule of law. Geoffrey wrote extensively both on the definition of abuse of power, and on standards and procedures for holding administrators to account. He advocated the development of a sophisticated body of administrative law for control of official decisions and actions, and supported the appointment of an Ombudsman. In 1976, he also supported a modified incorporation of the European Convention on Human Rights. His ideas here closely approximated various provisions of the Human Rights Act of 1998, although he was highly critical of the Act.

In the course of his efforts to advance the rule of law, Geoffrey not merely advocated better controls on police and also the growth and development of a general body of administrative law. He also elaborated and defended Dicey's concept of 'conventions of the Constitution' which, though enforceable neither in the law courts, nor by the presiding officers in the Houses of Parliament, are 'considered to be binding by and upon those who operate the Constitution'.[48] In *Some Problems* Geoffrey stressed that the definition of 'conventions' may be 'amplified by saying their purpose is to define the use of constitutional discretion'. He went on to say that 'conventions are non-legal rules regulating the way in which legal rules shall be applied'.[49] His stress on conventions may, however, be viewed as an extension of the rule of law, and thus also qualifies as a branch of that ancient subject of legal theory.

---

[47] Ibid., p. 110.
[48] *Some Problems of the Constitution*, p. 29.
[49] Ibid., p. 30.

Geoffrey opened his book *Constitutional Conventions—The Rules and Forms of Political Accountability* (1984) with a prefatory quote from Edward Freeman, author of *The Growth of the English Constitution* (1872):

> We now have a whole system of public morality, a whole code of precepts for the guidance of public men which will not be found in any page of either the statute or the Common Law but which are in practice held hardly less sacred than any principle embodied in the Great Charter or in the Petition of Right.

Geoffrey now stressed that although conventions 'do not always modify legal powers', the major purpose of domestic conventions 'is to give effect to the principles of governmental accountability that constitute the structure of responsible government'.[50] Geoffrey's book is without doubt the leading modern treatment of the subject.

Geoffrey closed the book with an illuminating discussion of 'the character of convention' in which he treated the vagueness of conventions, the justiciability of conventions, the obligation of conventions, and the changing of conventions. He emphasised that conventions are 'unlike both legal rules and ordinary moral rules. They are unlike legal rules because they are not the product of legislative or of a judicial process. They differ from ordinary moral rules because their content is determined partly by special agreement, and many of them govern matters that apart from such agreed arrangements would be morally neutral'.[51] Yet many conventions are rules, are thought to be obligatory, and can strongly and properly influence the exercise of legal powers and the discharge of legal duties. Geoffrey acknowledged that many conventions are general or vague, yet he emphasised that clear cases do arise for the application of conventions and they are in fact applied. Given the intimacy of conventions and law, it is appropriate to treat conventions and Geoffrey's illuminating writings on them as concerned with an important extension of the rule of law, even though disputes about the meaning or application of given conventions are not justiciable in courts.

A further subject that may also be viewed as a branch of that staple of jurisprudence and legal theory called the rule of law is statutory interpretation. Geoffrey saw that without a stable and uniform methodology for the interpretation of statutes, the rule of statutory law would at least be erratic if not impossible. In a substantial essay, co-authored with Robert S. Summers, Marshall advanced a number of important principles

---

[50] *Constitutional Conventions*, p. 17.
[51] Ibid., pp. 216–17.

that must be observed if an interpretive methodology is to be faithful to statutory law and uniform throughout the jurisdiction.[52]

VIII

Geoffrey played a full part in College and University affairs at Oxford, serving in the 1960s as a University representative on the City Council, and succeeding to the position of Sheriff in 1971. His duties included the prevention of unlawful grazing on Port Meadow and the destruction of ragwort. Between 1965 and 1977 he was Secretary to the Governing Body of Queen's. His tutorial fellowship was due to expire in 1996, but in 1993, on the retirement of John Moffat, he was elected to the Provostship of Queen's. He brought to the Provostship great knowledge of how the college operated and a real devotion to, and indeed love, of Queen's. He was a strong believer in the college system and did not flinch from being in a minority of one in university bodies when he thought that college autonomy was at risk. He sought to defend the college system and the tutorial system against the managers and bureaucrats who were seeking to destroy it. He took his duties as Provost seriously, and, though a life-long agnostic, attended chapel regularly. On his retirement in 1999, he was elected to an Honorary Fellowship, having devoted forty-two years of his life to his college. Geoffrey died on 24 June 2003, after being diagnosed with leukaemia.

Despite Geoffrey's massive scholarly achievements, he never lost his innate and natural modesty. He remained a man of great sweetness of dis-postion, totally lacking in pomposity or ambition. He was both reticent and uncompetitive, hating any form of display or self-advertisement, stridency of any sort. His modesty led many to underestimate the scale of his achievement. He was one of the most underestimated scholars of his generation. But he made a fundamental and permanent contribution to the study of the British Constitution, a contribution that is both searching and profound.

VERNON BOGDANOR
Fellow of the Academy

ROBERT S. SUMMERS
Cornell University

[52] Geoffrey Marshall and Robert S. Summers, 'The Argument from Ordinary Meaning in Statutory Interpretation', in *Northern Ireland Law Quarterly*, 43 (1992), 213 ff.

Note. This biography relies heavily on Vernon Bogdanor's 'Introduction' to the festschrift for Geoffrey Marshall, in David Butler, Vernon Bogdanor and Robert Summers (eds.), *The Law, Politics, and the Constitution* (Oxford, 1999), and the obituary notices in *The Times,* 26 June 2003, and *The Independent*, 1 July 2003. It has also benefited from the recollections of Mrs Pat Marshall and by Dr Martin Edwards, Fellow of the Queen's College, to whom many thanks are due; and from Geoffrey's own, typically humorous account of his life which he had prepared for his memorialist when he knew that he was dying.

JOHN ROSKELL

John Smith Roskell
1913–1998

JOHN ROSKELL'S lifetime work on the medieval English parliament had
the consistency of direction and solidity of judgement that were characteristic of his personality. Respectful of the long tradition of scholarship
in this field, he defended a broadly neo-Stubbsian view of parliament
against the revisionists, while making a more critical and balanced assessment of the role of the Commons in what his mentor, J. G. Edwards,
termed 'The Second Century' of its history, after 1377. He brought to his
work an unrivalled familiarity with the text of the parliament rolls, carefully scrutinising language and context to establish the development of
the procedures and powers of the House of Commons. In parallel with
this he constructed from the biographies of the members, a picture of its
composition and social and political background. Through this twin
track approach he sought to define the role of parliament in a political
society led and ruled by the king and aristocracy. His insistence on never
going a step beyond the evidence, his profound distrust of speculation,
and the down-to-earth commonsense of his Lancashire stock, gave his
conclusions a solidity that commanded assent. He steered to successful
completion the official history of *The House of Commons, 1386–1421*,
which bears the imprint of his approach.

John Smith Roskell was born on 2 July 1913 at Norden, near
Rochdale, where initially both his parents worked in the cotton mills. His
father, John Edmund, had some musical talent and was also organist at
St Paul's Church. After serving in the First World War, he became a piano
teacher and cinema organist in the Rochdale area. John Smith attended

Proceedings of the British Academy, **130**, 157–174. © The British Academy 2005.

the Norden village school, from which he won a county council scholarship to Rochdale municipal secondary school which he attended from
1924 to 1929. It meant a twice daily journey by tram into Rochdale, the
wearing of shoes rather than clogs, and learning first French then Latin.
After morning assembly one day, Dr Henry Brierley, secretary of the
Lancashire Parish Register Society, addressed the boys on the origins of
their surnames. 'Roskell', he explained, came from Hrosketel, reflecting
the Norse immigration of the tenth century along the river Wyre into the
area of Amounderness. To the attentive ear of the young John it was one
among other experiences which fed his awakening interest in history. This
was manifest when he gained distinctions in History, French and Latin in
the school certificate examination. At that point the family moved to
Clayton-le-Moors and John transferred to the nearby Accrington Grammar
School where he sat the entrance examination for Manchester University.
Interviewed by E. F. Jacob, he was awarded the Jones scholarship for two
years, to the value of £40 per annum, commencing at Michaelmas 1930.
The Manchester history school bore the distinguished imprint of T. F.
Tout and James Tait (who was still an honorary professor), with Jacob as
the current holder of the medieval chair. Lewis Namier arrived in 1931
but there is no indication that either his recently published work or his
personality made an impression on Roskell at this point. It was the capti-
vating lectures of W. A. Pantin which provided his baptism into medieval
history and Jacob who confirmed him as a late medievalist through the
special subject on the Conciliar Movement and Henry V, taken in his
third year. Supported by an internal scholarship, he achieved a first class
in 1933 and embarked on an MA thesis on 'The Knights of the Shire for
the County Palatine of Lancashire, 1377–1460'.

Meanwhile, however, the family's fortunes had worsened. The advent
of the 'talkies' made cinema organists redundant except for playing the
programme in; orchestras were disbanded, forcing his father to take a
series of small time commercial jobs. Eventually he secured appointment
as cinema organist in Douglas (Isle of Man) to which the family moved
in 1937. As a student, young Roskell commuted daily into Manchester by
bus from Clayton-le-Moors until in January 1933 he secured accommo-
dation in St Anselm Hall, a Church of England residential hall for
students, affiliated to the university. It was the beginning of a lifelong
attachment. Having completed his MA thesis (examined by Jacob and
Tait) in 1934, he was awarded the Langton fellowship, valued at £200 per
annum, to fund his doctoral research at Balliol College, Oxford where
V. H. Galbraith was a fellow. For an indigenous Lancastrian, Oxford was

an alien and not wholly welcoming or congenial world. But with Galbraith he established an immediate rapport. Writing to C. R. Cheney after their first meeting he reported that 'I like Galbraith immensely; for one thing he doesn't speak so differently from myself, as most people do up here.'[1] Later he wrote that Galbraith 'did my soul a power of good'. They met together once a week for a lunch at the Balliol buttery consisting of a Cornish pasty, a banana, and coffee, to discuss the 'finds' which he had made in his research. His confidence in his work grew, and he also integrated himself into the life of the college, playing in the second soccer eleven and rowing fifth oar in the second college eight. He began exploring the Oxfordshire countryside, with brass rubbing expeditions. But he lived frugally—'as near to the bone as possible'—even to the extent of cycling down to Oxford from Clayton-le-Moors every term, a two day journey. Out of the total £600 received from his Langton fellowship he thereby saved £120 to pay for his sister Jessie's training as a teacher.

From his Master's thesis, Roskell conceived the idea of investigating the composition of a single parliament, to obtain a snapshot picture of the range and diversity of its members and their contribution to its work. He chose that of 1422 because the complete returns were available and he was already familiar with the political background. In fact the parliament was untypical in two respects. Called to establish the form of government in the crisis after Henry V's premature death, it commanded the attendance of a higher proportion than usual of the military and political elite among the gentry, while for the same reason its preoccupation with weighty matters of state left little room for the more habitual concerns of the lower house. Nevertheless its exceptional importance and abundant documentation ensured that there emerged a substantial thesis. In 1937 Galbraith left Oxford for Edinburgh and John Roskell returned to Manchester to write up his thesis, again taking up residence at Anselm Hall, first as a tutor and then (in 1939–40) as sub-warden. In 1937 his MA thesis had been published as a volume in the Chetham society, setting a new standard for the composition of biographies of MPs.[2] On the strength of these achievements he was appointed an assistant lecturer when in 1938 Bertie Wilkinson moved to the chair of medieval history at Toronto. The story of the young Roskell's emergence from the industrial working class, through the encouragement of local teachers, the support

---

[1] Letter dated 15 Oct. 1935 from Balliol College.
[2] *The Knights of the Shire for the County Palatine of Lancaster, 1377–1460*, Chetham Society, NS, 96 (1937).

of county and university scholarships, and the ultimate patronage of the leading scholars in the subject, to follow his bent as a medieval historian was characteristic of the inter-war years. His own steady determination, self-discipline, and loyalty to his family were one element; the civic university recruiting the ablest members of the local working population and providing an intellectual training noted for its rigour and firmly empirical content was the other. By 1939 Roskell could look back in the knowledge that 'it had all worked out in the end'. In fact, of course, his world was soon to be transformed and further work on medieval history postponed *sine die*.

On 25 July 1940 John Roskell joined the Royal Navy in which he was to serve for the next five years. Here his Norse ancestry found fulfilment. He soon proved himself a natural seafarer, spending most of the war at sea, principally on smaller ships. Having been broken in as an ordinary seaman, he joined HMS *Rodney* as midshipman, and then became sub-lieutenant RNVR responsible for depth charges on HMT *Ronaldsay*, an Isles class minesweeping trawler based on Scapa Flow. When subsequently she moved to Gibraltar to form part of the task force for the 'Operation Torch' landings on the north African coast, Roskell was gunnery officer and claimed at least one straffing enemy aircraft. In December 1943 he was appointed first lieutenant on HMS *Dumbarton Castle*, a corvette then under construction on the river Tay and subsequently engaged on convoy duties and U-boat hunting on the Clyde–Gibraltar run. Roskell's wholehearted engagement in naval warfare left a lasting impression on him, surfacing in later years in his conversation and in his emphasis on duty and respect when he was again exercising authority as a departmental professor. In two brief interludes ashore he appeared in rating's rig before K. B. McFarlane and M. McKisack at Oxford for his D.Phil. viva in January 1941, and as a commissioned officer in August 1942 for his marriage to Evelyn Liddle, likewise a Manchester graduate, at Nelson parish church. On his demobilisation they set up house in Bury and 'JS' (as he now came to be known) returned to the university as a full lecturer.

He now had to read himself back into the subject from which he had been completely divorced for five years. For teaching he resumed his old stint though, following the departure of Jacob to Oxford, he shifted the special subject back to Richard II and the Great Schism. More work would be needed to prepare his thesis for publication, and he set himself to extend his knowledge of parliament by a systematic reading of *Rotuli Parliamentorum*, 'page by page, column by column'. During the inter-war years distinguished work on the medieval parliament had been published by a number of scholars working in the neo-Stubbsian tradition and mainly exploring the nature of representation and the electoral process in the period before 1400. However this had also come under fire from two flanks. The powerful scholarship of H. G. Richardson and G. O. Sayles was deployed to disparage the role of the Commons and to suggest that they were subservient to the Lords, while Tudor historians led by A. F. Pollard and J. E. Neale were claiming that only in their own century did 'parliament become a political force with which the crown and government had to reckon' as the Commons 'became the centre of parliamentary gravity'. In writing up his thesis into a book, Roskell felt bound to counter these claims. He mounted a twin-track defence of the independence and importance of the medieval House of Commons through detailed biographies of its members and a close scrutiny of its records. From the former he sought to demonstrate the political stature of those elected; from the latter the true significance of their parliamentary activity.

The Commons in the Parliament of 1422 was completed in 1952 and published two years later.[3] It begins with chapters on the procedures for elections in the counties and boroughs and an analysis of the parliamentary experience of those elected. Although the normal carry over in succeeding parliaments was only one in five, the average number of parliaments attended by the knights of the shires in 1422 was six, and as many as two-thirds had previous parliamentary experience, while their collective experience went back a quarter of a century. Thus, despite its transient existence a medieval House of Commons exhibited a continuous political identity and a collective will. Continuity among the borough members was less marked, but here Roskell was able to show that the influx of outsiders into the smaller borough seats had begun in the reign of Henry VI, half a century earlier than had been claimed, and that many of these were lawyers, officials, and members of the royal household with working connections to the political class. The Commons were, in fact, a rather more homogeneous body, representative of the middle strata of society, than their different categories suggested. Roskell had thus constructed the first profile of a medieval House of Commons, concluding that there was nothing to suggest that either within or outside parliament such men of affairs were the tools of the Lords. If, in this conclusion, he

---

[3] *The Commons in the Parliament of 1422: English Society and Parliamentary Representation under the Lancastrians*, Studies Presented to the International Commission for the History of Representative and Parliamentary Institutions, 14 (Manchester, 1954).

was endorsing the argument of McFarlane's two articles on 'Bastard Feudalism', this was reinforced by the lengthy biographical notes which comprised almost half the book. Roskell saw the representative principle as being at the very heart of parliament's purpose and unique authority. He readily acknowledged the pre-eminence of the nobility in government, but his demonstration that over the whole medieval period rarely more than half the peers attended parliament confirmed him in the view that the Lords were essentially summoned to meet the elected representatives of the realm.[4] In the circumstances of 1422, however, it fell to the Lords to assert that, in the absence of an effective king, the exercise of royal authority was vested in them, meeting in parliament or council, a doctrine to which the Commons assented. This countered the claim of Humphrey, duke of Gloucester, to exercise a regency under the terms of Henry V's will and codicil. When Roskell wrote, the text of this was missing, and its subsequent discovery vindicated his deductions about its terms in all points save the dating of the codicil.[5]

Although the book itself was not published until 1954, the preliminary articles had established Roskell as the leading exponent of the medieval English parliament in the post-war generation. In 1948 he was asked to become secretary of the British section of The International Commission for the History of Representative and Parliamentary Institutions in succession to Helen Cam, a post which took him to the quinquennial congresses at Paris (1950), Rome (1955), and Stockholm (1960). In 1949 he delivered a paper at the Anglo-American Historical Conference on 'The Medieval Speakers for the Commons in Parliament'.[6] The immediate post-war years were fruitful not only in his developing scholarship but in his teaching. Despite the fact that the number of students had doubled (but more on the science than the arts side), the university to which Roskell returned in 1945 did not differ greatly from that he had known in the 1930s. Long periods of English and European history were taught through twice-weekly lecture courses which filled the mornings, supplemented by shared essay classes once a week. Special subjects in the third year were largely the preserve of the professors, who not only ruled supreme in their departments but controlled the Senate,

---

[4] 'The Problem of the Attendance of the Lords in Medieval Parliaments', *Bulletin of the Institute of Historical Research*, 29 (1956).

[5] 'The Office and Dignity of Protector of England, with Special Reference to its Origins', *English Historical Review*, 68 (1953).

[6] 'Medieval Speakers for the Commons in Parliament', *Bulletin of the Institute of Historical Research*, 23 (1950).

leaving faculty boards with little role. It was 'a strongly hierarchical institution' in a very traditional mould. Most of the professors and senior
administrators were Manchester men, with less than a handful of women.
'Austere, utilitarian, and overcrowded', the university was nonetheless
entirely congenial to the young Roskell, to whom the 'bronchitic sub-
climate', the soot black architecture, and the surrounding streets of one-
up, one-down, back-to-back houses familiar to Engels, made it seem
home from home. He got on well with Christopher Cheney, Jacob's
successor, and found the returned war veterans, serious and committed
men, kindred spirits and perhaps easier to relate to than the new influx of
Oxbridge lecturers. But this post-war phase had come to an end by
1952, when the average age and the overall numbers of students had
both dropped and the first of the new universities at Keele, with new
educational ideals and new course structures, was beginning to break
the mould.[7]

At this point Jacob urged Roskell to apply for the newly established
chair of medieval history at Nottingham. It had not been in his mind, for
he was happily established at Manchester, with his young family, his book
completed and further research mapped out, and few administrative
responsibilities. He was well known to both the assessors, D. C. Douglas
and J. G. Edwards, but nevertheless was both surprised and a little dis-
concerted to be offered the post. Here too the syllabus was traditional. As
professor he taught the outline course in English history to 1485, along
with Stubbs, *Select Charters*, and a special subject. His sole assistant,
J. C. Holt, was assigned the outline course in European history but was
able to lay claim to a special subject of his own on the reign of King John.
Roskell quickly adapted to the more informal atmosphere in a smaller,
but very lively, department, appreciating the daily exchange of ideas over
coffee and the opportunity to develop broader theses at meetings of a
staff history society. It was here that 'Perspectives in Parliamentary History' had its origin. Manchester had retained the entrance requirement
for historians of Latin at O-level, but despite his efforts Roskell could not
get that accepted at Nottingham. He worked hard and successfully to
establish a strong medieval department, though research graduates were
few. Outside the department he proved an effective administrator, becoming chairman of the library committee and taking his turn as Dean of the
Faculty of Arts. He subjected the papers for Senate meetings to the same

[7] B. Pullan with Michele Abendstern, *A History of the University of Manchester, 1951–73*
(Manchester, 2000), pp. 1–31.

scrutiny as Stubbs, *Select Charters*, and came to be respected for his plain speaking and tenacity in upholding principles. Though insisting on his status, he could relax with his students taking them on brass rubbing expeditions to Strelley and other churches. He and his family found Nottingham congenial and eventually a wrench to leave when, in 1962, he was invited to return to Manchester to succeed J. M. Wallace-Hadrill. Roskell himself was temperamentally averse to making career moves and was principally moved to accept by the strong sense of obligation to his Alma Mater which had nurtured his early career and by a sense of homecoming to his native region.[8]

Despite the increased administrative burden at Nottingham Roskell pressed ahead with the study of the Speakers of the Commons, outlined in his earlier lecture and article. It was while at Nottingham that he began to compile and publish in the relevant local history journals a series of biographies of Speakers. These were full length studies of their public careers, detailing their connections, offices, military and political service, and rewards, drawing mainly on printed sources and selected PRO records. Twenty-six such articles had appeared by 1963, covering twenty-nine individuals.[9] These formed the extensive groundwork for the book published in1965.[10] It might have been expected that from these Roskell would have framed a profile of the kind of men who were elected Speaker, and he did indeed emphasise that they were pre-eminently chosen for their familiarity with rulers and government. But the more evidence he gathered of their personal connections, the more cautious he became of adducing political motivation from it. He felt on firmer ground in discussing the origins of the Speaker's office, the nature of his protestation, the circumstances of his election, and the scant evidence of his work. On a close scrutiny of the parliament rolls he concluded that Sir Peter de la Mare probably was the first to hold the office *eo nomine* in 1377; that his ritual protestation on taking office defined his responsibility as the mouthpiece of the Commons and did not assert freedom of speech; that the ambiguous evidence of his election points at different times to both the Commons' freedom of choice and the Crown's influence; and that he

---

[8] For this paragraph I am indebted to communications from J. C. Holt, H. G. Koenigsberger, and D. Welland.

[9] Subsequently collected and republished in *Parliament and Politics in Late Medieval England*, vols. 2 and 3 (London, 1981, 1983).

[10] *The Commons and their Speakers in English Parliaments, 1376–1523*, Studies Presented to the International Commission for the History of Representative and Parliamentary Institutions, 27 (Manchester, 1965).

acted as a chairman, in ordering debates and perhaps directing them to meet the agenda of the Crown. The first part of the book provides a masterly evaluation of the evidence on these problems to yield a definitive account of the early Speakership, as reflecting the corporate identity of the Commons. Here again the theme of the Commons' independence of mind was demonstrated through a convergence of individual biographies and institutional forms. The second and longer part seeks to place each Speaker in the context of his parliament(s) in a chronological narrative. In his introduction Roskell evinced some unease about the extent of the circumstantial detail in this, and it must be said that it adds relatively little to the preceding discussion on either the men or the office.

If it was a 'strong sense of filial destiny' that led Roskell to return to Manchester, the move brought less a fulfilment than a frustration of his pedagogic ideals. He remained staunchly loyal to the standards and methods of his own training in handling evidence and drawing conclusions, namely through a close study of texts and the formulation of a precisely articulated argument. For him the study of history was an end in itself: it lifted a curtain on a corner of the past, without any claim to illuminate or influence the present. His method and purpose did not match the mood of moral assertion and radical innovation of the years 1968–72. These were difficult years for Roskell, and there were several factors in the situation which made his position increasingly isolated and embattled. In 1965 Manchester University, though rapidly expanding to meet the postwar baby boom, was still largely governed by those, like Roskell, whom it had nurtured. At lecturer level there was an unusually large turn over, as numbers of those who had joined in the 1950s and now had books to their credit, moved back to Oxbridge or to the new universities. There were 250 resignations from the university in the session 1965–6 alone. At the same time there was a large influx of junior lecturers who had no attachment to the Manchester tradition and, frustrated with the hierarchical structures, tended to sympathise with the student programme of 'a community of learning'. All this made it difficult to bridge the gap, in age and outlook, between a traditionalist professoriate and student radicals. Student radicalism came to a head in 1968–70 with the occupation of Whitworth Hall and the administrative offices, boycotts of lectures, and verbal attacks on the Vice-Chancellor. There were demands for representation at all levels of university government and for the reshaping of teaching methods and syllabi. While these evoked some sympathy from the junior lecturers, Roskell as the senior professor in the department set himself firmly against all change to the structure and content of teaching.

Such inflexible conservatism at a time of rapid and challenging change in English universities exasperated some of his junior colleagues, the more so as he ruled the department in the traditional mode of Jacob and Cheney. Not surprisingly, he could not carry his colleagues with him nor stop the changes that ineluctably took place, the one he most deplored and fought hardest being the abolition of the Latin entrance requirement. With it went the obligatory paper on Stubbs, *Select Charters*. With the barriers down, medieval history began to lose its prestige and pre-eminence at Manchester, where it had been strongest. While authoritarian and rigidly opposed to the democratising tendencies in the department, his relations with 'his' lecturers were paternalistic and he was genuinely concerned for their well-being. Similarly, although out of tune with his students' radicalism, he exhibited an avuncular and personal interest in them as individuals. The primacy he accorded to disciplined learning and exactitude of expression won him their respect and gratitude. He was generous of his time, ready to repeat a whole special subject session for the benefit of a student who had missed it by attending a boycott. His insistence on correct grammar and syntax was appreciated, if only in retrospect. His special subject on Henry V attracted a small number of takers of high quality, some of whom became professional historians. He had enormous pride in the history department. Although he lectured formally in a suit and gown, he was not remote. With a genial manner and a humorous twinkle beneath the bushy eyebrows, he could relax in students' company, though quick to suppress any presumption or affront to the dignity of himself or others in authority. His transparent honesty, decency, and kindness helped to ease relations with those who disagreed with what he stood for.[11]

In the years that followed Roskell for the most part devoted himself, within the university, to his department and subject. He was a prime mover in establishing the Honours School of Medieval Studies in 1966 and his great love of books made him an ideal chairman of the library committee and of that of the University Press. He worked closely with the dynamic new University Librarian, Frederick Ratcliffe, to effect the merger of the John Rylands Library into the university. By the time the revised university charter and statutes came into effect early in 1973 most of the radicalism had disappeared. It provided enlarged lecturer representation on the main university bodies while at subject level the new

[11] For this paragraph I have drawn on Pullan with Abendstern, *University of Manchester, 1951–73*, chs. 5–10 and communications from I. Kershaw and R. G. Davies.

departmental boards were intent on exercising real influence. There 'debates were conducted with passion and votes were often taken' and in practice the professors usually accepted the verdict. However the student dream (shared by some of the younger lecturers) of flattening the hierarchy and creating a commonwealth of equality had faded. Academics wanted decent salaries, assured promotion, and regular sabbatical leave: the last only confirmed in 1977 as one year in ten.[12] Roskell never had any until the very last term of his tenure of the chair, when he had to spend part of the time in hospital.

He had celebrated his return to Manchester with a notable lecture in the John Rylands Library which put into perspective the development of parliament's control of government up to the reigns of the later Stuarts.[13] Acknowledging that parliament was, in origin, an instrument of the Crown, he countered the assertions of H. G. Richardson and G. O. Sayles that its primary function was judicial and that the Commons were generally subservient to the Lords, adducing the necessity of their assent to taxation and legislation, and the status and experience of their leading members. He equally challenged the claim by Tudor historians that parliament only achieved its place in the constitution through being made a partner in government under Henry VIII, when the House of Commons became the centre of parliamentary gravity. Taking a longer perspective, Roskell asked whether such views did not misplace the frontier between the medieval and modern constitution—between parliament as an occasional and extraordinary event ancillary to government and parliament as an indispensable and permanent part of government. Only in the latter condition could it exercise effective control over government. Reviewing in turn a series of criteria—parliament's right of regular assembly and control over its dissolution; the Commons' right to freedom of speech; their ability to control the crown's ministers; their authority to legislate, and to grant and control the spending of taxes—he argued that in all these matters the great divide came in the latter seventeenth century. It was then that 'the Crown lost the power to govern effectively without parliament'. 'Only then does parliament move into a significantly new phase of its history: the constitution of the *ancien régime* is now really at an end'. The conflicts of Crown and parliament in the late medieval and early Stuart periods, like its partnership with the Tudors were episodes in

[12] Pullan with Abendstern, *University of Manchester, 1951–73*, chs. 11–13; eid., *A History of the University of Manchester, 1973–90* (Manchester, 2004), pp. 36, 53–67.
[13] 'Perspectives in English Parliamentary History', *Bulletin of the John Rylands Library*, 46 (1964), 448–75.

building up its potentiality. 'Perspectives in Parliamentary History' was among the most effective of John Roskell's writings. While untypically broad in scope and combative in theme, it eschewed polemic and developed its argument lucidly, in detail, and with compelling force. He also, on his return to Manchester, took up the problem of the authorship and character of the *Gesta Henrici Quinti*. With the collaboration of Frank Taylor on the text, and the benefit of a journey to Normandy to retrace the route of Henry V's march, their joint conclusions appeared in a double article in 1971, followed by a fully annotated edition with introduction in 1975. From a careful and critical evaluation of the *Gesta*'s subject matter, Roskell convincingly argued that it was an original and skilful piece of propaganda, composed in the winter and spring of 1416–17 to support the English position at the Council of Constance and the alliance with the Emperor Sigismund. While disallowing the current attribution of authorship to Thomas Elmham, Roskell found insufficient evidence to suggest any other royal chaplain.[14]

In the last decade of his tenure of the chair Roskell served on a number of extramural bodies in which he found considerable fulfilment. He greatly appreciated being elected a Fellow of the British Academy in 1968, as much for the credit it brought to Manchester as to himself, and he assiduously attended the biannual section meetings. In Manchester he served on two bodies customarily associated with holders of the medieval chair. One was the presidency of the Lancashire Parish Register Society which he held from 1962 until 1984. Although professionally he had limited knowledge of parish registers and how they were being exploited by demographic historians, his academic standing and his enthusiasm for the publication of primary sources for Lancashire history were highly valued by the society. So was his methodical and unhurried conduct of its council and annual general meetings, 'slowly, properly, and very traditionally'.[15] He also, in 1972, succeeded Jacob as president of the Chetham Society, on the council of which he had served since 1950. With the cooperation of his colleague W. H. Chaloner as reader and editor, it was a period of remarkable vigour in publications, with volumes appearing in all but two of the years from 1965–85. Rising production costs led to a crisis in 1981–2 but by the time Roskell resigned in 1984 the society's finances had been put on even keel. Closely allied to this was his position

---

[14] 'The Authorship and Purpose of the *Gesta Henrici Quinti*', *Bulletin of the John Rylands Library*, 53 (1970–1), 54 (1971–2); J. S. Roskell and F. Taylor (eds.), *Gesta Henrici Quinti* (Oxford, 1975).

[15] Letter of Dr C. D. Rogers, 18 Nov. 2002.

as Feoffee of Chetham's Hospital and Library in succession to Wallace-Hadrill in 1963. He knew the library well, having studied there in the 1930s, and on the resignation of Gordon Rupp in 1967 he became chairman of its library committee. The Library, with its valuable rare book collection, was a semi-autonomous part of the Hospital founded by Humphrey Chetham (d. 1653) which was now an academically modest secondary school. Their relative position was confusing: there were two trusts with separate endowments managed by one board of twenty-four governors drawn from the university and the city. Here too Roskell conducted business slowly and systematically, ensuring that the proprieties were strictly observed. But in 1980 he was caught up in a controversy which reached national proportions. Throughout the 1960s and 1970s the finances of both institutions declined and plans were made for converting the Hospital, the wealthier of the two, into a specialist co-educational music school, for which new boarding facilities would have to be provided. This placed in jeopardy the rare book holdings as the largest realisable asset. Roskell strove to convince the Feoffees that the Library should be treated on an equal footing with the school; that its historic contribution to the cultural and scholarly life of the North-West must be maintained, and that the preservation of its holdings and buildings should be their top priority. Throughout the 1970s he secured annual grants from the university and city and compiled an historical statement for the Feoffees of their obligation under Chetham's will. But by 1979 the Library's deficit had risen to £11,000, and the decision was taken to sell a considerable number of the books at auction, mainly in the fields of cartography and illustrated works of medicine and natural history including some Arabic and Near Eastern manuscripts. The sale in November 1980 generated expressions of outrage in the national press and the resignation of one of the Feoffees.[16] The public criticism distressed Roskell, who was comforted by the support of his predecessor C. R. Cheney, but he had ensured that the Library's main holdings in the history and topography of the North-West remained intact, and the substantial sum raised (£600,000) enabled the Library and School to be put on a sound financial footing. The Library was transformed from a mere museum into a valuable working asset for scholars and on his retirement in 1990 he received public and private tributes to his achievement. His work for Chetham's Library gave him more pleasure and satisfaction than any other, for it

---

[16] Minutes of the meeting of the Feoffees, 23 Nov. 1990; Roskell's unpublished historical résumé for the Feoffees; letter from B. Pullan to Roskell 30 Nov. 1990.

evoked his strongest qualities, of integrity and determination, and his deepest convictions, of fidelity to a founder's intentions and to the history of the North-West.

He was likewise devoted to, and much enjoyed, his membership of St Anselm Hall, which had been integrated with the university in 1956. On his return to Manchester, he was appointed chairman of the Hall committee, where 'he was an attentive but un-interfering backstop to several wardens', sustaining their authority and guiding the committee with skill and wisdom in practical matters of finance and building. He cherished the ethos of the Hall as a single sex community, resisting attempts to make it solely a freshers' residence. Here student radicalism was comparatively muted, and Roskell, often accompanied by Evelyn, was welcomed as a regular attender at aularian occasions, such as plays, concerts, and old members' reunions.[17]

His relaxations were wholly in character. Foremost was his lifelong passion for cricket which he had played regularly as a schoolboy and student. On moving to Nottingham he joined the staff cricket club, as a middle order batsman. Usually a slow scorer, taking time to play himself in and scoring ones and twos rather than boundaries, he could be relied on to maintain one end through long periods. He also specialised in fielding in the deep near the square leg boundary, being particularly skilful in judging balls hit high and placing himself to catch them in two cupped hands. After returning to Manchester he ceased to play, but would umpire. Above all he loved watching the game, at Trent Bridge and Old Trafford, taking his lunch bag and binoculars, watching the match ball by ball, and keeping a score card. Not for him drinking in the pavilion; cricket was accorded the same respect and attentive scrutiny that he gave the parliament rolls. His gastronomic preferences were simple and traditional: a pork pie and pasty, or Lancashire black puddings and black peas, were favourites, washed down with a Guinness or bitter; he never touched spirits. John Roskell was essentially a homely and family man, taking the children to his parents at Douglas and later Fleetwood in the 1950s, and in the 1970s joining the family of his pre-war friend from St Anselm Hall, Charles Tremlett, on the Lleyn peninsula.[18]

When Roskell retired in 1979 the university put on record its recognition of his loyal service. The encomium spoke of his pride, combined with humility, in having been raised in the great medieval scholarly tradition of

[17] Obituary by R. G. Davies in *The St Anselm Hall Newsletter*.
[18] Information supplied by Edmund Roskell.

this university which he had notably sustained; of his being warm-hearted, generous, and staunchly reliable as a colleague; consistently devoted to the welfare of the university and his own students; a Lancastrian and Mancunian through and through. As he once remarked of Manchester, 'It's a large and dirty city, but I love it and it's home'.[19] His retirement was also marked by a volume of essays in his honour by fellow medievalists, edited by his colleagues R. G. Davies and J. H. Denton. The essays comprise a sustained review of the development of the English parliament throughout the middle ages, illuminating Roskell's own formulation of its 'participation in government at the sovereign's command'.

In the 1980s Roskell took up two academic projects which had occupied him persistently if intermittently over the last two decades. One was a detailed investigation of the articles of impeachment brought against Michael de la Pole, earl of Suffolk, in the parliament of 1386. Despite the fact that de la Pole was convicted of three of the seven charges, most historians had dismissed these as 'paltry', 'trivial', and 'frivolous'. Roskell sought to explain why the Commons were outraged at de la Pole's self-enrichment as chancellor and his cavalier treatment of undertakings given in the previous parliament. The book begins by establishing the context: the failures and frustrations of the war with France, the taxation granted for it, and the confusion and corruption in government that produced the Commons' demand for reforms. Richard II's refusal to implement these and his assertion that ministers were solely answerable to himself reflected a 'scheme for government by personal prerogative' which the impeachment was designed to challenge. Roskell then proceeded to a detailed consideration of the charges, dividing them into those on the dereliction of his duty as chancellor and those alleging peculation in that office. To the first, focusing on the failure to implement the reform ordinance of 1385 and the mishandling of the relief of Ghent, de la Pole pleaded that he shared responsibility with other royal councillors, the Commons responding that this did not exculpate him as chancellor. The second set of charges gave instances of how he had used his office for personal profit under royal favour and protection. Roskell examined in detail the honours and grants which de la Pole had received, concluding that, though these were technically defensible, 'royal partiality could hardly have gone further' in bending the rules. Roskell's demonstration of the thorough knowledge displayed by the Commons about de la Pole's affairs and the workings of the royal administration underlined his claim

---

[19] Resolution passed at the meetings of Senate and Council on 2 Oct. 1979 and 3 Jan. 1980.

that they were informed and independent critics, though he did not broach the wider question of what support they might have received from his enemies among the nobility or from within the government. On these questions, in a characteristic footnote, he declined to go a step beyond the evidence.[20] The unremitting concentration on the substance of the allegations makes demanding reading, for here as elsewhere Roskell was determined that the reader should be made aware, not only of the evidence for his conclusions, but of its limitations, and precisely what he had and had not established. If the book may be thought too narrowly focused, it is a superlative example of his investigative method and scholarly integrity.

The project that filled the major part of John Roskell's retirement was the volume in *The History of Parliament* covering the period 1386–1421. While he was still at Nottingham he had been asked—probably at the suggestion of J. G. Edwards—to undertake the section for 1377–1422. Launched in 1951, the *History* bore the imprint of Namier's belief that the key to politics lay in personalities, patronage, and connections, and that the determinant influences were local and personal rather than national and ideological. It was thus envisaged as primarily a register of the Commons, to be compiled by teams of scholars working over an extended period, together with 'an outline of its principal transactions'. That accorded well with Roskell's already well practised biographical approach, and his belief that 'the workings of any institution . . . are conditioned by the nature of those who take part in what it does'. The Trustees thought that a medieval section could be completed in five years; Roskell considered that it would take at least ten. In the event it took almost forty. With this in mind he encouraged research students at Nottingham and Manchester to do MA theses on particular shires, though never having more than two at a time. This meant that progress was slow, and in 1966 the Editorial Board (of which he was not a member) proposed shortening the period by starting in 1386; that would reduce the number of biographies by 3,000. Against his better judgement, and under the threat of the section being terminated, Roskell concurred, but it rendered useless a large number of biographies already completed for the earlier years. Even then it was an uphill struggle to get completed work from a series of temporary researchers and only after the appointment of two 'dedicated and energetic collaborators', Dr Linda Clark and Dr

---

[20] *The Impeachment of Michael de la Pole, Earl of Suffolk, in 1386 in the Context of the Reign of Richard II* (Manchester, 1984), p. 154, n. 111.

Carole Rawcliffe, on a permanent basis in 1975 was steady progress maintained.

The biographies and constituency surveys which they compiled in Tavistock Square were sent up to Manchester for his approval. He would read them carefully, crossing out and interlineating, and then go over all his corrections with them on his visits to London. Every statement had to be substantiated: 'I do insist on being presented with all the facts.' The biographies returned 'stamped with his inimitable style, with clauses and sub clauses, and a distinctive syntax, peppered with such expressions as the forenoon'. Yet as time passed inflexibility softened to dry humour. 'I am well aware' he once remarked to Carole Rawcliffe, a perceptible twinkle evident below the daunting eyebrows, 'that you disregard my amendments, and even find them ponderous [pause for effect], but I need you to know that I read every word.' He was ever paternalistic and avuncular towards his female research assistants of another world and generation, interested in them as persons as well as professional scholars, while maintaining formal decorum even over the cup of tea and clouds of tobacco smoke with which sessions ended.[21]

The volumes of the *History* already published for later periods had attracted criticism for being almost exclusively biographical. Roskell therefore resolved to use his retirement to write an extended introduction which would present the functioning of parliament as an institution. Into this he poured the accumulated knowledge and reflection of a lifetime, rapidly becoming absorbed in a task which 'once started I could not stop'. Describing it as 'a conducted tour of *Rotuli Parliamentorum*', which he had at his fingertips, he dealt, in turn, with the evidence for the composition of both houses, electoral practice, the judicial, petitioning, consultative, and taxing functions of parliament, the ordering of its business (*regimen parliamenti*), and the rights of its members. It is not only an impressive *tour de force* but a model of meticulous scholarship, precise reading, and judicious interpretation. Roskell finished the introduction at Easter 1988 and the four volumes were published in 1992.[22] At the launch party, appropriately held at the Speaker's House early in 1993, he was delighted to be welcomed in the cross-Pennine accent of the current Speaker, Betty Boothroyd. *The House of Commons, 1386–1421* was not only the crowning achievement of fifty-five years research into the

---

[21] C. Rawcliffe and L. Clark, 'A Personal Memoir of the Making of *The House of Commons, 1386–1422*', *Parliamentary History*, 17 pt. 3 (1998), 297–300.

[22] J. S. Roskell, Linda Clark and Carole Rawcliffe (eds.), *The History of Parliament. The House of Commons, 1386–1421*, 4 vols. (Stroud, 1992).

history of the medieval parliament but the culmination of a scholarly tradition reaching back to William Stubbs of which John Roskell was a proud and unashamed exponent.

He was deeply bereaved by the death of his wife, Evelyn, in 1989, after which he wrote nothing apart from an autobiographical memoir. He died in hospital at Stockport on 1 May 1998.

GERALD HARRISS
Fellow of the Academy

Note. In preparing this memoir I have been assisted by communications from Dr L. S. Clark, Professor J. H. Denton, Mr J. T. Driver, Professor Sir James Holt, Professor H. G. Koenigsberger, Dr J. R. L. Maddicott, Dr P. McNiven, Mr D. H. Pennington, Dr M. Powell, Dr C. Rawcliffe, Dr C. D. Rogers, Revd Dr S. S. Smalley, Dr J. Taylor, Mr C. Tremlett, and the late Professor D. Welland. I am considerably indebted to Dr R. G. Davies, Professor Sir Ian Kershaw, and Professor B. S. Pullan for information about the Manchester History department and to Mr Edmund Roskell for giving me access to his father's papers. I have to thank the Edinburgh University Press for permission to use verbatim extracts from *Parliamentary History*, 17, pt. 3 (1998), 293–300. Unattributed quotations are from J. S. Roskell's manuscript memoir deposited in the British Academy.

ISAAC SCHAPERA, IN THE FIELD AMONG THE TSWANA, MOCHUDI, IN 1929

Royal Anthropological Institute

Isaac Schapera
1905–2003

THE FOUNDING FATHERS of 'British social anthropology' were Bronislaw
Malinowski and A. R. Radcliffe-Brown. As an undergraduate at the
University of Cape Town, Isaac Schapera was introduced to the new discipline by A. R. Radcliffe-Brown. He then became one of the first members of Bronislaw Malinowski's post-graduate seminar at the London
School of Economics. At the age of thirty, he succeeded to Radcliffe-
Brown's position in Cape Town. Twenty years later, he found himself
sitting, literally, in Malinowski's own chair, in his office at the LSE. Yet he
was not greatly impressed by the theories of these masters. When his contemporaries divided between the two parties of followers of Malinowski
and followers of Radcliffe-Brown, he remained apart, occasionally snip-
ing at both sides, at least in private. He recalled that Malinowski had
dubbed him (presumably not altogether favourably) an eclectic ('whatever
that may be'), but his basic belief was that ethnography endured, while
theories came and went. Towards the end of his career he preferred to
describe himself as an ethnographer rather than as an anthropologist. Yet
he was not an ethnographer of the new type, pioneered by Malinowski in
the Trobriand Islands. Nor did he agree that functionalist ethnographers
necessarily did better research than the Junods or even the Livingstones.
In his work, as in his life, he was a loner.

And although he spent the second half of his long life in London,
Schapera also remained very much a South African, if a rather particular
type of South African—much more so than his friends Meyer Fortes and
Max Gluckman, who came to identify with England. Not that he insisted

Proceedings of the British Academy, **130**, 177–202. © The British Academy 2005.

too much on matters of identity, except when it came to sports events. (Anyone but England . . .) He let people label him as they wished. Raymond Firth always called him Isaac. To his English friends, he was 'Schap'. But to his intimates, his family and his South African cronies, he was 'Sakkie', which is the Afrikaans diminutive of Isaac.

His parents, Herman and Rosie Schapera,[1] immigrated to South Africa at the turn of the century from what is now Belarus, and settled in Garies, a small town in the semi-desert district of Little Namaqualand, in the Northern Cape. They came with their first two children: Max, who became a country storekeeper, and Annie. Another three children, all sons, were born in South Africa. Isaac, born in Garies on 23 June 1905, was the youngest.

Poor Jewish immigrants to South Africa from Eastern Europe at the turn of the century often made a start as peddlers in rural, Afrikaans-speaking districts. Herman worked as an itinerant peddler and for a while he kept a drapery store in Garies. The Schaperas would have had little to do with the disenfranchised 'non-whites'. In Namaqualand these were so-called Coloured people, some of whom were still identified as Hottentots. Yet even a modest white family had servants. Isaac had a Hottentot nanny. Herman moved his family to Cape Town in 1911, but the family went back to the *dorp* for their holidays, lodging with Annie, whose husband, Nathan Abrahamson, had a hotel in the town. During these holidays Isaac was befriended by a district surgeon, Laidler, who had an interest in local history and traditions, and who let the boy loose in his library.

In Cape Town, Herman tried various ways of making a living, without success. Rosie died in 1918, shortly after Isaac celebrated his bar mitzvah. He observed nine months of mourning and then told his father that the rituals did him no good and that he would not attend the synagogue any longer. His father said he was also not a believer, but had felt that his children should be given something of a religious background, including instruction in Hebrew. Isaac always spoke well of his father, but Herman remarried a year after Rosie's death, to a widow with seven children of her own, and Isaac's relationship with his step-mother was disastrous. At the age of fifteen he left home and went to live alone in a boarding house. He stayed on when he entered the University of Cape Town in 1921, at the age of sixteen, and for the rest of his life he lived in furnished rooms in boarding houses and hotels.

---

[1] The spelling of the surname was evidently peculiar to the South African branch of the family.

Despite this unhappiness at home, Isaac and his brother Louis were doing well at the South African College School, which claimed to be the oldest secondary school in South Africa and was certainly the leading grammar school in Cape Town. Isaac was a year ahead of another son of poor immigrants, Meyer Fortes, who also became a well-known anthropologist. He told me that Fortes came first in his class at school, while he himself was always runner-up to 'a boy named Solly Zuckerman'.

In 1924 Herman went bankrupt, and in 1925 he committed suicide. Schapera's only sister, Annie, now became the central figure in the family. Her husband had helped to support Louis and Isaac at the University of Cape Town. Louis qualified as a doctor and then emigrated to England. When Isaac arrived in London as a post-graduate student, he and Louis were estranged from each other—Isaac was inclined to blame the break on Louis's new wife—but he always felt close to his sister Annie and in time to her children, grandchildren and great-grandchildren, in particular his great-niece Carol, who came to live in London.

At the University of Cape Town, Schapera started a degree in law. ('Jewish family tradition. My older brother became a doctor, second brother goes into law . . .)[2] There was provision for the student to take an outside subject in the second year of study. Having been introduced to archaeology and ethnology in Laidler's library, he elected to follow a course in social anthropology, and found himself fascinated by the lectures of A. R. Radcliffe-Brown, who had been appointed to the newly established Cape Town chair in social anthropology just as Schapera entered the university.

Cape Town had not only acquired a new professor: it was pioneering a new discipline. This was the first established chair in social anthropology anywhere in the British Empire.[3] Moreover, the science, as he called it, that Radcliffe-Brown introduced in Cape Town was very different from the established South African ethnology of the missionary anthropologists like Junod and Bryant, who were strongly influenced by Frazer. It was also a new development in the tradition of British anthropology. Although Radcliffe-Brown was selected for the Cape Town chair by an advisory committee of the anthropological establishment, Haddon, Marett, Frazer and Rivers, he repudiated their conception of anthropology.

---

[2] Adam Kuper, 'Isaac Schapera—a conversation', Part 1, *Anthropology Today*, 17 (6) (2001), 3–7. Citation p. 4.
[3] See I. Schapera, 'The Appointment of Radcliffe-Brown to the Chair of Social Anthropology at the University of Cape Town', *African Studies*, 49 (1) (1990), 1–13.

In his inaugural lecture, Radcliffe-Brown announced that social anthropology was the comparative study of social structures. Social structures were integrated systems. Any change in any part would have repercussions for the rest of the system. He then drew the moral for South Africa. The traditional social systems of the African peoples had been transformed by European interventions: 'we inaugurated something that must change the whole of their social life'. In consequence, 'segregation is impossible'. This did not imply that South Africa could be governed as a moral unity: the different communities based their laws on different principles, the Europeans, for example, relying on contract, while African people referred rather to ideas of debt.[4] But although he favoured gradual change—it was, he said, 'a law of sociology' that slow change was best—Radcliffe-Brown prophesied that in South Africa 'a new product of civilisation' would combine black and white elements. In his farewell lecture, in 1926, which was fully reported in the *Cape Times*, he concluded that 'South African nationalism must be a nationalism composed of both black and white'.[5]

The African academic and politician, D. D. T. Jabavu, praised Radcliffe-Brown in the *Cape Times* for his 'unbiased racial outlook',[6] but he made the establishment nervous, especially when he challenged the policy makers. Giving evidence to the Economic and Wage Commission of the Union Government in 1925, Radcliffe-Brown testified that:

> The process of the assimilation of the natives, i.e. their absorption into the European system, not only economically but also politically, in religion, by education, has been now proceeding for some time and has gathered considerable momentum, and that this process is only to a comparatively slight extent capable of control by legislation.[7]

He insisted that Africans had the same educational potential as whites. When a member of the Commission asked him whether an urban black man was entitled to equal rights with a white man, he replied: 'I cannot see any possible argument to prevent it once he has been brought into our economic system.'

[4] *Cape Times*, 25 Aug. 1921, reprinted as an Appendix (pp. 35–9) in Robert Gordon, 'Early Social Anthropology in South Africa', *African Studies*, 49 (1990), 15–48.
[5] Cited by George W. Stocking, Jr, *After Tylor: British Social Anthropology 1888–1951* (Madison, WI, 1995), p. 327.
[6] D. D. T. Jabavu, 'Science and the Native', *Cape Times,* 24 Mar. 1924, cited in Gordon 'Early Social Anthropology in South Africa', 20–1.
[7] Radcliffe-Brown's evidence to the Economic and Wage Commission, Cape Town, 29 Oct. 1925, File no. 44, pp. 4855–924.

Schapera described Radcliffe-Brown as 'an extremely good lecturer'.

> He never lectured from notes, but was so lucid that you just copied everything
> down . . . With graduates, though, he did not know what to talk about. He had
> said it already. So he made me do archaeology and courses in the psychology of
> language and physical anthropology. Also, he was thoroughly detached. The
> only time he became human was when my father committed suicide. It was in
> the newspaper. Radcliffe-Brown had just been lecturing to me on Durkheim's
> theory of suicide. He apologised the next day . . . it was the only spark of
> humanity I ever found in him.[8]

Radcliffe-Brown lectured on legal anthropology, which as a law student would have appealed to Schapera,[9] but his main course of lectures
provided a routine ethnological survey of South Africa, interspersed with
brief favourable references to Durkheim and put-downs of the evolution-
ists. Schapera would later pass his lecture notes on to Radcliffe-Brown's
successor, T. T. Barnard, who had come to Cape Town without any
knowledge of Africa. Barnard gratefully used them as the basis for his
teaching. In due course they constituted the model for Schapera's own
lectures, both at the University of Cape Town and subsequently at the
LSE.[10]

Schapera was in the running for a Rhodes Scholarship, but according
to his sister Annie he was passed over because candidates were required
to have 'an outside interest', and he evidently had none. In the event,
Radcliffe-Brown took charge of the next step in his career.

> I was completing my MA at Cape Town and Radcliffe-Brown, it was his last
> year in Cape Town, said to me: 'Schapera, if you get a distinction you get a
> scholarship, and then you go either to Malinowski in London or Lowie in
> California.'

He opted for London and the LSE in 1925, just a month after his father's
suicide. However, Malinowski claimed that he had no room for a new
student. 'Seligman is Africa', he told Schapera. 'You come from Africa.
Would you be a student of Seligman?'[11]

---

[8] Jean Comaroff and John Comaroff, 'On the founding fathers, fieldwork and functionalism: A
Conversation with Isaac Schapera', *American Ethnologist*, 15 (1988), 554–65
[9] In a letter to Haddon, in Dec. 1922, Radcliffe-Brown reported that he was 'working on the
origin of law as illustrated by the African native legal systems. I lectured on the subject last year,
and shall make a book of it when I can'. Radcliffe-Brown to Haddon, 18 Dec. 1922. Haddon
Papers, Envelope 4, University Library, Cambridge.
[10] Schapera passed his notes on to me, and I have deposited them in the library of the London
School of Economics.
[11] Adam Kuper, 'Isaac Schapera—a conversation', Part 1, p. 5.

'Sligs' Seligman, whose portrait was to hang in Schapera's office in Cape Town, was a veteran of the Torres Straits expedition. He later carried out survey work in the Sudan on behalf of the Sudan government. Seligman purveyed an old-fashioned form of ethnology, short on ideas though long on detail, and mixing cultural, linguistic and biological observations. He was increasingly isolated at the LSE, as Malinowski's influence grew, but his students shared an affectionate regard for him, and he took care of them as best he could. When Schapera's scholarship ran out after two years, Seligman arranged for him to be appointed to an assistantship in the department for a further year so that he could finish his thesis.

Schapera's thesis was based on library sources rather than on fieldwork. He worked up the material in the British Museum, seated alongside Raymond Firth, who was writing a dissertation on the economics of the Maori, which was also based mainly on secondary sources. (Seats L5 and L6, Firth recalled). Shortly afterwards, Audrey Richards undertook a reanalysis of the literature on Southern Bantu nutrition for her dissertation.[12] Richards and Firth were working under the direction of Malinowski, and they organised their studies with reference to functionalist ideas. Schapera's thesis, however, avoided sociological or historical arguments. Very much in the Seligman mode, it provided a synthesis of what was known about the Bushmen and Hottentot peoples of Southern Africa. (He adopted the umbrella term Khoisan, which had been coined by the German biometrician Leonhard Schultze in 1928, and intended as a biological label.) The thesis was published in 1930, when Schapera was twenty-five years old, with a dedication to Radcliffe-Brown, and it remained the standard reference work for a generation. It was intended as the first volume of a series to be edited by Schapera and Jack Driberg, another student of Seligman, which would 'provide in a scientific manner a comprehensive survey of what is at present known about the racial characters, cultures, and languages of the native peoples of Africa'.[13]

Seligman's students, Schapera, Evans-Pritchard and Driberg, became close friends and they remained loyal to their supervisor. However, Malinowski was transforming anthropology at the LSE, with his functionalist doctrines and Trobriand examples. Even Seligman's students

---

[12] In her Foreword to the published thesis, Richards thanks Schapera, who 'gave me useful advice from his specialized knowledge of South African cultures', Audrey Richards, *Hunger and Work in a Savage Tribe* (London, 1932), p. vii.

[13] I. Schapera, *The Khosian Peoples of South Africa: Bushmen and Hottentots* (London, 1930), p. v.

attended Malinowski's seminars. They tended to react against his over-bearing personality and his dogmas, but Malinowski 'asked you questions', Schapera recalled, 'and you had to think. Now Radcliffe-Brown never made you think. He just dictated. Beautifully clear but—you never thought. Malinowski made you think.'[14] He kept thinking for many years about Malinowski's ideas, but was decidedly ambivalent about the man himself. He recalled travelling with Firth to join Malinowski in Oberbozen, in the Tyrol, during the university vacation in 1927, where one of his duties was to scrub Malinowski down with medicines while he lay naked ('except for a modest piece of cloth covering his genitals') and discoursed on the psychology of kinship.[15] He also said that Malinowski once advised him to change his name, and that he replied that he would do it if Malinowski first changed his. (This was a particularly sensitive matter, since his brother Louis did change his name when he established himself as a physician in London.) Malinowski took him on twice as a research assistant, but sacked him both times. According to Schapera, the first sacking was because he refused to take Malinowski's shoes to be repaired. The second time, Malinowski sent Schapera to the British Museum to find a quote which would prove that Freud had suggested responses to his patients. 'I spent a fortnight reading Freud, came back, and said, "I cannot find anything". He said, "You! Get out!"'[16]

Schapera often spoke of these tensions between Malinowski and himself, and he would refer one to the American edition of *Married Life in an African Tribe*, to which Malinowski had contributed a preface (something Schapera discovered only when he received a copy of the book). Here Malinowski stated that Schapera had been a student of Seligman. ('You see! Not a student of Malinowski at all!') However, Malinowski had written to the publisher to praise the monograph, and the quarrel may have been more complicated than he admitted, since Schapera later felt some remorse—or perhaps apprehension. In June, 1931, he wrote from Mochudi in the Bechuanaland Protectorate to congratulate Malinowski on the award of the Rivers medal, and to apologise:

> I am afraid that I left London feeling rather bitter against you, but subsequent reflection has convinced me that I was to blame throughout for the strained nature of our relationship. I feel ashamed to admit that I allowed my youthful conceit to run away with me then, and I can only hope that you will be able to forgive me for the intolerable rudeness I displayed towards you. I have regretted

[14] Adam Kuper, 'Isaac Schapera—a conversation', Part 1, p. 6.
[15] Comaroff and Comaroff, 'On the founding fathers', p. 556.
[16] Ibid., p. 557.

it bitterly ever since I came out here, especially as I have begun to realize how very much I owe to your kindness and to the stimulus of your teaching.

He went on to describe his research.

The BaKgatla among whom I am working have been affected to a very considerable degree by European influences, and I have got a good deal of interesting data on the nature of the changes brought about by this type of culture contact. What has impressed me most is the fact that although the old tribal ancestor-worship has been well-nigh completely displaced by Christianity, magic still flourishes very strongly, and even church members of high standing still resort to the magician at the beginning of the agricultural season, when they are building new houses, when they are in need of rain, and so on. . . .[17]

Replying with unusual promptness, Malinowski wrote: 'I am extremely glad that you are tackling the changing African.' He went on to accept Schapera's apology. 'I shall not attach any undue importance to past events, which I associate with the state of your health. In this connection may I tell you that you ought to have at least one or two hours exercise every day, graduated Swedish gymnastics are far the best.'

Schapera had started to do fieldwork soon after his return to South Africa in 1929. His decision to situate his research in the Bechuanaland Protectorate, a British colony bordering South Africa, came about largely by chance. Mrs Hoernlé, the anthropologist at the University of the Witwatersrand in Johannesburg, disposed of some government funds for research. She had been intrigued by reports of an initiation ceremony that was due to take place among the Kgatla in the Transvaal. She had also heard that a new chief was being installed among the Kgatla at Mochudi in the Bechuanaland Protectorate. Schapera was despatched to Mochudi. He turned up with the Resident Commissioner for the formal installation in the afternoon, only to learn that the traditional ceremonies had been completed early that morning. He had to rely on the report of a young journalist, whom he would later describe as his first informant. His name was Laurens van der Post. But the plan to move on to the Transvaal Kgatla was abandoned. That afternoon he met the retiring regent, Isang Pilane, who readily fell in with his suggestion that he should make his study in Mochudi.

And two or three days later I was sitting in his house, and he was acting as an interpreter. There were two older women he had called to give me information

[17] This letter and Malinowski's reply, and also Malinowski's correspondence with the American publisher of *Married Life in an African Tribe*, are in the Malinowski collection in the LSE library.

on gods and magic. I was full of magic then. Malinowski had just written a book on that. Then a message comes through to the chief: the missionary wants to see him. He says: 'Tell the missionary to go away. I'm busy writing a book with Dr Schapera.' So when the man treats you like that you don't say: I have got to go to the Transvaal to study backward peoples. And you see that accounts for the sort of anthropology I did. Isang wanted his tribe put on the map.[18]

The following year, 1930, Mrs Hoernlé took a year off from the University of the Witwatersrand, and Schapera was engaged to teach her classes. Among his students were Max Gluckman, Ellen Hellmann, Eileen Krige and Hilda Kuper, all of whom became important figures in the discipline. They had been attracted to the subject by Mrs Hoernlé. A large part of the appeal of her teaching was her engagement with political issues. She was at this time active in a liberal think tank, the South African Institute of Race Relations. Max Gluckman and Hilda Kuper were sympathetic to the Communist Party, Ellen Hellmann was a liberal. According to Max Gluckman, the whole cohort 'either before or after they did field research, believed in the integration of Africans and Whites—and other ethnic groups—within a single social system based on equality of all men'.[19] And this was a fraught political moment. In 1929, after an election that was dominated by the race question, an Afrikaner nationalist government had come to power, with a programme of Afrikaner cultural revival, ethnic mobilisation in politics, job reservation for whites, and racial segregation. It was also to be sympathetic to the Nazi movement in Germany.

Schapera's lectures must have touched on current affairs, or at least on issues of social change, since he claimed that Eileen Krige once walked out of the class complaining that he was teaching sociology and not anthropology.[20] Hilda Kuper recalls, however, that he 'was not an inspiring lecturer, but had wonderful material—you had to tell yourself, "Don't go to sleep, what he is saying is good"'. She added that she remembered best his lectures on law, which contrasted the theories of Radcliffe-Brown and Malinowski.[21]

During the vacation, Schapera took these students (plus a visiting member of Malinowski's seminar, Camilla Wedgwood) into the field, to

---

[18] 'Isaac Schapera—a conversation', Part 1, p. 6.
[19] Max Gluckman, 'Anthropology and Apartheid: The work of South African anthropologists', in Meyer Fortes and Sheila Patterson (eds.), *Studies in African Social Anthropology* (London, 1975).
[20] Kuper, 'Isaac Schapera—a conversation', Part 1, p. 7.
[21] Hilda Kuper, 'Function, History, Biography', in George W. Stocking, Jr (ed.) *Functionalism Historicized* (Madison, WI, 1984), p. 196.

Mochudi. Hilda Kuper says that the students found it 'a strange experience', since they had just been reading Malinowski's *Argonauts*, with its romantic account of fieldwork. They discovered that this was not Schapera's style.

> Staying usually in a trader's home, Schapera would sit on a chair in the sunshine, working at a table with his main informant, whom he would get to collect others, and they would discuss and debate. He was very good at asking demanding questions, and he also went to the courts to listen to cases, but it was an approach very different from Malinowski's. Schapera told us to write down what we saw and heard, but asked us to stay away from his best informant.[22]

His note-keeping was, indeed, remarkably meticulous. Many of his neat files have been deposited in the library at the LSE, and in a note to the archivist when he deposited the notebooks he added a brief explanation of the conventions adopted.

> As a rule each entry is headed by the name(s) of the informant(s) and the date of the interview. In the rare instances of its use, 'o.o.' refers to an 'own observation' (i.e., by I.S.) though usually such observations were recorded separately.
> Entries scored through (in pencil, etc.) were subsequently transcribed again, in classified form, on to typed sheets, according to subject matter. These sheets were the main sources used in preparing books or papers for publication.

Schapera worked almost entirely with informants, either specialists (rain doctors, chiefs, elders, etc.) or through the agency of literate assistants, who interviewed their neighbours, friends and relatives on his behalf. These assistants were typically schoolteachers who were temporarily suspended, generally (or so he liked to say) for having made a school-girl pregnant. Schapera paid his assistants and some of his informants a daily rate equivalent to their usual salaries. His assistants collected census and genealogical data, carried out interviews, and wrote essays on topics that interested him. As time went on, and his command of the language improved, he collected more texts in Tswana. He also copied all the documents that came his way, including court records, which he was to mine for many years.

Not only did Schapera depend relatively little on participant observation. His field expeditions were also less extensive than those of the Malinowskians. Between 1929 and 1934 he made annual visits to Mochudi, the Kgatla capital, usually in university vacations, spending just over fourteen months in the field over this period of fifteen years. One

---

[22] Hilda Kuper, 'Function, History, Biography', in George W. Stocking, Jr (ed.) *Functionalism Historicized* (Madison, WI, 1984), p. 196.

advantage was that he gradually achieved a sophisticated command of Setswana. Another was that he could work up historical materials while pursuing ethnographic research. Initially he collected oral histories, village censuses, and genealogies, and focused particularly on marriage, magic, and Christianity. In 1934 he began to do applied studies for the Bechuanaland administration, on law, migrant labour and land tenure. He spent a further four months in 1934 among the Ngwato, and between 1938 and 1943 he made intensive research visits to the Ngwaketse, Kwena and Tawana, and brief visits to the Tlôkwa, Malete and Rolong.

In 1930, Schapera had joined T. T. Barnard at the University of Cape Town, and settled, once again, in a boarding house, the Mount Nelson hotel. The new discipline Radcliffe-Brown established in Cape Town had survived the rumpus provoked by his political opinions, but it was not in robust health. Barnard was a dilettante, more interested in horticulture than in anthropology. He did no research in South Africa. Students could opt for elective courses in social anthropology over two years of the BA degree, but classes were small. At the undergraduate level, teaching was exclusively in the form of lectures.

In 1935, Barnard retired to Bournemouth, where he devoted himself to growing bulbs, and Schapera succeeded to the chair of social anthropology, at the age of thirty. He did not introduce any radical changes to the syllabus, and seems to have been a dutiful rather than a dedicated university professor. His lectures were concerned largely with South African ethnology, eked out with examples from Kenya, which he had visited briefly on behalf of the International African Institute. David Hammond-Tooke, who came to the department as a master's student in 1947, recalled that Schapera 'seldom raised theoretical issues', though in broad terms endorsing the theories of Radcliffe-Brown. 'We did not hear an awful lot about Malinowski'. The text books he prescribed for undergraduates were Goldenweiser's *Anthropology*, Linton's *Study of Man* and Seligman's *Races of Africa*. During the war years he made a point of addressing racist theories. (He came up with a definition of the Aryan as a man with a white skin, a thick skin, and a foreskin.) However, issues of government policy and social change were handled by Jack Simons, a member of the South African Communist Party.[23]

He was more active in broader academic circles, particularly in the national network of what was called 'African Studies' or 'Bantu Studies'.

[23] W. D. Hammond-Tooke, *Imperfect Interpreters: South Africa's Anthropologists 1920–1990* (Johannesburg, 1997), pp. 39–41.

The prime minister, Jan Smuts, had begun to provide funds for African studies in the early 1920s, although the anthropologists complained that he gave much more money for archaeology than for ethnography. However, the Hertzog government that came into power in 1929 was deeply suspicious of liberal academics. In 1931 it discontinued support for the Union Advisory Committee on African Studies and Research, which had brought together the main academics in the various universities to disburse the government block grant. The academics now established the Inter-University Committee for African Affairs, which affiliated itself to the International Institute of African Languages and Cultures in London. Led by Rheinhallt Jones, director of the liberal Institute of Race Relations, who had launched the journal *Bantu Studies*, the Committee brought together representatives of English and Afrikaans language universities, and included Jabavu from the Fort Hare Native College. Schapera served a term as chairman, and seems to have maintained good relations with all sides, but strains were soon apparent between the liberal faction from the English-language universities and the leaders of the Afrikaner team, Eiselen and Lestrade.[24] These became more urgent as the new government developed plans for thorough-going racial separation. G. P. Lestrade, who had established the Ethnological Section of the Department of Native Affairs in 1925, advocated separate development for the black population. Werner Eiselen became an advocate of separate 'Bantu' education. The radical historian Macmillan issued a blanket denunciation of the anthropologists as 'paralysed conservatives'[25] but Hoernlé and Schapera did articulate an alternative perspective, which recalled Radcliffe-Brown's view of South Africa.

During this fraught period, Schapera edited two survey volumes, *Western Civilization and the Natives of South Africa: Studies in Culture Contact*, which appeared in 1934, and *The Bantu-Speaking Tribes of South Africa: An Ethnographical Survey*, published in 1937. Both were written largely by members of the Interuniversity Committee on African Affairs. His Preface to the volume on Western Civilization opened with a restatement of Radcliffe-Brown's thesis: 'Europeans' and 'Natives' 'have exercised a steadily growing influence upon each other's lives . . . It is no longer possible for the two races to develop apart from each other.'

---

[24] The material in this paragraph is drawn from Hammond-Tooke, *Imperfect Interpreters*, pp. 45–8.
[25] H. Macmillan, '"Paralyzed Conservatives": W. M. Macmillan, the Social Scientists and the Common Society, 1923–1948', in H. Macmillan and S. Marks (eds.), *Africa and Empire: W. M. Macmillan, Historian and Social Critic* (London, 1989).

Lestrade, and the Native Economic Commission, had advocated a policy of strict segregation, euphemistically dubbed 'adaptation'. Schapera argued that segregation, premised on the revival of 'traditional culture', was impractical in South Africa. Inexorable changes had been in train for over a century. There was no way in which this process could be stopped, or even controlled, short of imposing totalitarian rule.

> The successful pursuit of an adaptationist policy must of necessity involve complete authoritarian control of all possible influences by the administration. Changes in one aspect of culture inevitably react upon other aspects; and there is little purpose in the Administration's attempting to bolster up the Chieftain-ship and Native legal institutions, the family and parental control, when the sanctions and privileges upon which they rest are at the same time being steadily undermined by the missionary, the teacher, the trader, the labour recruiter, and the farmer . . .
>
> A thorough-going policy of adaptation thus calls for complete segregation of the Native under absolute administrative control extending to every aspect of life. As things now are in South Africa, this condition is not likely to be realized. Moreover, even if the policy were feasible, what is to be its final outcome? What place is to be given ultimately to the Native in the social and political system of the country? This question the Native Economic Commission shirks completely.

He concluded that: 'Bantu culture will change and develop, drawing most of its impetus from the elements of our own civilization, no matter what we can now do or how we attempt to control it. The best we can hope to achieve is so to regulate our active participation in the process of change as to avoid conflict and disaster.'[26]

Most of the chapters in the volume *Western Civilization* were stud-iedly neutral in tone, but some contributions reflected the full range of perspectives on African policy. Eiselen attacked the British missionaries who had been promoting assimilation of the Africans; an economist, W. H. Hutt, prophesied that capitalism would bring about a free labour market; while Jabavu contributed a chapter entitled (though perhaps not by his own choice) simply 'Bantu Grievances'. In his contribution to *The Bantu-Speaking Tribes*, the historian J. S. Marais wrote that 'the position of Natives throughout the country has become worse since 1910. Rights they formerly enjoyed have been abolished or have become precarious; the principle of anti-Native discrimination has been extended into a number of new fields, and new ways of enforcing it have been devised.'[27]

---

[26] I. Schapera, 'Preface' to I. Schapera (ed.) *Western Civilization and the Natives of South Africa: Studies in Culture Contact* (London, 1934), pp. ix–xiv.

[27] J. S. Marais, 'The Imposition and Nature of European Control', in I. Schapera (ed.), *The Bantu-Speaking Tribes of South Africa: An Ethnographical Survey* (London, 1937), p. 355.

Schapera summed up his own views in a chapter entitled 'Cultural Changes in Tribal Life':

> Of the Bantu as a whole it can be said that they have now been drawn perman-
> ently into the orbit of Western civilization. They do not, and probably will not,
> carry on that civilization in its purely European manifestations. It is more likely
> that in certain directions at least they will develop their own local variations. But
> these variations will be within the framework of a common South African civi-
> lization, shared in by both Black and White, and presenting certain peculiarities
> based directly upon the fact of their juxtaposition. Already such a civilization is
> developing, a civilization in which the Europeans at present occupy the position
> of a race-proud and privileged aristocracy, while the Natives, although econom-
> ically indispensable, are confined to a menial status from which few of them are
> able to emerge with success. There has grown up among the Europeans an ideal
> of race purity and race dominance, according to which the integrity of White
> blood and White civilization must be maintained at all costs. And so we find spe-
> cial legislation and usages of social intercourse directed on the one hand against
> miscegenation and on the other erecting artificial barriers against the cultural
> advancement of the Blacks. But despite all this, the Bantu are being drawn more
> and more into the common cultural life of South Africa . . .[28]

Yet the battle-lines were not drawn simply between the segregationists and the assimilationists, and Schapera's position was not without its ambiguities. Malinowski, who visited South Africa in 1934, as a guest speaker at a conference of African education, discerned a process of cul-tural syncretism at work. Perhaps influenced by the first studies of Africans in Johannesburg, which had been carried out under the direction of Mrs Hoernlé,[29] he argued that a dynamic mixed culture was emerging in the city slum yards, and would spread.[30] This view was endorsed by Z. K. Matthews, a professor at Fort Hare Native College who studied with Malinowski and became a leading figure in the ANC.[31] It was, how-ever, rejected by Radcliffe-Brown, who insisted that the crucial develop-ments were in the field of social organisation, tribal societies being drawn into national political and economic relationships.[32] Schapera developed

[28] I. Schapera, 'Cultural Changes in Tribal Life', in I. Schapera (ed.), *The Bantu-Speaking Tribes of South Africa: An Ethnographical Survey* (London, 1937), pp. 386–7.
[29] Ellen Hellmann undertook the first study of an African slum, in the early 1930s, and she was soon followed by E. J. Krige and Hilda Beemer. The most significant of these studies was Hellmann, *Rooiyard: A Sociological Survey of an Urban Native Slum Yard* (published in 1948 by the Rhodes-Livingstone Institute, but based on a thesis submitted in 1934).
[30] Bronislaw Malinowski, 'Introduction' to *Methods of Study of Culture Contact in Africa*, London: International African Institute, Memorandum XV, 1938.
[31] Z. K. Matthews, 'The Tribal Spirit among Educated South Africans', *Man*, 35 (1935), article 26.
[32] See especially A. R. Radcliffe-Brown, 'On Social Structure', *Journal of the Royal Anthropological Institute*, 70 (1940), 1–12.

Radcliffe-Brown's perspective in his contribution to the volume on 'cultural change' in Africa that was published by the International African Institute in 1938 under Malinowski's direction.[33]

But Malinowski also endorsed 'a sophisticated nationalism or tribalism' that 'can still draw full strength from the enormous residues of old tradition'.[34] He formed an alliance with the Swazi King, Sobhuza, who had been influenced by the Zulu cultural movement, Inkhata, which was established in 1922, and who was promoting a neo-traditionalist policy.[35] Sobhuza came to the education conference in Johannesburg to press for the revival of Swazi initiation ceremonies. He argued that they would provide young Swazi with a sense of identity and discipline. His initiative faced opposition from missionaries, and some educated, Christian Swazi, but Hoernlé and Schapera had visited Swaziland earlier in 1934 at the invitation of members of the administration, and written an official report which recommended the revival of the regimental system.

Malinowski may have been influenced by sympathy for the nationalist movements within the old Austro-Hungarian Empire, but in Africa the endorsement of particularist ethnic movements generally implied support for authoritarian chiefs, and might even be taken as lending support to policies of segregation. These choices were less stark in the economically undeveloped British Protectorates than in the Union, and the implications were different in Swaziland, where Sobhuza was a neo-traditionalist, and in Bechuanaland, where the major chiefs were active modernisers (although Schapera's friend Isang also encouraged the selective preservation of traditional values and tried to foster tribal patriotism).[36] But whatever their views on Christianity or education, these chiefs were united in their support of their prerogatives. In his essays on political institutions and on the law in *The Bantu-speaking Peoples*, Schapera insisted on the primary authority of the Chief, and he generally represented the Tswana chiefs as agents of progressive change, although he did criticise some of their excesses. (However, when he gave me his copy of the pamphlet on the administration of Bechuanaland that had been published in 1932 by the radical commentators, Margaret Hodgson and W. G. Ballinger, I found that he had marked up passages in which they criticised the administration's reliance upon the chiefs, who, Hodgson and

---

[33] I. Schapera, 'Contact Between European and Native in South Africa' in *Methods of Study of Culture Contact in Africa*, London: International African Institution, Memorandum XV, 1938.
[34] Bronislaw Malinowski, *Dynamics of Culture Change* (New Haven, 1945), p. 158.
[35] Paul Cocks, 'The King and I', *History of the Human Sciences*, 13:4 (2000).
[36] I. Schapera, *Married Life in an African Tribe* (London, 1940), p. 351.

Ballinger wrote, 'seem to have had only one idea, to preserve their own powers, and consequently to preserve the conditions on which these powers are based.')[37]

Schapera's ethnography is nevertheless free of the celebration of traditional leaders that characterised some contemporary South African studies, notably *The Realm of a Rain-Queen* (1943) by E. Jensen Krige and J. D. Krige, and Hilda Kuper's *An African Aristocracy* (1947). Nor did he defend British policy in the Protectorates. His first significant papers on the Kgatla dealt with the complex but largely detrimental consequences of labour migration and with the sometimes perverse effects of mission policies, which undermined family values and eroded traditional safeguards on sexual morality.[38]

More broadly, his research in the 1930s and 1940s was distinguished by a concern with 'social change', a focus endorsed in South Africa by Mrs Hoernlé and, latterly, by Malinowski in London. Malinowski's *Argonauts of the Western Pacific*, published in 1922, had opened with a lament for the 'cruel irony that just as the importance of the facts and conclusions of ethnological research is . . . becoming recognised, . . . the material of our science is vanishing'. In a paper published in 1929 in *Africa*, entitled 'Practical anthropology', Malinowski abandoned this elegiac tone and demanded an 'anthropology of the changing native'.[39] This reflected the fact that the Colonial Office was at last showing an interest in social and legal research in Africa. Schapera was soon to profit from the new agenda.

The Colonial Office had begun to reform the system of indirect rule in Africa, and in 1934 the Bechuanaland administration duly issued two reform bills, the Natives Tribunal Proclamation and the Natives Administration Proclamation. These substantially limited the powers of the chiefs, and introduced new tribal councils and a hierarchy of customary

[37] Margaret L. Hodgson and W. G. Ballinger, *Bechuanaland Protectorate*, Britain in South Africa (no. 2) (Alice, Eastern Cape, 1932).
[38] I. Schapera, 'Premarital pregnancy and native opinion: A note on social change', *Africa*, 6 (1) (1933), 59–89; 'Labour migration from a Bechuanaland Native Reserve, Part 1', *Journal of the African Society*, 32 (1933), 386–97; 'The BaKxatla BaxaKgafêla: A preliminary report of field investigations', *Africa*, 6 (4) (1933), 4–2–12; 'Economic conditions in a Bechuanaland Native Reserve', *South African Journal of Science*, 30 (1934), 633–55; 'Labour migration from a Bechuanaland Native Reserve, Part 2', *Journal of the African Society*, 33 (1934), 49–58. See also his two essays in a general journal, *The Critic*, 1933, 'The native as letter-writer' (2: 20–28), and 1934, 'The aspirations of native school children' (2: 152–62). This series of essays was to foreshadow much of his more extensive publications in the next decade.
[39] B. Malinowski, 'Practical anthropology', *Africa*, 2 (1929), 22–38.

courts. In the years immediately prior to the Proclamations, the administration had been particularly exercised by disputes with Tshekedi Khama,
regent of the largest tribe, the Ngwato. Tshekedi and other influential
chiefs now feared that their authority was under threat. They certainly
had grounds for their concern. The new High Commissioner, Lt-Col. Rey,
had written in his diary soon after taking office in 1929 that the chiefs
'practically do as they like—punish, fine, tax and generally play hell. Of
course their subjects hate them but daren't complain to us; if they did
their lives would be made impossible.'[40]

This was the background to Schapera's first commission from the
Bechuanaland Protectorate administration, but there was also a more
specific impetus. In debates in the Native Advisory Council, representatives had remarked that a young generation of chiefs were coming to
office who were ignorant of Tswana traditions and would need guidance
in the administration of the law.[41] It was partly in response to these concerns, and partly in order to help magistrates in their work, that the
administration decided to commission a handbook of Tswana law.
Schapera volunteered to take this on, and began work in 1934.

In his introduction to the *Handbook*, Schapera remarked that it was a
book of laws and not a study of the role of law in society. He would therefore not deal with theoretical questions. He also 'had to resist the temp-
tation' to discuss 'the extent to which various laws are actually enforced
or obeyed in practice, the many subterfuges employed to circumvent the
law, the occasional violation of recognised court procedure and principles
of justice by autocratic, biased, or venal Chiefs or headmen, and the
surreptitious exercise of power and rights now declared illegal by the
Administration'. To treat such matters, he noted, would cause resentment. In any case, these machinations were 'after all, abuses of the law
and not part of the law itself'. But he promised a further study (which he
never wrote) that would deal 'with Tswana government and law as
actually seen in practice, and not merely as represented in the statement
of formal principles here given.'[42]

He also noted that there was not a single body of customary law that
applied throughout Bechuanaland. Individual chiefs had introduced

[40] Cited by Diana Wylie, *A Little God: The Twilight of Patriarchy in a Southern African Chiefdom*
(Hanover, NH, 1990), p. 114. Wylie gives an excellent account of these measures and their
political context, pp. 107–17.
[41] See Rey's 'Introduction' to I. Schapera, *A Handbook of Tswana Law and Custom: Compiled
for the Bechuanaland Administration* (London: 1938).
[42] I. Schapera, 'Preface' to *A Handbook of Tswana Law and Custom: Compiled for the
Bechuanaland Administration* (London, 1938), p. xi.

regulations of their own, some for instance, banning bridewealth, others insisting on it, and even setting rates of payment. (In practice, the *Handbook* noted mainly divergences between the Kgatla and the Ngwato. He did not have adequate information on other tribal courts.)

Finally, he explained that the *Handbook* was not a compilation of the ancient body of Tswana law. His aim was to give a statement of the laws that were in force at the time. This was the most original feature of Schapera's codification, the insistence on the emergence of a modern Tswana law, fed by traditional principles but also by tribal and governmental legislation, and responsive to social changes in the society. The creative role of tribal legislation was documented in another study, which he rewrote many years later to illustrate the principle that individual chiefs could and did influence the direction of social change.[43]

Yet while Schapera did his best to avoid theoretical debates in the *Handbook*, he could not evade some fundamental problems.[44] He cited no authorities, but his view of law was based on the familiar positivist dictum of Oliver Wendell Holmes and Roscoe Pound that law is what the courts enforce. The Tswana had two relevant terms: *mokgwa*, and *molao*.[45] He translated the first as custom and the second as law, and submitted that the Tswana distinction reflected the fact that courts punished breaches of law but not of custom.[46] He admitted, however, that this distinction was difficult to maintain. In the absence of a published code of law, the courts 'have to deal with customary rules of behaviour, with traditional usages habitually followed by the people and regarded as more or less binding and obligatory'. It was therefore 'impossible to isolate legal rules absolutely from other rules of conduct'. He suggested that the criterion for identifying a law should be the probability that the court would enforce a particular rule, but had to concede that this was a straightforward calculation. Different tribal courts followed their own precedents, and even a single court was not always consistent. In practice, Schapera himself implicitly decided which rules should be codified as laws.[47]

---

[43] I. Schapera, *Tribal Legislation among the Tswana of the Bechuanaland Protectorate: A Study in the Mechanism of Cultural Change*, London School of Economics, Monographs on Social Anthropology, 9 (1943). This was substantially recast and reissued in 1970 under the title *Tribal Innovators: Tswana Chiefs and Social Change 1795–1940*, London School of Economics, Monographs on Social Anthropology, 43.

[44] But see Simon Roberts, 'Introduction' to new edition of *Handbook of Tswana Law and Custom* (Münster, 1994).

[45] He was to use these terms in the title of a collection of texts on Tswana custom published in Tswana. I. Schapera, *Mekgwa le Melaô ya Botswana* (Alice, Eastern Cape, 1938).

[46] Schapera, *A Handbook of Tswana Law and Custom*, p. 36.

[47] Ibid., pp. 37–8.

The internal classification of laws raised similar problems. 'In practice, although not in theory,' Schapera remarked, 'Tswana law is divided by the people themselves into two main classes', corresponding to the conventional distinction between civil and criminal matters. However, a variety of cases were resolved by the award of civil damages and by the imposition of criminal penalty. If law was what the courts enforced, then Tswana law was not neatly divided into criminal and civil departments.[48]

Special copies of the *Handbook* were distributed to chiefs and magistrates, interleaved with blank pages to allow them to write comments. Tshekedi was particularly upset by the occasional aspersions on the chiefs, but he and his colleagues were more exercised by the limitations on their judicial authority imposed by the Proclamations. These were watered down in 1943. In the meantime, the *Handbook* itself became a widely used source both in Tswana courts and in political disputes.[49]

The Bechuanaland Administration was content with his *Handbook*, and Schapera was given two other major commissions, one to report on labour migration, the other on problems of land tenure. He made several reports to the government on specific problems of land tenure, some of which are reported in the book, which also provides a masterly overview of the Tswana laws and practices regarding property. But the monograph on *Land Tenure* is perhaps notable chiefly for its final chapter, in which Schapera explored the problems raised by the Tswana habit of living in large towns. Chiefs insisted that this concentration of the population was necessary for the maintenance of order. Indeed, if a prominent man moved his family out of the town this could be interpreted as a sign of incipient revolt. There were economic and environmental arguments on the other side. Schapera reviewed the issues with judicious neutrality.[50]

His report on labour migration brought together and analysed all the available statistical data. He insisted on the role of the chiefs in stimulating migration (from which they profited through various payments and impositions), and assessed the mixed economic and social consequences. As ever, Schapera offered a balanced account of costs and benefits. Finally, he considered possible remedies, emphasising particularly that the government should address the 'push' factor that drove people out of the country to seek work. He suggested that the chiefs' right to demand unpaid labour should be curtailed. He recommended a reduction in the

---

[48] Ibid., pp. 46–7.
[49] See, e.g., Wylie, *A Little God* (1990), p. 172.
[50] I. Schapera, *Native Land Tenure in the Bechuanaland Protectorate* (Alice, Eastern Cape, 1943), especially ch. XV.

tax burden that forced many men to go abroad, and remarked that rural development projects might make it easier to earn money at home. However, he refused to support any statutory restrictions on labour migration.[51]

In 1940, Schapera published another and very different study of social change, his one attempt to reach a broader audience. *Married Life in an African Tribe* was surely inspired by the success of Malinowski's *Sexual Life of Savages*. Published in 1929, just when Schapera made his first visit to Mochudi, it had caused something of a sensation, although Malinowski's book did not match the sales of Margaret Mead's *Coming of Age in Samoa*, which had appeared a year earlier, in 1928. Schapera presented his own study as a 'social history'. He did not intend, he wrote, to contribute to theoretical debates on family and marriage. 'My object has been rather to describe in a straightforward manner how the Kgatla family has changed and what sort of life it leads today.'[52] Drawing on letters and often startlingly frank personal statements (usually collected by his assistants) Schapera described in unprecedented detail courtship, love affairs, and sexual practices, including masturbation and homo-sexuality, and documented the day-to-day life of married people. But while Mead and Malinowski had celebrated the sexual freedom of Trobrianders and Samoans, Schapera painted a bleak picture of the love life of the Tswana.

> If I appear to have stressed the unhappy marriages too much, and to have paid little attention to the happy ones that do also exist, it is because the latter, so far as I could judge, are comparatively rare. Few of the women I got to know well enough to talk to on this topic pretended to be living harmoniously with their husband. Almost always there were complaints of sexual ill-treatment or of infidelity, and the characteristic female attitude was one of resignation rather than of happiness. . . . the polygamous ideal still prevails and the virtually enforced monogamy of to-day has not been accompanied by the true companionship upon which a successful union should rest.[53]

Not only were husband and wife frequently at odds. Parents demanded obedience from their children, in the old style, but modern children were often financially independent and had gained an education that distanced them from the older generation. 'The conditions of modern Kgatla life

---

[51] I. Schapera, *Migrant Labour and Tribal Life: A Study of Conditions in the Bechuanaland Protectorate* (London, 1947).
[52] I. Schapera, 'Preface' to *Married Life in an African Tribe* (London, 1940), p. 7.
[53] Schapera, *Married Life in an African Tribe*, p. 212.

almost inevitably produce strained family relaltionships.'[54] Domestic discord was fostered by migrant labour, the schools, and the perverse influence of the missionaries on domestic institutions. 'Western civilization, through the changes it has produced, must be held mainly responsible for the lack of happiness and contentment now so frequently observed in married life, although there is little to suggest that even in the old days these emotional satisfactions were a common feature of the Kgatla family system.'[55]

The book caused some local controversy. Tshekedi Khama was shocked by its sexual frankness, and so was the Archbishop of Cape Town. Schapera received a radio call in the field from the Principal of the University of Cape Town: 'Serious complaints have been made on account of your book. Will you please come back to answer them.' In retrospect Schapera said the problem was that 'according to my description of sexual intercourse amonst the Kgatla, it was very much like the way the civilized, Europeans committed sex. There was nothing exotic about this. That's what . . . annoyed the serious crowd in Cape Town.'[56] In any case, the fuss blew over, but despite the best efforts of the Archbishop, the book never became a best-seller,[57] perhaps precisely because of the lack of exoticism, but also because the Tswana did not seem to be having more fun than anyone else. On both counts, *Married Life* was a striking, perhaps dispiriting contrast to the popular studies of sex and marriage produced by Mead and Malinowski.

In his contribution to *African Systems of Kinship and Marriage* (1950), Schapera described the pattern of cousin marriage among the Tswana, relating it to the political structure of the tribes and documenting changes over four generations.[58] This was one of the very few studies of preferential marriage in Africa that was backed up by good statistics. He also published studies of the demographic studies of Tswana wards, and a monograph on *The Ethnic Composition of Tswana Tribes* (1952). Many years later he published a short monograph on magic, *Rainmaking Rites of Tswana Tribes* (1971), which provided an insight into the manipulation of magical objects to sustain power within Tswana royal families.

[54] Ibid., p. 273.
[55] Ibid., p. 355.
[56] Adam Kuper, 'Isaac Schapera—A conversation', Part 2, *Anthropology Today*, 18 (Feb. 2002), 16.
[57] It was reissued by Penguin in 1971, but did not catch on.
[58] I. Schapera, 'Kinship and Marriage among the Tswana', in A. R. Radcliffe-Brown and D. Forde (eds.), *African Systems of Kinship and Marriage* (London, 1950).

He also had an interest in ethnohistory, collecting oral traditions and editing ethnographic reports dating from the earliest days of contact to the diaries and letters of nineteenth-century missionaries. This historical curiosity was exceptional in British social anthropology at the time, although it fitted into a well-established tradition of research in South Africa. He published ethnographic and historical notes in Tswana that were popular with local readers, and in 1965 he edited and annotated a collection of the praise poems of the Tswana chiefs.[59]

Taken together, his publications on the Tswana represent the most complete individual contribution to the ethnography of an African people. They provide the baseline for modern studies of Botswana, and are valued by the educated people in the country. Suzette Heald, who taught anthropology at the University of Botswana, remarked that in Botswana 'his name lives on in many ways—in a road named after him in the capital Gaborone, and in his "home" village of Mochudi where he was patron of the Phuthadikobo Museum, which effectively stands as a memorial, displaying many of his photographs. One of the first acts of the newly formed University of Botswana, in 1985, was to award him an honorary doctorate, and a photograph of this event is reproduced in the current University prospectus.'[60]

By the late 1940s Schapera's fieldwork days were over, and in 1950 he moved from Cape Town to London. Smuts's wartime government had been defeated by the Afrikaner Nationalist party in elections in 1948. The new government introduced a rigorous policy of segregation, under the intellectual guidance of two former professors at the University of Stellenbosch, Hendrik Verwoerd and the ethnologist Werner Eiselen. Schapera would later deny that his move to London had anything to do with the change of regime in South Africa. In the accounts of his move that he gave after his retirement he would represent himself as having passively responded to the initiatives of his friends. Evans-Pritchard had encouraged him to apply for the vacant Cambridge chair, though later switching his support to Fortes, who was appointed. At the same moment, without evidently advising him, Firth had put Schapera up for a professorship at the LSE. (In both cases, incidentally, Audrey Richards had been shut out.)

---

[59] I. Schapera, *Mekgwa le Melaô ya Botswana* (Alice, Eastern Cape, 1938); *Ditirafalô ya Botswana ba lefatshe la Tshireletsô* (Alice, Eastern Cape, 1940); *Praise Poems of Tswana Chiefs* (Oxford, 1965).

[60] Suzette Heald, 'The legacy of Isaac Schapera', *Anthropology Today*, 19 (6) (2003), 18–19.

Schapera found a serviced room in the White House Hotel off the Euston Road, where he was to remain for half a century. A new routine was established. Mornings would be spent at the LSE, where he would lunch. He then walked home and spent the afternoons at his desk. In the evenings he would drink whisky and read. Where possible weekends would be spent with old friends, especially the South Africa connection, Meyer Fortes, Max Gluckman and Joe Loudon (who had been his student in Cape Town). Evans-Pritchard would sometimes camp on his floor when he visited London, and share his whisky. (*Witchcraft, Oracles and Magic among the Azande* was the only ethnographic monograph Schapera kept by his bedside.) The Firths would have him to their home in Highgate for Sunday lunches. Every year he would visit Holland to spend a week with a former student, Hans Holleman, who was Professor of African Studies at Leiden University, and when I succeeded Holleman, Schapera would come across and spend a week with each of us.

But while he could be warm and entertaining, he had the set habits of the confirmed bachelor. He had once been briefly engaged to be married to Hilda Beemer (Kuper), but he had no enduring love affairs. There was a time when his drinking would cause trouble, particularly with the wives of his friends, and he became lonelier than ever as his friends died— Evans-Pritchard in 1973, Gluckman in 1975, Fortes in 1983. On a visit to Cape Town shortly after his retirement he had an emergency operation on a suspected cancer that resulted in permanent damage to his vocal chords. This made him self-conscious and reluctant to meet new people. But he became friendly with younger colleagues at the LSE and with the new generation of ethnographers and historians in Botswania. And his great-niece Carol offered him a home from home.

At the LSE he was a loyal lieutenant to Firth. He would complain that Firth was too interested in personal power, although Schapera was ready to use patronage to help friends. He felt that Firth underrated his achievement, but their relationship was generally smooth. Firth was the central figure in the national anthropological institutions, and when Schapera dutifully served terms as President of the Royal Anthropological Institute and Chair of the Association of Social Anthropologists, he would consult Firth on important questions, and he supported Firth's policies in the British Academy to which he was elected in 1958.

His most enduring contributions in his London years were the collection of praise poems of Tswana chiefs, some going back several hundred years, and his editions of David Livingstone's letters and journals. Five volumes appeared between 1959 and 1972[61] and they became essential sources for Livingstone studies. Although he continued to teach and to write about South Africa, he would now confine himself largely to comparative essays based on the traditional ethnographic materials.

His teaching at the LSE followed the pattern of his courses in Cape Town. He would synthesise South African ethnography under various conventional headings, and sometimes test sociological theories against this ethnographic record, usually to destruction. In 1950, shortly after arriving in England, he delivered the Josiah Mason Lectures at the University of Birmingham. Invited to discuss 'politics and law in primitive society', he chose to confine himself to

> the forms and functions of primitive governments, which in contrast with law are still a relatively unexplored field of study. I have also confined the range of illustrative material to four separate groups of peoples living in South Africa. This I have done in the belief that detailed and systematic comparison of even a few different types of society, all occurring in a single region, is likely to provide a more satisfactory basis for generalization than scattered and fragmentary citations of the kind originally attempted and still far too common in the literature of social anthropology. In effect the book is now a study of primitive governments in South Africa, not of 'primitive government' in general . . .[62]

This focus on 'primitive government' was in marked contrast to Schapera's studies on the effects of colonial rule, but British social anthropology was now moving away from 'applied' research. *African Systems of Kinship and Marriage*, published in 1950, was a collection of timeless accounts of 'traditional' institutions. This was true even of the chapters by Schapera and Richards, both of whom had written about the great changes in marriage and family life. There was a vogue for what was termed 'theoretical work', and this was distinguished by the avoidance of any consideration of colonial realities. However, *Government and Politics in Tribal Societies* did raise some pertinent questions about conventional theories (for example, demonstrating that Gluckman was quite wrong to suggest that rebellions in 'tribal society' seldom resulted in tribal fission).

---

[61] I. Schapera (ed.), *Livingstone's Private Journals, 1851–1853* (London, 1960); *Livingstone's Missionary Correspondence, 1841–1856* (London, 1961); *Livingstone's African Journal, 1853–1856*, 2 vols. (London, 1963); *David Livingstone's South African Papers, 1849–1853* (Cape Town, Van Riebeeck Society, 1972).

[62] I. Schapera, *Government and Politics in Tribal Societies* (London, 1956).

And Schapera's method of regional comparison, though by no means original, was persuasively defended and it influenced other scholars.[63]

Schapera took early retirement from the LSE in 1969, bored with teaching (never his forte), and unsympathetic to the student insurgency of the time. Orderly and ascetic, lonely, liable to depression, he had a way of erasing the past. He never kept letters, and the only review of any of his books that was found among his papers was a rare unfavourable appreciation, by Eileen Krige. He seldom returned to the places in which he had spent the important years of his life. After completing his research in Mochudi in 1934, he returned to the town only once, for a week. After leaving South Africa in 1950, he went back on visits only three times to Cape Town (once to receive an honorary doctorate from the University), and only twice to Botswana, all brief visits. He rarely visited the LSE after his retirement. But a new generation of loyal friends visited him regularly, and he enjoyed gossiping about anthropologists, and keeping up with new research on South Africa.

His work had been the centre of his life, and he felt diminished when, well into his seventies, he found he had stopped writing. He never stopped reading, however. Although he was eclectic in his tastes, he favoured nineteenth-century English novels, Pepys's diaries, and the Bible, all of which he liked to read as ethnographic documents (he published essays on Cain's sin, and on the use of kin terms in Jane Austen's novels).[64] He regretted that he had forgotten his Hebrew, but he forgot little else. To the very end he would effortlessly quote poetry (the Victorians again), reel off scholarly references when asked for help, copy-edit one's essays with intimidating precision, and tell pointed anecdotes of his teachers and contemporaries, stories that tended to improve with each retelling.

He was frail but in good health to the end. He died from a heart attack, apparently while cooking himself breakfast, on 26 June 2003.

ADAM KUPER
Fellow of the Academy

---

[63] I. Schapera, 'Some comments on comparative method in social anthropology', *American Anthropologist*, 55 (1953), 353–62.

[64] I. Schapera, 'The sin of Cain', *Journal of the Royal Anthropological Institute*, 85 (1955), 33–43; *Kinship Terminology in Jane Austen's Novels*, Occasional Paper of the Royal Anthropological Institute, No. 33 (London, 1977).

Note. I am grateful to Carol Sensky and Allan Lichtenstein for information on Isaac Schapera's family background.

A complete bibliography of Schapera's published work has been compiled by Suzette Heald, and is available on the internet. (Isaac Schapera: A Bibliography. http://www.thuto.org/schapera/resource/bibl.html.)

BEN SEGAL   *J. Appel & Co*

Judah Benzion ('Ben') Segal
1912–2003

I

BEN SEGAL had a long career as a teacher of Semitic languages, all of it at the School of Oriental and African Studies, London University. His principal interest was in Aramaic and Syriac—in addition, of course, to Hebrew and the other main Semitic tongues. Before his teaching career he was employed in the Sudan Civil Service and, during the Second World War, his service was frequently behind the enemy lines in North Africa.

Ben Segal was born at Newcastle (where his father was a Rabbi for some time) on 21 June 1912. His father, Moses Hirsch (Zvi) Segal (1876–1968), was born in Lithuania and was educated in London and Oxford where he served as tutor in biblical and Semitic studies under the great S. R. Driver. In 1926 he transferred to Jerusalem where he became a lecturer in Bible (full professor in 1939), and in that capacity he was the present writer's teacher. He also wrote a grammar of Mishnaic Hebrew which is unsurpassed to the present day. He married a daughter (Hannah Leah)[1] of Aryeh Leib Frumkin (1845–1916) who was Ben's mother. Ben's elder brother Samuel (1902–85) was a physician and politician (Labour Member of Parliament) and one of the first life peers. The Frumkins were early residents of Palestine, and Aryeh Leib founded Petach Tiqvah ('gate of Hope') near Tel Aviv.

---

[1] Cf. an article about her in the *Jewish Chronicle Literary Supplement*, 25 Dec. 1961.

Proceedings of the British Academy, **130**, 205–212. © The British Academy 2005.

Ben was educated at Magdalen College School, Oxford, and at St Catharine's College, Cambridge. He was John Stewart of Rannoch Scholar in Hebrew, 1933; and obtained a first-class in the oriental languages Tripos in 1935. In 1936 he was Tyrwhitt scholar and Mason prizeman, and received his Cambridge BA in 1935 (MA 1938). Those who knew the peaceful and self-effacing Ben well, must have been surprised that he was a boxing blue, though when the occasion demanded it there could be steel in his temperament. From 1936 to 1939 he was Mansel Research Exhibitioner at St John's College, Oxford, as well as James Mew Scholar in 1937; he received his Oxford D.Phil. in 1939.

After his university education he joined the Sudan Civil Service as Deputy Assistant Director, Public Security, 1939–41. In 1940 he came on leave to Jerusalem to visit his parents. His father, my teacher, introduced me to his son who was eight years my senior. Both having studied similar Semitic languages, the beginnings of a friendship developed between us which lasted in increasing measure (later including our wives) to his dying day.

During the 1939–45 war he was attached to GHQ Middle East Forces (1942–4) to carry out, thanks to his knowledge of Arabic, secret operations ahead of Montgomery's Eighth Army and behind Rommel's lines. He had been introduced to David Stirling, founder of the SAS; and with some others Segal was conveyed behind the German and Italian fronts to lay up for three months, in very primitive conditions, to radio back to Cairo all intelligence on enemy tank and aircraft movements. His team would move from cave to cave to avoid detection; they used informers to obtain details of enemy plans. With the help of local Arabs he seized the key Libyan town of Derna. He crowned that achievement by flying from a town-hall window the Union Jack—rapidly sewn together from his handkerchief and a collection of colourful rags. This is now on view in the Imperial War Museum. His feat, a combination of high courage and practical prowess, was recognised by the award of the Military Cross.

In his last little book, entitled *Whisper Awhile*, he refers to these operations—but in so self-effacing a manner that the connection between those exploits and the MC is mentioned only in the publishers' blurb. *Whisper Awhile*, in all its chapters, is a gem of a book. Segal and his group had several close escapes from German and Italian search parties, but they managed to report back, often walking hundreds of miles from hideout to hideout. Though given 'licence to kill' any spies among the Arabs, Segal preferred to move his hideouts rather than taking a life. At Derna he had succeeded in releasing some Allied prisoners of war. To protect his identity he was referred to as Captain Seagrim.

On his return to civilian life he joined SOAS, at first principally as lecturer in Aramaic and Hebrew. In 1961, when the Chair of Semitic languages fell vacant, on the retirement of Professor C. J. Gadd, the appointing committee had difficulty in reaching a unanimous decision about his successor. Both Gadd and his predecessor, Sidney Smith, were essentially Assyriologists and had come from the British Museum. The external referees favoured a similar decision and strongly urged the appointment of Donald Wiseman to the Chair of Assyriology, while the internal referees suggested a distinguished Semitist, Ben Segal. The externals eventually prevailed, and Wiseman became a highly successful holder of the Chair of Assyriology. Sir Cyril Philips, the Director of SOAS, then got in touch with me at Manchester (where I occupied the Chair of Semitic languages) and asked me whether I would be able to make a convincing case for Ben Segal to be appointed to an *ad hominem* Chair of Semitic languages. No easier task had ever been entrusted to me, and Segal's elevation to the Chair occurred without delay in 1961; it remained in his charge until 1979 when he reached the age of retirement.

In those days the distinction between established chairs and *ad hominem* ones was still in place, and I considered the Semitics Chair of greater significance than my, by then, established Chair of Ethiopian Studies at SOAS. My proposal was acted upon and the two Chairs were amalgamated. At the present time there is no Chair of Semitic languages at SOAS—and indeed anywhere in Britain in the full sense—except at Cambridge where it is occupied most worthily by Professor Geoffrey Khan, one of the ablest graduates of SOAS, a pupil of both Segal and myself. From 1961 to 1968 Segal was Head of the Department of the Near and Middle East. After retirement he became an Honorary Fellow of SOAS. He was particularly pleased, especially as a Jew, to be called as a Visiting Lecturer to Ain Shams University, Cairo, in 1979.

Afterwards he accepted the principalship of the Leo Baeck College (1982–5), a liberal training institution for rabbis and Jewish studies in general. He was also an active member of the Council of Christians and Jews and President of the North Western Reform Synagogue as well as of the British Association for Jewish Studies (1980). An unusual honour was the bestowal on him of the Freedom of the City of Urfa, in Turkey, in 1973—the 'blessed city' of Edessa on which Segal had written a mighty tome. In 1968 he was elected a Fellow of the British Academy whose meetings he attended deep into his eighties.

The first of his major publications was *The Diacritical Point and the Accents in Syriac* (1953), an important work but aimed at the specialist rather than the general reader. This limitation is decidely not the case as regards *The Hebrew Passover* (1963). Segal himself says in his preface that 'the influence of the Passover on the ritual and thought of Judaism and Christianity has probably been more profound than that of any other festival'. He discusses in detail the sources and the tradition based on the historical documents as well as modern theories on the origins and early development of the Passover, including the 'primitive Passover' and the 'Passover in Canaan'. Altogether this is a book of absorbing interest.

His *Edessa* book (1970) is a work of large format running to over three hundred pages and may probably be considered his *magnum opus*. It is beautifully written and richly illustrated. Pope Eugenius III wrote to King Louis VII of France in 1145 of 'The city [of Edessa] that was ruled by Christians and alone served the Lord when, long ago, the whole world in the East was under the sway of pagans.' The book is the outcome of five visits to Urfa (the modern name of Edessa) between 1952 and 1966. His chapters deal with Edessa under the Kings; the blessing of Jesus and the triumph of Christianity; life at Edessa, AD 240–639; and the last five centuries, 639–1146.

One of Segal's other abiding interests concerned the Jews of Cochin whose history he published in 1993. They form a tiny community on the Spice Coast of south-west India and have done so for some two thousand years. According to legend, the apostle Thomas found a Jewish presence in this area. The earliest extant record is an inscription, dated AD 1000, in Malayalam on copper plates, by which Indian princes granted exemption from taxation to one Joseph Rabban. At about the same time a largely autonomous Jewish principality was set up near Cochin. The Cochin Jews probably never numbered more than two thousand. When Indian independence was closely followed by the establishment of the State of Israel in 1948, most of the community emigrated to the new state. Today only a handful of Jews remain in Cochin.

The last massive volume from Segal's pen is a *Catalogue of the Aramaic and Mandaic Incantation Bowls in the British Museum* (2000). In an excellent review of this remarkable work, John Healey writes (*Journal of Semitic Studies*, 48, autumn 2003) that 'this is one of those books which has been long awaited by scholars in the field, but the wait was well worth it. Here we have the definitive publication and study of one of the world's most important collections of incantation bowls, apparently surpassed numerically only by the collection of the Iraq Museum' (if that still exists in a usable state). 'The volume is set to become a primary source of reference in Aramaic studies and script development.'

I must briefly revert to *Whisper Awhile*, his last book, running to seven unconnected chapters of some ninety pages altogether. Each chapter has an autobiographical flavour, but the word 'I' is used in an almost impersonal sense, for self-effacement was the core of Segal's personality. The book was never intended for sale, but was given to family and close friends. When he told me that the supply had been exhausted, I approached an acquaintance in the Oxford University Press, for the original publishers were no longer in business. The OUP were immensely helpful and produced some three hundred copies photographically for a largely notional remuneration.

Like many of us, Ben could also be quirky: on one occasion he invited a colleague from another college and asked me to join them at lunch at SOAS. Once the colleague had departed I handed to Ben the money I owed him for my lunch. He accepted it, but the next morning he telephoned to say that we could not meet, the two of us with our wives, as had been arranged for that evening, because he felt so hurt that I had paid him the money for my lunch. I urged him to forgive me, for I had done that quite innocently. He forgave me and we agreed to reinstate our meeting that evening, on the express condition that he would pay and that I would promise not to do so. When the waiter handed the bill to me, I immediately pushed it towards Ben. He rummaged in his wallet but could not find what he wanted. He then turned to me and asked me to pay after all. I said I could not possibly do so, since he would not expect me to break my word . . .

Altogether Ben was that rare scholar whose character and learning shone in equal measure. He and his wife Leah (Seidemann), with their two daughters, Miriam and Naomi, had a happy and serene relationship. Ben died of cancer and cardiac failure in London on 23 October 2003, aged 91.

There were detailed obituaries in *The Times*, *The Guardian*, and *The Independent*. That in *The Independent* was by Arthur Irvine and is particularly good and exhaustive.

A memorial service took place in his synagogue on 30 November. There were three brief addresses before a large congregation. The Qaddish prayer is normally said by a son or the nearest male relative. On this occasion it was beautifully recited by his daughter Naomi, a most salutary departure from the usual compulsory restriction to males.

II

It will probably be in the area of Aramaic studies that Ben Segal will be best remembered in the academic world. Here his interests and abilities were unusually wide-ranging: whereas most scholars in this field specialise in one particular dialect of Aramaic or one particular period or topic, Segal's publications range in date from Imperial Aramaic texts of the sixth to fifth century BC to Modern Aramaic proverbs of the twentieth century AD,[2] and they cover in between Hatran[3] as well as Syriac and Mandaic from the first millennium AD; the topics he chose to write on were likewise admirably varied: language, palaeography, epigraphy, history, and religion. Though two of his major publications, the meticulous edition of the lamentably fragmentary Aramaic texts of the Achaemenid period from Saqqara,[4] and his catalogue of the British Museum's collection of Mandaic magic bowls,[5] concern dialects other than Syriac, it was in the area of Syriac studies that much of his most important work was done.

His early *The Diacritical Point and the Accents in Syriac* (London, 1953), based on early manuscripts in the British Library's exceptionally fine collection of Syriac manuscripts, will doubtless continue for a long time to provide the essential starting point for the subject. A series of visits, in the 1950s, to Urfa, ancient Edessa, in south-east Turkey and the discovery of pagan Syriac inscriptions resulted in several important articles, in *Anatolian Studies* (1953) and elsewhere. Hitherto the number of Syriac inscriptions from the first to the third centuries AD had been extremely meagre; Segal's discoveries, and their careful publication, increased their number significantly, and many of the inscriptions now collected in H. J. W. Drijvers and J. F. Healey's *The Old Syriac Inscriptions of Edessa and Osrhoene* (1999) had received their initial publication by Segal in the *Bulletin of the School of Oriental and African Studies.*

His work on the early Edessene inscriptions led to an interest in the history of this ancient centre of Syriac culture; this culminated with the

---

[2] 'Neo-Aramaic proverbs of the Jews of Zakho', *Journal of Near Eastern Studies*, 14 (1955), 251–70.
[3] 'Arabs at Hatra and the vicinity: marginalia on new Aramaic texts', *Journal of Semitic Studies*, 31 (1986), 57–80.
[4] *Aramaic Texts from North Saqqara with some Fragments in Phoenician* (London, 1983). The various different points of interest that these unpromising scraps offer are usefully drawn out by H. G. M. Williamson in his review in the *Journal of Egyptian Archaeology*, 73 (1987), 265–9.
[5] *Catalogue of the Aramaic and Mandaic Incantation Bowls in the British Museum* (London, 2000).

publication, in 1970, of his best known and most widely read book, *Edessa, 'the Blessed City'*, covering the history of the city up to its capture by Zangi in 1146. This is an eminently readable work, and one based on a close famil-iarity with the scattered Syriac sources; its one drawback for the scholar is that the references to the many different chronicles quoted are left non-chalantly vague, and so anyone in search of these who does not share Segal's intimate knowledge of the sources is likely to find this aspect of his work not a little frustrating. For the more general reader, however, this is not a great problem, and it is perhaps thanks to the absence of pages over-burdened with references that the book has reached a wider readership, and has been translated into both Turkish and Arabic (1988); it also earned its author the Freedom of the Municipality of Şanliurfa.

Side products of the intimate knowledge he had gained of the Syriac chronicles can be seen in a series of valuable articles, 'Mesopotamian Communities from Julian to the rise of Islam',[6] 'Syriac chronicles as source material for the history of Islamic peoples',[7] 'The Jews of North Mesopotamia before the rise of Islam',[8] and 'Arabs in Syriac literature before the rise of Islam'.[9]

In September 1987 Segal visited Kerala in order to attend the First International Syriac Conference at the recently founded St Ephrem Ecumenical Research Institute (SEERI), in Kottayam (Kerala), which specialises in the Syriac tradition of the indigenous Churches of Kerala. One outcome of this visit to India was his history of the Jews of Kerala, mentioned by Professor Ullendorff. At the conference itself he returned to the topic he had started out with, namely the diacritical point, though here he dealt with an important feature which he had deliberately not touched on in his earlier monograph, namely the use of the point to indi-cate *Qushshaya* ('hardening') and *Rukkaka* ('softening'). Though his paper was published among the other conference papers in SEERI's own periodical *The Harp: A Journal of Syriac and Oriental Studies* (1:2/3 (1988), 13–20), a longer (and more accurately printed!) form subsequently appeared in a rather more accessible place.[10] This return to the beginning, as it were, proved to be his last contribution to Syriac studies. At the time of Segal's first publications in Syriac studies this was an academic field

---

[6] *Proceedings of the British Academy*, 41 (1955), 109–39.
[7] In B. Lewis and P. M. Holt (eds.), *Historians of the Middle East* (London, 1962), pp. 246–58.
[8] In the Festschrift for his father, M. H. Segal, edited by J. M. Grintz and J. Liver (Jerusalem, 1964), pp. 32*–63*.
[9] *Jerusalem Studies in Arabic and Islam*, 4 (1984), 89–128.
[10] *Journal of Semitic Studies*, 34 (1989), 483–91.

that was little cultivated: the very considerable revival of interest that the last three decades have witnessed is in no small part due to the stimulus provided by two books, one being R. Murray's *Symbols of Church and Kingdom. A Study in Early Syriac Tradition* (1975), and the other, Ben Segal's *Edessa, 'the Blessed City'*, of five years earlier.

Part I   EDWARD ULLENDORFF
Fellow of the Academy

Part II   SEBASTIAN BROCK
Fellow of the Academy

SIR JOHN SMITH

John Cyril Smith
1922–2003

JOHN CYRIL SMITH, Emeritus Professor of Law at the University of Nottingham, Fellow of the Academy since 1973 and chairman of the Law section in the early 1990s, was born on 15 January 1922. The second son of Bernard and Madeline Smith, he spent his early years in County Durham, where his father had an engineering business, and John went into the family business on leaving St Mary's Grammar School at Darlington. He worked as a civil engineer until joining the Royal Artillery to fight in the war. It was during his military service, in which he rose to the rank of captain, that he attended a lecture on law, and that sparked the interest that he went on to pursue to such outstanding effect in Cambridge. He took a First at Downing after the war, progressed to the LL B, and then went straight into teaching at Nottingham. He was made Head of the Department of Law in 1956 and promoted to Professor in 1957, and he led the Department for thirty years almost without a break until his retirement in 1987. In 1957 he married Shirley Anne Walters, who died in 2000. They are survived by their two sons and a daughter.

The Law of Contract

After a couple of years of teaching at Nottingham J. C. Smith was awarded a Commonwealth Fund Fellowship at Harvard University in 1952–3. He became impressed by the casebook method of teaching, common in the United States but little known in this country. Its essence is

Proceedings of the British Academy, **130**, 215–223. © The British Academy 2005.

that students prepare for a class by reading reports of assigned cases, and then during the class they are asked questions about the cases and about their views of the judge's reasoning, which they have to defend in front of all the others. J. C. Smith not only encouraged colleagues at Nottingham to adopt this interactive approach, but set out (with J. A. C. Thomas) to construct a casebook for use in his own Contract course. The result was *A Casebook on Contract*, a book composed of extracts from case reports, pertinent questions and linking text. The book has now gone into eleven editions,[1] and was tremendously influential in the 1950s and 1960s in encouraging law teachers to experiment with more interactive methods of instruction.

Evidence and procedure

When he retired from his chair in 1987, Sir John said that the only subject he had taught every year throughout his career was Evidence. His deep understanding of the law was apparent in his case commentaries on the subject for the *Criminal Law Review*, although by the mid-1980s he was handing over many Evidence cases to his colleague and former student Diane Birch for commentary—a good example of his supportive treatment of able young lecturers. However, there were several issues in Evidence that continued to intrigue him. Perhaps it was his first career as an engineer that led him to be fascinated by the operation of computers: certainly he wrote effectively on the subject of computer-generated materials as evidence,[2] and the subsequent development of the law owed much to his demystification of the processes at work and their relevance to evidentiary concepts. Sir John was a strong advocate of the presumption of innocence, in the form of the principle, advocated by the Criminal Law Revision Committee in its notorious report on Evidence,[3] that the only burden that should be imposed on defendants in criminal cases is an evidential burden (i.e. the burden of producing sufficient evidence to raise the issue, which the prosecution must then disprove), and that the burden of proving an issue to

---

[1] (London), 1st edn., 1955, 11th edn., 2000.
[2] Most influential was 'The Admissibility of Statements by Computer', [1981] Criminal Law Review, 387.
[3] Criminal Law Revision Committee, 11th Report, *Evidence (General)*, Cmnd 4771 (London, HMSO, 1972)—notorious because of the recommendation that adverse inferences from silence be permitted, and the furious reaction to this from many parts of the legal profession. Sir John was not a member of the CLRC at this time.

the court should never be imposed on the defendant. He was therefore a critic of the many statutory provisions that appeared to ignore the principle, and also of the decision of the House of Lords in *Hunt*,[4] which drew from him a learned and much-cited article on 'The Presumption of Innocence'.[5] He also made telling contributions over the years to the development of criminal procedure, a subject much neglected by academic lawyers. A fine example is his article on 'Satisfying the Jury',[6] teasing out the procedural issues where the members of the jury are agreed on some issues in a case but not others. Another example would be his writings on the bill that became the Criminal Appeal Act 1995, where he pointed out the problems that would be created by the reduction of the grounds for allowing an appeal against a conviction to the single and unembellished word 'unsafe'—and, of course, he was right about this.[7]

Criminal law

It is chiefly for his work on the substantive criminal law that Sir John Smith will be long remembered. When the *Criminal Law Review* was founded in 1954, J. C. Smith was among the first contributors, with several articles in the first few years. Most of these articles concerned the law of larceny, and his tremendous command of the authorities on this subject led the Criminal Law Revision Committee to co-opt him to the subcommittee formed to propose 'a simpler and more effective' law of theft. The Committee's report on the subject acknowledges his assistance,[8] and he went on to write a monograph, *The Law of Theft*,[9] that ran into eight editions and was much cited in the courts. Sir John was sharply critical of many judicial decisions on the interpretation and application of the Theft Acts, reserving his strongest condemnation for the reasoning of the House of Lords in three leading cases.[10]

---

[4] [1987] Appeal Cases 352.

[5] (1987) 38, *Northern Ireland Legal Quarterly*, 223.

[6] [1988] Criminal Law Review, 335.

[7] See, for example, 'The Criminal Appeal Act 1995: (1) Appeals against Conviction', [1995] Criminal Law Review, 920, and his commentary on *Mullen* [1999] Criminal Law Review, 561.

[8] Criminal Law Revision Committee, 8th Report, *Theft and Related Offences*, Cmnd 2977 (London, HMSO, 1966); see particularly para. 2.

[9] (London), 1st edn., 1968; 8th edn., 1997.

[10] *Morris* [1984] Appeal Cases, 320, commentary at [1983] Criminal Law Review, 813; *Gomez* [1993] Appeal Cases, 442, commentary at [1993] Criminal Law Review, 304; *Hinks* [2001] 2 Appeal Cases 241, commentary at [2001] Criminal Law Review, 162 ('At least the House of Lords got the question right . . . Pity about the answer').

Much of Sir John's groundwork on the law of larceny was accomplished in the late 1950s and early 1960s, when he began work on a new textbook on criminal law. At that time only Kenny's *Outlines of the Criminal Law* served as a student text, and that was beginning to show its age, having had its first edition as long ago as 1902. The demands of modern university learning pointed to the need for a more rigorous, detailed and up-to-date text. In the early 1960s J. C. Smith invited his colleague at Nottingham, Brian Hogan, to join him in the project on which he had already embarked, and the result was the publication in 1965 of the first edition of Smith and Hogan's *Criminal Law*. This immediately became the leading textbook in the field, being both widely used in university law schools and greatly relied upon throughout the legal profession and in the courts. Those parts of the text dealing with larceny had to be extensively rewritten for the second edition, in the light of the Theft Act 1968. Since then the book has grown considerably in size, partly in response to the needs of practitioners, and (after the untimely death of Brian Hogan in 1996) Sir John completed the last two editions on his own. After the publication of the tenth edition in 2002,[11] Sir John decided to place future editions of the work in the hands of Professor David Ormerod of Leeds, whom he had nurtured as a junior colleague at Nottingham in the 1990s.

Why has 'Smith and Hogan' been so successful? Its initial success probably derived from the close attention to detail, the clarity of its analysis of the law, a willingness to encourage critical reflection on the development of the law, and its reference to (and interaction with) scholarly writings on the criminal law. In later years Sir John admitted to a lack of sympathy for much modern writing on the criminal law—he was not impressed by the increasingly philosophical analysis of fundamental concepts, and had no time for 'critical legal studies' approaches—and the book's engagement with current scholarship fell away. But it has retained its own critical tone in respect of many legal developments, and remains the first port of call for teachers, students and practitioners who want an authoritative statement of the law on a certain point. It is much used in the universities, often in conjunction with Smith and Hogan's *Criminal Law: Cases and Materials*.[12]

From what perspectives did Sir John criticise the criminal law? His position was that of the old-fashioned liberal, and this committed him to a strong strain of subjectivism. But by no means all his criticisms of

---

[11] (London), 10th edn., 2002, by Sir John Smith.
[12] (London), 8th edn., 2002, by Sir John Smith.

statute and case law stemmed from this source: he was a fierce defender of consistency and logic in legal propositions, often in the face of judicial decisions that found it convenient to dispense with such values when it was a matter of upholding the conviction of a villain, and his great respect for the historical development of the criminal law led him to criticise decisions that ignored the purpose behind certain legislative provisions. One characteristic critique of this kind is to be found in his commentary on the decision of the House of Lords to the effect that, despite the enactment of the Criminal Attempts Act 1981, impossibility could still afford a defence to a charge of criminal attempt: 'The House of Lords has done it again. Confusion and uncertainty have been substituted for the orderly and simple solution of this longstanding problem intended by Parliament.'[13]

This particular example brings us back to the theme of subjectivism—the principle that a person should only be liable to conviction of a criminal offence if he or she intended or knowingly risked causing the prohibited harm, and that a person should be entitled to be judged on the facts as he or she believed them to be. Sir John had embraced this principle in the context of the law of attempts in one of his earliest and best-known articles, 'Two Problems in Criminal Attempts', published in the *Harvard Law Review*.[14] There he developed a normative argument in favour of allowing recklessness to be a sufficient fault element for a criminal attempt, contrary to the prevailing orthodoxy that limited the fault to intention alone in the context of attempted crimes. He also argued in favour of convicting a person of an attempt even though the acts done could not, on the facts as they were, have led to the commission of the full offence—such as trying to pick a pocket by putting a hand into a pocket that turned out to be empty. (This line of argument was accepted by Parliament in the Criminal Attempts Act 1981, and explains Sir John's blunt condemnation of the House of Lords when they interpreted the Act otherwise.)[15] The same normative arguments were advanced in a more general context in his 'The Element of Chance in Criminal Liability'.[16]

This vigorous subjectivism led Sir John to oppose not only strict liability in the criminal law (i.e. those offences for which a person may be

[13] [1985] Criminal Law Review, 504.
[14] (1957) 70 *Harvard Law Review*, 422; a few years later he revisited the topic and focused on the precise points of disagreement with Glanville Williams: 'Two Problems of Criminal Attempts Re-Examined' [1962] Criminal Law Review, 135 and 212.
[15] See the text at n. 13 above.
[16] [1971] Criminal Law Review, 63.

convicted without proof of fault) but also any requirement that a mistaken belief should have been held on 'reasonable grounds'. He was therefore a great supporter of the decision in *Director of Public Prosecutions v. Morgan*,[17] which held that a man should not be convicted of rape if he mistakenly believed that the victim was consenting, and that there should be no requirement of reasonable grounds for such a belief. That decision, combining the subjective principle with what Lord Hailsham described as 'inexorable logic', stands as a fine example of the approach that Sir John had been advocating for years. On the other hand, a few years later came a decision of the House of Lords that embodied just the approach that Sir John thought unacceptable: in *Caldwell*[18] the House held that a person may be held to be 'reckless' not only by knowingly risking the prohibited consequence but also by unwittingly risking it, if it was a risk that should have been obvious. Sir John criticised this decision because it introduced an objective standard and allowed the conviction of someone who was unaware of a particular risk, and also because it failed to follow the intention of Parliament (and of the Law Commission) on the matter. Shortly after his death, the House of Lords overruled its decision in *Caldwell*,[19] accepting the criticisms that Sir John and others had made at the outset.

Quite apart from his general writings on the criminal law, Sir John devoted scholarly attention to the history and future development of some particular topics. His pre-eminence in the law of theft has already been mentioned. He wrote two original and searching papers on the law of complicity,[20] and his concern for the intellectual development of complicity was evident in his powerful response to the Law Commission's proposals on the subject.[21] In the late 1980s he delivered the Hamlyn Lectures on the subject of defences to criminal liability, and the resulting monograph is a treasury of careful analysis and thoughtful criticism,[22] although without engagement in the debate about the concepts of justification and excuse that was enthusing many scholars at the time.

---

[17] [1976] Appeal Cases, 182.

[18] [1982] Appeal Cases, 341.

[19] *R. v. G.* [2003] 3, Weekly Law Reports, p. 1060.

[20] 'Aid, Abet, Counsel or Procure', in P. R. Glazebrook (ed.), *Reshaping the Criminal Law* (London, 1978), p. 120; and 'Secondary Participation and Inchoate Offences', in C. F. H. Tapper (ed.), *Crime, Proof and Punishment* (London), p. 21.

[21] 'Criminal Liability of Accessories: Law and Law Reform', (1997) 113 *Law Quarterly Review*, 453.

[22] *Justification and Excuse in the Criminal Law* (London, 1989).

Public service

In addition to his three decades as Head of the Law Department at the
University of Nottingham, and all his academic writings, John Smith
gave considerable time to official committees and other public service
work. He was appointed as a member of the Criminal Law Revision
Committee in the late 1970s, having already served as a co-opted member
on at least three references since the early 1960s. After his 'retirement' he
was appointed Special Adviser to the House of Lords Select Committee
on Murder and Life Imprisonment (1988–9), and subsequently an asses-
sor to Sir John May's inquiry (1989–92) into the Maguire case, otherwise
known as the case of the Guildford bombing. At the request of the Royal
Commission on Criminal Justice (1991–3) he prepared a simplified
exposition of the laws of evidence, which was subsequently turned into an
excellent introductory text.[23]

Undoubtedly Sir John's greatest contribution to the public service,
and probably the single piece of work for which he would most wish to be
remembered, is his chairmanship of the small group of academic lawyers
that produced the first draft of the criminal code. English law is unusual
in having an uncodified criminal law, differing in this respect not only
from most other European legal systems but also from most of the
Commonwealth and United States systems that are based on English law.
The code team was constituted in 1981, and produced a report and a draft
Criminal Code Bill which the Law Commission published for consultation in 1985.[24] It was slightly modified as a result of consultation with the
profession, and then issued as a Law Commission report in 1989[25] after
further discussions with Sir John and his team. The code team had to per-
form a far more extensive exercise than perhaps even they anticipated.
English criminal law was and is difficult to restate, not merely because of
a proliferation of statutory provisions enacted at different times in differing contexts, but also because much of the general part and some specific
offences remain undefined and exist only at common law. There were
committee recommendations for the reform of some parts of the law,
such as offences against the person and sexual offences, but in other areas
the code team decided that the common law was simply too chaotic and
contradictory to restate, and therefore resolved to incorporate their own

[23] *Understanding the Law of Evidence* (London, 1994).
[24] Law Com. No. 143, *Codification of the Criminal Law: a Report to the Law Commission*, H.C.
270 (London, HMSO, 1995).
[25] Law Com. No. 177, *A Criminal Code for England and Wales*, 2 vols. (1989).

recommendations. Thus the draft code produced by the team had a significant normative content, about which debate was inevitable. The code was also innovative in its style of drafting. The code team did not have parliamentary counsel to assist them, and they resolved to adopt a far less complex approach to drafting than is customary. 'We have adopted, so far as possible, a simple relatively spare style, avoiding redundant expressions. Statements should not be longer than they have to be; and even when unavoidably long, they should be easy to read.'[26] The difference in style is striking, and the team's efforts are much to be commended.

The problem, however, has not been the drafting. It has been a dire absence of political will. In the early 1990s the government showed little or no enthusiasm for codification. There was a suggestion that the draft code would be too large for Parliament to deal with—a statement that was unconvincing at the time, and which has been falsified by Parliament's handling of several mammoth bills since then. The Law Commission responded in 1993 by producing a draft bill on offences against the person, with a view to prompting the enactment of the code part by part, but this was received with no official enthusiasm at all. In the meantime Sir John Smith was working tirelessly to promote the draft criminal code, referring to it in his case commentaries in order to illustrate the respects in which the law and its administration would be improved by its enactment. The change of government in 1997 led to some optimism, and the Home Office swiftly published a further draft bill on offences against the person. But, again, nothing actually happened. Recent years have seen some strong official statements about the need for a criminal code,[27] but Sir John was becoming weary about the widening gap between aspirational statements and real progress.

Sir John Smith died on 14 February 2003, at the age of 81. He had been President of the Society of Public Teachers of Law in 1979–80, was knighted in 1993 and was awarded honorary Doctorates of Laws by Sheffield, Nottingham, Villanova and De Montfort universities. He was always a modest man, and ever courteous in his dealings with others, particularly students and young colleagues. He was one of the giants of academic law in the second half of the last century, and without his out-

---

[26] Law Com. No. 143 (see above, n. 24), para. 2.20.
[27] e.g. Home Office, *Criminal Justice: the Way Ahead*, Cm 5074 (London, The Stationery Office, 2001), para. 3.59; Lord Justice Auld, *Review of the Criminal Courts in England and Wales* (London, The Stationery Office, 2001), pp. 20–2.

standing application and advocacy the project of codifying the criminal law of England and Wales would be much further from fruition. As it is, the epitaph that the enactment of the Criminal Code would provide cannot yet be written.

ANDREW ASHWORTH
Fellow of the Academy

RICHARD WOLLHEIM

Richard Arthur Wollheim
1923–2003

RICHARD ARTHUR WOLLHEIM was born on 5 May 1923 in London, the younger son of Eric Wollheim, of a German Jewish family, and Constance Baker, whose family came from the West Country and for centuries were peasants. His father was a theatrical impresario, who from 1918 acted as the Diaghilev ballet's London manager. His mother was a Gaiety show-girl, who performed as an actress playing to the troops during the First World War, but at her husband's insistence left the stage when she married. In his posthumously published memoir of his childhood, *Germs* (2004), which begins with his tottering out through the front door into the light at the age of two, Richard traces the roots in childhood of a variety of emotions he experienced in later life—resentment against calm, quiet places, the lure of danger, shame at the unreliability of his body, certain fears of inundation—and paints vivid pictures of his parents' opinions, routines, behaviour and character. His father was emancipated and although he embraced no religious faith—indeed, considered all religion to be folly, he insisted that Richard was brought up as a Christian, an encumbrance Richard freed himself from when he grew up, from then on regarding all religions as harmful illusions, and, like Hume and Nietzsche, believing that religions tend to be worse the further they stray from polytheism.

At the age of 13 he went to Westminster School as a King's Scholar. It was the first time that he had been away to boarding-school, something he had been looking forward to but which turned out to be very different from what he had expected. Before he went to Westminster, he later wrote,

Proceedings of the British Academy, **130**, 227–246. © The British Academy 2005.

he had lived entirely in books and the past. When he arrived there, he was, by his own account, a prig and physically weak and he did not believe in defending himself. He was very frightened by the boys he found himself among and he quickly sought refuge in the company of a small group of somewhat older boys, the aesthetes, by which he meant those passionate about art. In his first year, influenced by Aldous Huxley's *Encyclopaedia of Pacifism*, one of a number of Huxley's pamphlets that he found one afternoon in the Army and Navy Stores after he had faked illness in order to avoid games, he ardently embraced a qualified form of pacifism and as a result left the Officers Training Corps. This qualified pacifism admitted the possibility of a just war — Richard regarded the Spanish Civil War as a just war — but regarded war as just only in exceptional circumstances. He already detested patriotism, as he did throughout his life. It was over pacifism that he had his first quarrels with his father, who, although he was liberal and speculative in his thoughts about the arts and sciences, was fiercely conservative about life and politics, and had preached to Richard a doctrine of total obedience to one's parents for as long as one continues to live with them. At the end of his first year he discovered politics and soon became a socialist — a life long commitment. When he was 15 he applied to join the Communist Party, but received no reply — a stroke of luck, he remarked, but one of which he was a little ashamed.

At the outbreak of the Second World War, his pacifism was such that he could not believe that a war fought solely by the great imperialist powers could be just. But his mind was changed by the German attack on the Soviet Union and in 1941 he volunteered for war service. This enabled him to spend a year at Balliol College, Oxford, where, on the advice of a friend, he applied to join the Inniskilling Dragoon Guards. After surviving the unpleasant rigours of a friendless pre-OCTU and then an equally friendless OCTU (Officer Cadet Training Unit), he found himself sent to the Inniskilling Fusiliers, the regiment he had in fact been accepted by but which lacked the amusing company his friend had led him to expect in the Dragoon Guards. Soon he was posted to a battalion of a West Country regiment, where he became an object of ridicule and hostility and endured a very miserable time. Things went from bad to worse until an unexpected turn of events provided a solution. An adverse report recommending a change of employment led to his being arraigned in front of the Brigadier. This meeting not leading to a successful resolution of the issue, a few weeks later he found himself up before the Brigadier again. This time, however, the Brigadier sprang a surprise by saying that although it might be the most foolish idea he had ever had, he thought that he would like to have on his headquarters someone who could talk about Proust. This resulted in Richard's leading, with some misgivings, what he regarded as a rather sheltered war, despite his taking part in the Normandy landings, being captured by the Germans in August 1944 but escaping after five days to rejoin his unit, and, a few months later, rather fortuitously capturing a German officer and corporal.

Returning from war service to Balliol in 1945, he obtained two first class BA degrees, one in History in 1946, the other in Philosophy, Politics and Economics in 1948. His entry into academic life was effected by Freddie Ayer, whom he had met at Oxford in 1946 and saw socially from time to time over the next two years. Freddie, who had become Grote Professor of Philosophy of Mind and Logic in the University of London and Head of the University College Philosophy Department, amazed him by announcing that he intended to give Richard a job at UCL if he did well enough in Schools, and, when he did, promptly had him appointed to an Assistant Lectureship, even though, having read shortened PPE, he had studied philosophy for just four terms. A year later, in 1950, he married Anne Powell, with whom he had twin sons, Bruno and Rupert. Richard was already so well-read that, as Anne told me, it seemed to her as if he knew everything, and, in contrast to his friendless childhood, he now had a wide circle of friends—a circle that continually expanded throughout his life. Richard was convivial and greatly enjoyed conversation and many evenings were spent entertaining their closest friends. John Richardson, one of Richard's most long-standing friends, has written that some of the most stimulating evenings of his life were spent at Anne and Richard's Pelham Crescent house.

His first substantial piece of work, *F. H. Bradley* (1959), notable for the elegance and lucidity of its writing and its unrivalled mastery of Bradley's philosophy, was immediately recognised as the best book on its subject and in the revised edition published a decade later has remained the standard work on Bradley. Nearly everyone has found Richard's interest in Bradley puzzling, especially because Richard acknowledged the obscurity and paradoxical nature of Bradley's thought, some parts of which he confessed to finding incomprehensible. What could have attracted him to Bradley's metaphysics and logic, demanding yet unrewarding, which too often advance extravagant positions or abstruse doctrines by means of entangled, unacceptable arguments? It is true that Richard attributed perennial appeal to the doctrine of Monism, proposing an analogy 'between the metaphysical attachment to the idea of an undivided Reality, and the desire to establish "whole objects" which is of such crucial importance in infantile development'. And the highly personal style, caustic in Bradley's earlier books, ardent always, clearly appealed to him. But this does not suffice to account for the labour involved in unravelling, expounding and assessing the arguments that issue in Bradley's Absolute Idealism. The likeliest explanation comes from one of his friends, David Pears, who occupied the same house as Richard when Richard was switching from Medieval History to PPE, and who saw Richard as needing some relief from 'the contemporary philosophical diet' and as having 'a taste for unlikely systems with a baroque structure and, with it, a strong sense of the absurd'.[1]

There is, however, one part of Bradley's philosophy that Richard certainly admired: his ethical thought—the only aspect of Bradley's philosophy to which he seriously returned. Because he already held that an important constituent of moral philosophy is moral psychology, Richard approved of Bradley's proposing a theory of moral development in the individual. In a later paper he aligned Bradley's reflections on the good and the bad self with ideas of Melanie Klein, arguing for a conception of moral philosophy according to which its central task is 'to explore the nature or structure of that process whereby our propensities, supremely our desires, are modified or selected, our attitudes to them are developed, so that we are then capable of being appropriately moved to moral action', moral action being thought of as self-realisation in the sense accorded it by Bradley—true self-realisation being the realisation of the good, as opposed to the bad, self.

Richard's later thoughts about morality and the proper nature and scope of moral philosophy, which stemmed from his commitment to a naturalistic conception of morality as being primarily a part of the psychology of a person, the norm of development and the vicissitudes it is liable to having been uncovered by psychoanalysis, were both highly unusual and problematic. In fact, he claimed to take seriously the question 'whether there really is such a thing as morality, or whether it is a dream, or perhaps a nightmare'. And in more than one place he wrote of his scepticism about morality. But as it stands this does not accurately reflect his real view. His naturalism about morality maintains that 'morality originates in certain natural movements of the psyche, which do not themselves require reference to morality either to describe or to explain them. More specifically, it originates in our primitive capacity to tolerate certain conditions and our primitive incapacity to tolerate other condi-

---

[1] Private communication.

tions of ourselves.' From morality's being primarily a part of the psychology of the person, he drew the conclusion that moral philosophy
must be pursued as moral psychology, and for him that form of moral
psychology that studies the moral sense as it develops in the typical life-
history of the individual—diachronic moral psychology—penetrates
deepest into the nature of morality. And he held that the central contribution of moral psychology to moral philosophy is its establishing that
obligation and value have fundamentally different sources in an individual's psychology, the first—the feeling or thought of being under an obligation—deriving in a particular way from introjection of the figure or
figures that form the superego, the second—the conception of something
as being good or valuable—arising from a certain form of so-called complex projection in which satisfied love, 'archaic bliss' (the oceanic feeling
sensed at the breast) is projected onto an object. Accordingly, evolved
morality has a composite character: morality broadly conceived is an
amalgam of morality understood in a narrow sense with obligation at its
core and the sense of value, of what is good and bad. Morality in the
narrow sense, based as it is on the superego, has a number of baneful features—'asceticism', 'inwardness', 'delinquency' and 'moral masochism'
(the first two being intrinsic to morality, the second common deformities
of it)—which can be weakened but not entirely thrown off, and this is
what Richard had principally in mind in claiming that 'morality has a
pathological aspect as well as a benign aspect'.

If morality is conceived of as possessing a specific place in the life-
history of the individual, the criterion of a person's belief, decision or
sentiment really being moral is whether it appropriately descends from
the relevant part of the person's psychology. Richard was ready to
embrace the conclusion that certain of a person's beliefs, even though the
person himself thinks of them as being moral beliefs, and despite the fact
that they can be formulated only by using terms drawn from what is often
taken to be exclusively the language of morality—terms such as 'duty'
and 'obligation'—might fail to satisfy the criterion and so in fact constitute no part of the person's morality. For example, a belief about the
proper distribution of goods in a society, acquired by finding a certain
argument compelling, might lack the necessary credentials for being a
moral belief. And he held that obligation is primarily self-directed in that,
whereas the thought that someone morally ought to do something can be
appropriate as a self-addressed response since there can be a warrant for
it in our psychology, if addressed to others it lacks any psychological warrant and so is always inappropriate—so that thoughts that are genuinely

about what others ought to do, having no clear root in our psychology, do not express obligations. There is, of course, one important thing missing from this account of morality: while it provides a criterion for whether a belief, decision or sentiment is moral—part of the person's morality—it does not engage with the question whether a person's moral judgement or response is acceptable or unacceptable. Richard regarded acceptability as being a psychological notion, but it is to be regretted that he never seized the opportunity to elucidate the idea and indicate what the appropriate criteria of acceptability might be.

Richard considered the intellectual's prime duty to be social criticism. Accordingly, in the numerous radio talks and occasional writings of his earlier years he discussed a large range of social issues: pornography, homosexuality, equality of opportunity, freedom of opinion, advertising, state patronage of artists or museums and galleries and tax benefits for the donation of works to public institutions, private and public education, the environment, religion, universities, feminism, cities, inequality of income, the quality of work, the limits of state intervention in the lives of citizens, varieties of democracy—he considered that John Stuart Mill's case for proportional representation as an essential ingredient of representative democracy remained unanswered—the proper relation of law and morality, the use of violence in a democratic society for political ends, among others. About 1960 Richard, Ayer and Stephen Spender, inspired by a chance remark of Hugh Gaitskell's, started an informal group of intellectuals of the left which dined fortnightly in each other's houses and discussed social issues. But not so much as they hoped for came out of the group. He was a member of the Labour Party Commission on Advertising, which was set up in 1962, and contributed a paper on 'Advertising and Values'. He regretted the fact that the excellent report of the Commission was never properly discussed. He served as a panel-member of the Summerson Council (the National Council for Diplomas in Art and Design) in 1962–3 and resigned in disagreement with the Council's policy.

Underlying his concern with social issues was one of the deepest commitments of his life, 'devotion to the cause of socialism', and it is in the final section of his Fabian Society pamphlet *Socialism and Culture* (1961), where he raises explicitly what has been the implicit theme of the pamphlet, that his own conception of socialism becomes clear. Richard understood 'culture' in a wide sense, to mean the quality of life in a society—the relations between people, the character of their work and leisure, their knowledge, their interests, their arts, their freedoms, and so on—and the question is whether a socialist society should be a culturally single society, or whether it should be multicultural. His answer is that it should be culturally plural, various cultures existing side by side without any social prestige attaching to one rather than another. His argument for this conclusion is twofold. Negatively, he faults arguments for an integrated and cohesive society derived from the nature of culture and from each of the first two of the great ideals of progressive or radical politics, Equality, Fraternity and Liberty. Positively, he rests his case on the third of those ideals, Liberty. For a liberalised society is one in which people fulfil themselves according to their own view of life, provided that in doing so they do not inhibit the self-fulfilment of others, and this requires freedom from the constraints both of established authority and of social pressure, free access to the main ideas about the conduct of life that have evolved in human history, and the freedom to engage in what John Stuart Mill referred to as 'experiments in living'. Richard distances himself from the view that a socialist reconstruction of the forms of social life will erase human unhappiness and misery, but regards it as being, in a number of ways, conducive to self-realisation, and expresses his belief that 'the historical mission of Socialism is to introduce to the world a form of society where the individual may realise himself by drawing at will upon the whole range of human culture which is offered up for his choice freely and in its full profusion'.

It would be misguided to attempt to pin down the precise content of his socialism. For although he was certainly a democratic socialist— understanding the first business of a political democracy to be the defence of the rights of all and a socialist government as one 'that is ultimately prepared to wage war on all those forces in society which cramp and impoverish the lives of man'—and he maintained that inequalities in society could not be justified if the least privileged members of the society did not benefit from these inequalities, he advocated what he called 'political empiricism', a political empiricist being one who holds general social principles, the principles of Equality, Liberty and Fraternity, for example, but who is prepared to reject any principle he holds if given proof—proof of its disastrous consequences if applied in its categorical or unqualified form. So the principles of '89, like the principle of democracy itself, need to be elucidated, applied and tested and possible clashes between them acknowledged and assessed, a lifelong task. What can be said, however, is that Richard perceived his commitment to socialism as being rooted in his belief in a common human nature, the thought of a common human nature giving sustenance to the principles of '89, whatever elucidation of them and assessment of conflicts among them Richard might have favoured, universal human needs and general desires sustaining liberty and equality (of resources, opportunity, or whatever), fraternity being the acknowledgement of the nature we share with other human beings.

Nineteen sixty-two was a momentous year in his life. It was in this year that, after much hesitation and heart-searching, he took the decision to separate from his wife. Another important development was his entering into a Kleinian analysis with Dr Leslie Sohn, an analysis that lasted for more than eight years and to which Richard owed a great deal, especially the furthering of what he esteemed most in life, 'innermost knowledge of the self'. And in late July, afflicted by various conflicts in his life, with nowhere to live in London, he drove down to a cottage his niece had lent him and began work on his novel, *A Family Romance*, the title advertising to Freud's description of the fantasies a young boy devises to dispute or evade his father's authority, the novel's protagonist engaging in such a refashioning of his mistress's life. It had been a childhood ambition to write a complete novel, an ambition which stretched into maturity. But he had kept this secret; despite strenuous efforts he had been unable to fulfil it; and it caused him to feel shame in the presence of novelist friends he admired. However, this time he was better prepared to succeed, for his thoughts eventually crystallised about a linked set of ideas: the interdependence of form and content; the desire to set down what he had learnt from his analysis, not specifically about himself, but about those patterns of emotion in which our psychology manifests itself and which sometimes we project onto others; the adoption of diary form; the desire that the novel should be fully determined, everything in it having its reason; and the desire to distance himself from a prevailing view of criminal responsibility by illustrating the ideological message that people by and large do what they believe to be right, however objectionable their ideals may be. (He later wrote that in the last difficult days of writing the novel he had tried to console himself with the hope that at least one reader would welcome it as a tract against criminal justice.) This new conception, he felt, would make it possible for him to write a finished novel. When he returned to London in the autumn he had written twenty-seven of the hundred sections of the work, and, devoting to it whatever time he could spare from his teaching duties and philosophical writing, the novel occupied him for another four years, some of his time being taken up in what he described as 'a frenzied cultivation of low life, in which I pursued, for its own sake, an encyclopaedic knowledge of pubs and clubs frequented by prostitutes and young burglars, transvestites and insomniacs', not wanting anything to go on in such places that he was unfamiliar with. *A Family Romance* was finally finished in Cairo in the spring of 1967 and published two years later. The book was fairly well-reviewed but made no real impact and was soon forgotten. Although it has sometimes been described as a *roman-à-clef*, and it certainly lost him friends who seemed to recognise themselves in it, Richard claimed that in each case they were mistaken. He later confessed that he had not wanted the novel to be a very bookish book, but that is what it turned out to be. No later attempt at writing a finished novel was successful.

It was also in 1962 that his acquaintanceship with Adrian Stokes, which until that time had been rather slight, began to develop into very close friendship. He had met Stokes for the first time in 1958 at the private view of the Royal Academy's exhibition 'The Age of Louis XIV', having got interested in his work a few months before; and it was through his review of Stokes's *Greek Culture and the Ego*, which was published that year, that he had come to know Mrs Klein (whom Stokes had been in analysis with), who had only eighteen months to live and whom Richard described as 'the most impressive human being I have known'. But it was only with the start of his own analysis that he came to know Stokes very well. Stokes's house in Church Row, Hampstead, was, conveniently, on what they called 'the analytic route', and Richard called in usually once, sometimes twice a week, to talk with him. Richard greatly admired Stokes's writings on art: he regarded Stokes as the deepest contemporary critic of the arts and, with Meyer Schapiro, the most illuminating (Richard owned paintings by each of them). He later wrote a Preface to Stokes's *The Invitation in Art*; he reviewed three more of Stokes's books; he edited and wrote an Introduction to a selection of Stokes's writings (*The Image in Form*, 1972); he wrote a number of essays about Stokes's work; and he held that nothing could be better on the virtues of architecture than Stokes's *Venice*. Most importantly, he regarded the psychoanalytically inspired Tavistock books as displaying a superior psychoanalytic approach to art to Freud's own in his essays on Leonardo and on the *Moses* of Michaelangelo. Freud's concern, which requires access to material obtainable to the requisite extent only within the process of analysis, is solely with the (alleged) content of a work, a content that it might well share with things that are not art, and so fails to illuminate the work of art *qua* work of art or to engage with the nature of art. As opposed to this is an approach that is concerned with identifying the roots of artistic Form, meaning all the specifically artistic features of works—an approach exemplified above all in the later writings of Stokes, which exploit the extension of psychoanalytic theory effected by Mrs Klein—and which, construing certain formal characteristics as the natural correlates of certain organisations or relationships of the ego, the structural features of a work mirroring structural features of the person, constellations of feelings and dispositions, has no need of voluminous biographical material. For anyone looking to psychoanalysis to throw light on art, and who, as Richard did, both embraced Klein's development of Freudian theory and held that we can actually *see* the ego-states that correspond to them *in* the formal aspects of art, Stokes's work provides the paradigm, and its effect on Richard's own thoughts about art was marked. He could, he wrote, think of no better words to describe Stokes as a critic of the arts than those of Dante about Virgil: 'Poeta che mi guidi'.

In 1963 Richard was elected to the Grote Chair and became Head of the Department of Philosophy, positions he held throughout the rest of his time at UCL. There had been just three other members of staff when he arrived at UCL, but under Ayer's leadership it had gained in numbers, strength and reputation. Richard continued the transformation of the department, attracting to it outstanding talent and fostering an intellectual climate in which such talent could flourish. Many years later, soon after he had left the department, he paid this tribute to it: 'Throughout the time I have known it the department has always exemplified to a high degree the values that happen to please me most: audacity, toleration, a concern for tradition, and disregard for authority.' The credit for this state of the department was due not only to Richard but, as he would have been the first to acknowledge, to Ayer, whose leadership Richard greatly admired. Richard was made an Honorary Fellow of UCL in 1994.

Richard's first major statement on the philosophy of art and his principal contribution to analytic aesthetics, *Art and Its Objects* (1968), immediately established him as one of the world's leading aestheticians. It is marked not just by its sophistication, the wide range of problems it deals with, its exceptional command of the main terrain of the philosophy of art, the deep understanding and wide knowledge of art and art-historical writing it displays, its comprehensive mastery of the philosophical literature and the lucid style in which it is written, but by the distinctive conception of the philosophy of art it articulates—a conception that was further elaborated in the second edition, which contains six supplementary essays, and in other later writings, especially those collected in *On Art and the Mind* (1973) and *The Mind and Its Depths* (1993).

Richard acquiesced in the view that the central concern of aesthetics or the philosophy of art is to clarify the nature of art. But he rejected all standard approaches to the issue, in particular the simplistic idea that the right way to engage with the question 'What is art?' is to search for an illuminating reductive definition of 'art' or 'work of art', the complexity of the concept of art being such as to make such a search inappropriate. The leading idea of his own approach arises from his rejection of a spectator-oriented aesthetics: to grasp the nature of art it is necessary to see it from two points of view, that of the spectator and that of the artist, these points of view overlapping, spectator and artist not being different classes of people but roles that can be fulfilled by the same person, the distinctive function of the spectator being that of understanding art, the perspective of the artist, which commands pride of place, being a matter of seeing art and the artist's activity in the light of the intentions that guided his activity in making a work. Hence it is necessary to focus, not on works of art themselves, but on the so-called aesthetic attitude, where this is understood as all that is involved in regarding something as a work of art, which must be seen as linked with the complementary attitude of producing something as a work of art. And what this examination leads to is the suggestion that art is, in Wittgenstein's sense, a form of life, which requires, for artistic activity and appreciation to be possible, the existence of practices and institutions, and which issues in the conclusion that art is an essentially historical phenomenon, of necessity changing and its changes affecting the conceptual structure that surrounds art.

So there are two aims integral to art. The aim of the artist is to endow his work with a meaning determined by the intentions that guide his activity, the notion of intention being construed generously so as to include more or less any psychological factor—desires, beliefs, emotions, commitments and wishes, for example—that motivates him to work in a certain way. The aim of artistic criticism, the objective study of art, is to understand works of art. To understand a work is to grasp what the artist meant, which requires a cognitive stock that includes knowledge of its 'diachronic setting' or the aesthetic tradition of which it is a part, and that will often require very much more—knowledge of artistic conventions, various truths about the nature of the world, certain facts about the artist's life, for example. And any information, whatever its provenance or content might be, can properly be drawn upon if it enables the spectator to experience some part of the meaning of the work that otherwise he might have overlooked. But to grasp what the artist meant, to retrieve his intention, is not a cognitive achievement that consists in recognising that the artist intended a spectator to have a certain experience in engaging with the work. Such recognition is unnecessary. If the artist fulfilled his intention, all that is required is that a spectator, in engaging with the work, should undergo the experience the artist intended his work to provide: understanding a work is essentially experiential—it is understanding by acquaintance.

In addition to his psychological account of the meaning and under-standing of a work of art, two other psychological accounts figure large in his aesthetic thought. Again and again he returned to two important topics, the nature of pictorial representation and the nature of artistic expression, each, he held, depending on an exercise of both the spectator's and the artist's role, and for each he proposed a psychological account.

From his earliest writing on the topic of pictorial representation, he held two views, one flowing from the other. The first is that seeing an opaque marked surface as a representation involves seeing it in such a manner that one thing (a plane of colour, say) is seen as being behind or in front of another. The second is that pictorial representation is not restricted to figurative representation, for most abstract paintings demand this kind of perception. At first he elucidated pictorial represen-tation in terms of 'seeing as', but later he thought it necessary to replace this with 'seeing in', where seeing one thing in another consists of a conjunction of two visual experiences, one of seeing a surface and one of seeing, in looking at the surface, one thing in front of or behind another. A final change consisted in conceiving of seeing-in as, so to speak, the fusion of these two kinds of experience, so that seeing-in is an auto-nomous perceptual capacity, an experience of seeing-in being a single experience which has two aspects, one (the configurational) of seeing a marked surface, the other (the recognitional) of seeing in this surface something in front of or behind something else. Now he never sought to give a full explanation of what he took seeing-in to be, believing that since it was such a common experience he needed to do no more than gesture towards it for his meaning to be understood, and he was sceptical that it could be elucidated further than he had done. But adherents of alterna-tive accounts of pictorial perception, based on the idea of perceived resemblance or the idea of imagining seeing something—accounts that Richard continued to argue against to the end and the elements of which he refused to countenance in his own conception—have remained unconvinced that the notion of seeing-in, as Richard thought of it, is coherent, for it appears impossible, given his rejections, to explain the idea of seeing something in front of something else, seeing in a marked surface 'things three-dimensionally related', the 'awareness of depth', the 'effect' of three-dimensionality, that is intrinsic to pictorial perception. For Richard the recognitional aspect of an experience of seeing-in is a visual awareness of the object depicted, and the crucial issue is whether any reasonable sense can be made of this consonant with his denial that this visual awareness is an illusion, an experience of resemblance or one of imagining seeing something.

His conception of artistic expression—a work of art's being expressive of psychological states or processes—which always included the idea of the perception of a 'correspondence' between a work and a psychological state, the work seeming to us to match what we experience when in that state, received many partial elucidations before finally crystallising into an analysis based on the idea of the projection of emotion onto a work, where projection, again, is not simple but complex, the work's expressive properties being so-called projective properties. The analysis exists in two forms, the first of which requires the observer to be experiencing the emotion projected onto the work, the other dropping this requirement: in both forms the projected emotion 'colours' the observer's perception of the work. Only the second form is consistent with Richard's long-standing opposition to the idea that an artist, in creating a work as an expression of emotion, or an observer, in appreciating it as an expression of emotion, must feel the emotion that the work expresses. In any case, Richard was prepared to concede that the crucial concepts involved in his theory, even in its final form, suffer from indefiniteness, so that the theory is merely programmatic (although he wondered, not unreasonably in the case of painting, whether this might well be true of all philosophical theories of expression, the subject being still in its infancy). Although he never explicitly advocated a theory of the evaluation of art, it is clear that he favoured a projective theory of the status of artistic value. But, leaving aside the inadequate characterisation of the notion of complex projection, it is clear that the variety of artistic value would require a more nuanced projective theory than the one proposed for moral value, where what is projected is 'archaic bliss'. Richard would, I am sure, have acknowledged this.

Of the arts, his greatest love was painting, his memory for paintings that he had seen being exceptional. Nicholas Poussin, whom he discovered at the 1932–3 Burlington House exhibition of French paintings when he was only nine, remained his ideal of art, as the magnificent dust jackets that adorn his books declare. He had a strong feeling for architecture, understanding the perception of architecture—more generally the built environment, whether of the town or countryside—to involve corporeal projection, fine architecture sustaining the projection of good ego-states, poor architecture encouraging crude aggressive part-object fantasies. And so he considered good architecture to be 'not a luxury but a necessity'. He had a lifelong love of literature in all its forms, preferring poetry to the novel in his youth, his first love in fiction being Scott, whom he venerated throughout his life, Scott's novels being full of characters who embrace ideals that consume them, unlike the English novel of shared manners, which he did not favour. He described himself as 'somewhat unmusical, in some respects violently antimusical'. On one occasion he explained to me that in general he found music too emotional to listen to. But in fact his reaction was more specific than this would indicate. For one of the fears of inundation he suffered from throughout his life was inundation in the sound of music: his experience of music was too often one of drowning in a sea of sound. His struggle to come to terms with music was, he wrote, the hardest battle he had fought in his life. His two favourite composers were Monteverdi and Debussy. Despite his father's connection with Diaghilev, he was no enthusiast for the ballet, and he regarded the film as having failed to graduate as an art-form.

His marriage to Anne having been dissolved in 1967, in 1969 Richard married the American sculptor and potter Mary Day Lanier, step-daughter of Dwight Macdonald (one of whose books Richard had reviewed), whose artistic and political interests harmonised with his own. Their daughter, Emilia, was born in 1983: Richard adored her throughout his life.

Nineteen seventy-one saw the publication of his principal work on the theory of psychoanalysis, *Freud*, a lucid, precise and economical exposition of the development of Freud's theory of the mind, displaying an astonishing mastery of the details of Freud's theories of dreams, parapraxes, symptoms, jokes, neuroses, sexuality and other topics, at each stage of their evolution, indicating Freud's changes of mind and any unclarities or uncertainties in Freud's thought, not just expounding these theories but raising and answering objections that have been or are likely to be brought against them, and correcting a variety of misapprehensions of Freud's thought. It is especially notable for the emphasis that Richard places on the *Project for a Scientific Psychology*, a manuscript Freud wrote in 1895 putting forward a theoretical model of the mind and mental processes, both normal and pathological. Richard undertakes the heroic task of extracting from this difficult manuscript the main elements of Freud's picture of the mind and proceeds to demonstrate its powerful influence on Freud's thinking throughout the rest of his life and, despite his neither completing nor publishing it, its enduring importance for him. And the work concludes with an examination of a rather neglected aspect of Freud's thought, his reflections on the value of human civilisation—whether, given the conditions essential to the existence of a stable society, the fruits outweigh the burdens, and whether there could be a form of society which so mitigated the renunciations necessary to a civilised life that the outcome would be positive for nearly everyone.

Given his commitment to the leading ideas of psychoanalytic theory as developed by Freud and extended by Melanie Klein, this development being for him 'the most exciting, the most courageous, the most poignant adventure in the history of Western ideas', it is unsurprising that elements of the theory of psychoanalysis came to inform, to a greater or lesser extent, all his writing, lightly touching some works, saturating others, and this greatly contributes to its distinctive character. His knowledge of psychoanalytic theory was unrivalled, encompassing both the contributions of the main figures and the alternatives proposed by the principal 'revisionists' and deviators. In 1982 he was elected an Honorary Associate of the British Psychoanalytical Society (the first non-analyst to be honoured in this way), and in 1994 to honorary membership of the San Francisco Psychoanalytic Institute. In 1991 he was given an award for distinguished services to psychoanalysis by the International Psychoanalytical Association.

In spring 1982 he gave the William James Lectures in Philosophy at Harvard, which he revised and greatly expanded into *The Thread of Life* (1984). He held that 'the primary task of philosophy vis-à-vis psychoanalytic theory is to articulate the kind of understanding—the diversity of understanding, we might say—that psychoanalytic theory promises of human nature'. His lectures investigate the nature of the process that mediates between a person and the life he or she leads—the leading of a life—and he conceded that a characterisation of their ideology might identify their aim as a philosophy of mind of a kind that psychoanalytic theory requires. The unargued assumption of psychoanalytic theory and frequent recourse to elements of it dismayed reviewers sceptical of or antipathetic to psychoanalysis. But even if the aspects of psychoanalytic theory that Richard exploits were not to be viable, the book is saturated with thoughts and arguments that derive, not from the theory of psychoanalysis, but from profound reflection on human life—on the significance in the way we lead our lives of imagination, memory, fantasy, self-examination, self-concern, friendship, madness and death—and these and the sophisticated conceptual apparatus through which they are developed would, by themselves, be sufficient to render it invaluable. He argues for this account of friendship: 'The essence of friendship lies, I suggest, in the exercise of a capacity to perceive, a willingness to respect, and a desire to understand, the differences between persons. Friendship lies in a response to the singularity of persons, and a person's friendship extends only as far as such singularity engages him.' His own talent for friendship, one of his most endearing qualitites, illustrates this conception perfectly. Richard was an astute observer of humanity, relishing or tolerating a very wide range of ways in which those he engaged with might diverge from him, and he was unconcerned to control or change them. In return, people were attracted to him by his extraordinarily rich and curious mind, his wit, his humour, his passions, and the attraction was strengthened by their recognition of his interest in and respect for their idiosyncracies. For Richard, as for John Stuart Mill, whom Richard greatly admired, individuality was one of the supreme values in life, a value he celebrated in his teaching: he encouraged students who dissented from his views to articulate their reasons or express their own point of view and accommodated immovable disagreement gracefully, recognising how harmful an insistence on the merits of his own position was likely to be.

After thirty-three years in the Philosophy Department at UCL, the last nineteen as Head of Department, in 1982 Richard left for the USA, residing first in New York as Professor of Philosophy at Columbia University, then moving to California in 1985, where he remained, as Mills Professor of Intellectual and Moral Philosophy at the University of California, Berkeley, until 2002, being Chair of the Philosophy Department from 1998–2002, and between 1989–96 splitting his time between Berkeley and the University of California, Davis, where he was Professor of Philosophy and the Humanities.

In November and December 1984 he delivered the Andrew W. Mellon Lectures in the Fine Arts at the National Gallery of Art in Washington, which he greatly revised and enlarged into *Painting as an Art* (1987), and which is, arguably, his masterpiece. Richard was not an admirer of the art-historical manner in which painting was currently studied and he hoped that the theory of painting he advances would encourage an alternative approach. In the book he applies his psychological account of artistic meaning and understanding to the art of painting—a painting's meaning (each painting having one and only one meaning) being visual, revealed in the experience induced in an adequately sensitive and informed spectator who looks at the surface of the painting as the fulfilled intentions of the artist led him to mark it—and argues that a painting is a work of art in virtue of the way in which the activity from which it issues is practised; he advances a generative conception of individual pictorial style, distinguishing the set of characteristics associated with an individual style from the style itself, the style itself having psychological reality, a practical capacity lying deep in the artist's psychology, having been formed in the artist's mind and causing the characteristics associated with it to be as they are, and enabling the artist to fulfil his intentions; he distinguishes five main varieties of primary pictorial meaning or content that a work can achieve—representational, expressive, textual, historical and metaphorical—each specified with greater precision and a finer sense of aesthetic relevance than had previously been attained, and he identifies what he characterises as secondary meaning, which is what the act of giving a picture its primary meaning meant to the artist; and he illustrates his argument with a remarkable series of challenging interpretations of works by some of the painters he most admired—Bellini, Friedrich, Ingres, Manet, Picasso, Poussin and Titian, amongst others.

On the last page of the book he responds to a self-addressed challenge, asserting that his reply is 'the simplest, and the most important, thing' that he has to say in the lectures. The challenge is to explain what reason there is to believe that, if he has the right sensitivity and information, his own experience of paintings, which has been the basis of his interpretations, gives him a correct understanding of the fulfilled intentions of the artist. His response is to argue that all great art presupposes a universal human nature through which pictorial meaning works: only this can explain the survival of painting as an art. And this elucidates his claim at the beginning of the book that 'all art, or at any rate all great art, presupposes a universal human nature'. And at both the beginning and the end of the book he announces the locking together of two of his deepest commitments, the love of painting and loyalty to socialism, by the common ground in which they are rooted—a common human nature (to the understanding of which psychoanalysis, another of his deepest commitments, has made a major contribution). This locking together, which Richard does not elaborate, should not be misunderstood. In the first place, there is an asymmetry here that Richard does not mention: whereas great art presupposes a common human nature, Richard never argued that this is true of socialism. However, if socialism is derivable from there being a universal human nature, then, given the existence of great art, socialism follows—but only if the elements of human nature through which pictorial meaning works are the same as or imply the basic needs and desires which sustain socialism. Secondly, the locking together of these commitments did not incline him to embrace the view that a painting should be a true mirror of the social conditions of its age, the art of a socialist society reflecting the distinctive features of such a society, nor the view that the artist should further the cause of the progressive elements of his society. And he explicitly rejected the social explanation of pictorial works of art, that is, the assignment to them of a social function, or a limited set of social functions—reflecting, idealising, criticising or compensating for social conditions, say—one that all paintings necessarily discharge. However, maintaining that it is in the tradition of the great aesthetes—those passionate about art and best able to articulate their response to it—to be social critics, he argued that in fact there is a natural connection between the role of aesthete and that of social critic, so that it is the cases in which an aesthete is indifferent to the conditions of his society that require explanation. For, in the first place, aesthetes have a 'heightened awareness of the power of the environment upon us, and hence of its significance for us'. And, secondly, there is a natural link between aestheticism and utopianism—the demand that 'the outer world should exhibit a degree of harmony or integration comparable to that which man tries to establish within himself'—so that those aesthetes who recognise humanity wherever it occurs will be socialists, recognising the harmful forces on 'many of our fellow human beings' of 'advertising, the degradation and disintegration of the urban environment, the survival of religion, the proliferation of partial and therefore crude sexual imagery'.

His final book, *On the Emotions* (1999), a thoroughly revised, rewritten and massively expanded version of the Ernst Cassirer lectures that he delivered in the Philosophy Department at Yale University in the autumn of 1991, offers an account of the emotions, the most sophisticated account we have, which is held up against imagined cases and illustrated by well-chosen literary examples. It 'repsychologises' the philosophical study or conception of the emotions, attributing to them 'psychological reality'—which is to represent them as mental dispositions that cause their manifestations. It assigns to them a particular role within the psychology of the person—that of providing the person with an attitude to the world—and it sketches and then develops in great detail a characteristic history, proceeding from the originating condition to internal and external manifestations and other outcomes, a history not followed by every occurrence of emotion but one the recognition of which is essential to understanding what an emotion is. For two of the so-called moral emotions, shame and guilt, which deviate from the characteristic history, he identifies a different originating condition and outlines a different history, not just of any instance of them but of the emotions themselves as they develop in the life of the individual, incorporating the psychoanalytic notion of fantasy as an essential ingredient of his account. And in conclusion he proposes the view, although this is not developed sufficiently to be assessed, that the essence of any kind of emotion—what distinguishes it from any other—is its distinctive attitude, the identity of which lies in the character of the emotion's life, formed of the interactions between the world and the emotion. Like all Richard's books, *On the Emotions* has a character that distinguishes it from nearly all philosophical writing of the last century: not only does it display the highest qualities of abstract thought, it possesses great human interest.

In 2003, having for nearly twenty years accepted constantly renewed invitations to teach at Berkeley, he left the USA and returned to London, where he bought a spacious loft in Bermondsey. In Autumn 2002 he had begun to experience pain in one or another part of his body and in September 2003 his condition deteriorated and he was admitted to hospital. At first it seemed that the cause of his suffering might well be secondary cancer from melanoma—in the last couple of years he had had two moles removed from his skin—and Richard accepted the prospect of imminent death sweetly and calmly; but when the diagnosis was changed to multiple myeloma he looked forward to a longer life in which he would be able to carry out further projects. Feeling terribly sick after radiotherapy, he insisted on discharging himself from hospital and soon moved into his flat, which his wife had worked valiantly to prepare for his inhabiting, with his spirits high. But three weeks later he died of heart failure in his home before dawn on 4 November 2003.

Richard was one of the most original, creative and courageous philosophers of his time. It is unsurprising that he attracted invitations to give many of the world's most prestigious lectures. In addition to the three already mentioned, he was the Ernest Jones Lecturer, Institute of Psychoanalysis, London, 1968, the Power Lecturer, University of Sydney, 1972, the Leslie Stephen Lecturer, Cambridge University, 1979, the H. L. A. Hart Lecturer, Oxford University, 1985, the Gareth Evans Memorial Lecturer at Oxford 1996, the Roland Penrose Lecturer at the Tate Gallery 1998, the Werner Heisenberg Lecturer at the Bavarian Academy 2001 and the Lindley Lecturer at the University of Kansas 2001. Two Festchriften in his honour were published, in 1992 and 2001, the second containing his responses to the contributors. He was elected a Fellow of the British Academy in 1972 and a Fellow of the American Academy of Arts and Sciences in 1986. He was the greatest aesthetician of his generation and his contribution to the philosophy of his favourite art, painting, dwarfs all others. In the last fifteen years of his life he wrote regularly about painting (and drawing and architecture), especially for *Modern Painters*, of which he was a member of the Editorial Board, interviewing artists, reviewing exhibitions and engaging in art criticism. Each of his final philosophical publications was on the nature and art of painting. In his last years he had come to focus on the topic of pictorial organisation, about which he intended to write a book, which, in addition to some of his previously published views, would include his thoughts about the organisation of the paintings of Ruisdael, Bellotto and Monet (whose work he adored). It might appear extravagant to characterise the death of an 80-year old man as untimely. But Richard was exceptional: the passing of the years left his powerful and creative mind undimmed, his intellectual curiosity as keen as ever, his passion for painting, both new and old, undiminished. His death has deprived us not just of his company.

MALCOLM BUDD
Fellow of the Academy

Note. I would like to express my thanks to the late Anne Wollheim, who kindly gave up the time to talk with me about her life with Richard, and to Mary Day Lanier Wollheim, who allowed me to read Richard's memoir of his childhood, *Germs*, long before it was published, and with whom I had a number of enjoyable and informative meetings in Richard's Bermondsey flat.